Legal Translation between English and Arabic

Ali Almanna

Legal Translation between English and Arabic

palgrave
macmillan

Ali Almanna
Interpreting and Translation Studies
Hamad bin Khalifa University
Doha, Qatar

ISBN 978-3-031-14837-8 ISBN 978-3-031-14838-5 (eBook)
https://doi.org/10.1007/978-3-031-14838-5

This Palgrave Macmillan imprint is published by the registered company Springer Nature Switzerland AG.
The registered company address is: Gewerbestrasse 11, 6330 Cham, Switzerland

Contents

List of Figures

PART I

Theoretical Considerations

CHAPTER 1

Setting the Scene

Legal Translation

How would you define legal translation?

Legal translation is defined by Šarčević (1997: 13) as a type of translation in which the translator translates not only from one linguistic system into another, but rather, s/he translates "from one legal system into another". In other words, the translators should take into consideration the differences between the source legal system and the target legal system. This view adopted here is advocated by El-Farahaty (2015: 6) who holds that legal translation, as it is "bound by each language's culture", is not "merely the transcoding between the [source language] SL and the [target language] TL". To elaborate, translating legal texts, in particular legislative texts, is different from other types of translation as it requires the translator to be an insider in both cultures and systems, i.e. s/he needs to be an insider in the SL culture and system in order to understand, and an insider in the TL culture and system in order to encode the socio-cultural experiences in the TL (for more details on the perspective of insider/outsider, see Almanna 2014: 55–59).

Categories of Legal Texts

The interest of linguists in English legal discourse is relatively recent and regretfully scarce as yet. From both Mellinkoff's (1963) and Crystal and Davy's (1969) attempts towards systematization in the sixties, up to the

A. Almanna, *Legal Translation between English and Arabic*,
https://doi.org/10.1007/978-3-031-14838-5_1

Fig. 1.1 Bhatia's classification of legal texts

modern studies carried out by Bhatia (1993) on legislative texts, Kurzon (1986) on cohesive structures and, in Spain, Alcaraz Varó (2009) on the peculiarities of the English legal structure and its language, among others, the emphasis has been increasingly placed on the need to define and describe the legal discourse in its own context. Therefore, far from considering the legal text solely from its grammatical and semantic point of view, and, no doubt, influenced by the pragmatic flavour of other previous multidisciplinary analyses (see Danet 1980 and O'Barr 1982 for example), the objective of these studies has taken into account the extra-linguistic purposes of the text itself.

Bhatia (1982; also discussed in Sabra 2003: 15) classifies legal texts into three main types, as shown in Fig. 1.1 above.

Can you identify the type of this legal passage according to Bhatia's classification? "Civil law refers to the body of laws of a state or nation regulating ordinary private matters, as distinct from laws regulating criminal, political, or military matters".

Academic legal texts include the language of academic magazines, books specified for teaching law, and others. Juridical texts, by contrast, cover judgements issued by courts, the books which deal with legal cases, reports in that respect, and the like. Legislative texts, however, encompass a wide range of writing, such as legal documents, contracts, conventions, treaties, decrees, orders, and others.

Legal language is classified by Trosborg (1997: 20) into five types, namely

1. Language used in legal documents covering legislative writing, contracts, deeds, etc.
2. Language used in the courtroom covering the language used by judge, lawyers, witnesses, prosecutors, and the like.
3. Language used in textbooks covering, as stated above, academic books, magazine, and the like.
4. Language used by lawyers outside the courtroom covering their speech with other lawyers and lay people.
5. Language used by lay people when talking about law.

Can you identify the type of this legal passage according to Trosborg's classification?
قال ليّ المحامي إن وضع ابني في القضية ضعيف جدًا ويحتاج قدرة قادر كي يخرج منها بسلامة.

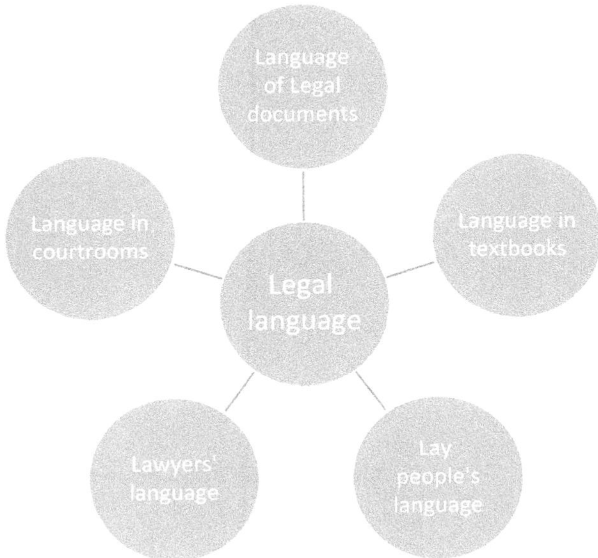

Fig. 1.2 Trosborg's classification of legal texts

Trosborg's classification can be modelled here to make the point clear (Fig. 1.2).

More recently, legal texts have been classified by Cao (2007: 9–10) into four types, as modelled below (Fig. 1.3).

As one may observe, Cao's classification is somehow similar to Bhatia's classification with the exception of legislative texts which are sub-divided into two types by Cao, namely legislative texts covering treaties, multilingual laws, domestic statutes, and the like, and private legal texts covering contracts, wills, tenancy agreements, etc.

Legal Translation between English and Arabic concentrates on all types of legal texts, regardless of their classification. However, legislative texts, which have "acquired a certain degree of notoriety, rarely equalled by any other variety of English" are given serious consideration (Bhatia 1993: 101). In any variety of language, there are some social factors that affect people's choice of language. Among these factors, as Holmes (1992/2013) points out, are the relationship between the participants, the setting or the social context in which the language is used, communicative purpose and the topic. Like other varieties of language, legal language includes a wide range of text types depending on

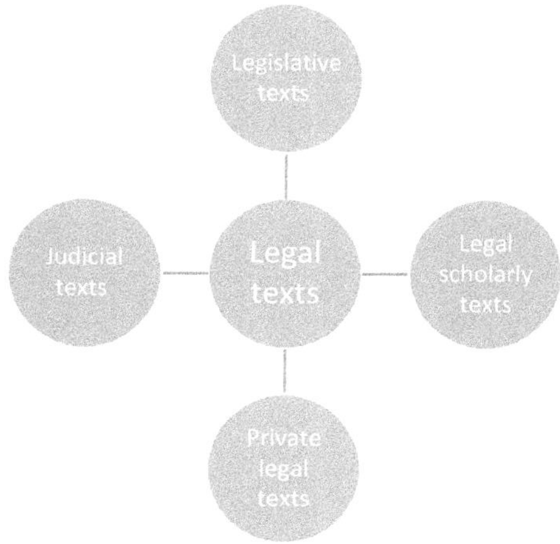

Fig. 1.3 Cao's classification of legal texts

the social factors mentioned above. So, for instance, when the relationship is between a solicitor and a client at the solicitor's office during working hours to discuss a legal matter, we will have a certain text type, which is definitely different from that between, for example, a judge and a witness giving his/her testimony in a court case. Accordingly, we can conclude that legal writing covers several text types, one of which is legislative texts, in which the communicative purpose, relationship, setting and topic are totally different not only from those of other varieties of language, but from those of other text types within the legal domain itself.

How would you translate the lexical item 'solicitor' *into Arabic? If you go for* محام*? How would you translate* 'lawyer' *and* 'barrister'?

In what follows, we will concentrate on the most important features that distinguish legislative texts from other legal texts, on the one hand, and from other varieties of language, on the other. These features are the communicative purpose, the position of the draftsman and the readership.

Communicative Purpose

According to the communicative purpose, legal texts are classified by Cao (2007: 10) another classification, which is different from the one based on the subject matter. Legal texts, according to their communicative purpose, are classified by Cao into '*normative texts*' covering

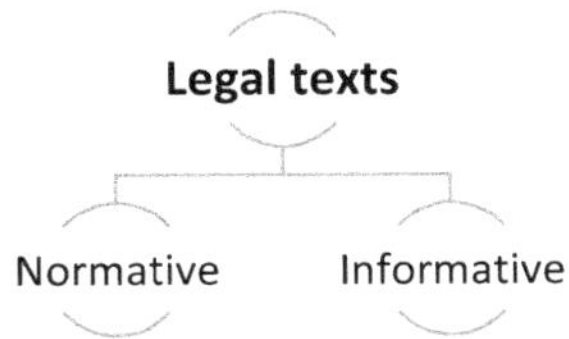

Fig. 1.4 Cao's classification of legal texts according to their communicative purpose

Is the following article taken from the UK Constitution, article 11 no 1 normative or informative?

"Everyone has the right to hold opinions without interference".

binding texts, such as legislative texts, contracts, treaties, etc. and 'informative texts' covering the language used in courtrooms, lawyers' language outside courts, lay people's language when talking about law, and the like as modelled above (Fig. 1.4).

Legislative writing, as Bhatia (1993: 102) indicates, is "highly impersonal and decontextualized, in the sense that its illocutionary force holds independently of whoever is 'the speaker' (originator) or 'the hearer' (reader) of the document". By examining all types of legislative writing, one can easily recognize that it is a type of writing whose function is to impose obligation and prohibition, confer rights and give permission, etc. (see Chap. 5 of this book for more details). So, the general function of such a kind of writing is directive (giving instructions to the addressee). Building on this, legal texts can be classified according to their communicative purpose into two types, namely '*directive*' (e.g. legislative texts, private legal texts) and '*informative*' (e.g. language used in courtrooms, lawyers' language used outside courtrooms, lay people's language, language used in textbooks, etc.).

The Process of Writing and Draftsman's Position

Legislative writing, as Bhatia (1993) points out, differs from other varieties of language not only in the communicative purpose, but in the way in which it is created as well. In any other kinds of written language, the originator and the writer of the text are embodied in one person, but in legislative writing the writer, which is the draftsman, will not be the originator of the legislative provision. In other words, in legislative writing, there are two stages: a text has to be originated, which is from the deliberations of parliament and then the text should be written in a specific way, which is done by the draftsman. So, what is intended by the originator is not necessarily the same that the writer conveys in his/her way of writing the provisions. In order to avoid such situations, draftsmen have to endeavour to use, what Bhatia (1993: 103) refers to as, "linguistic and discoursal strategies" to make their writing not only "clear, unambiguous and precise", but also "all-inclusiveness". This definitely makes the task of the draftsmen more difficult than that of those who are able to write down their own ideas, and for whom there is, to a considerable extent, a degree of freedom in directing and determining the aspects of the text that they write.

Readership

One of the crucial factors that play a significant role in determining the final shape of the target text (TT) is "the translator's need to take into account the target reader's expectations. This requires translators to take a number of fundamental decisions concerning the levels of acceptability and accessibility" (Almanna 2014: 108). The TT acceptability does not "depend on how closely it corresponds to some state in the world", but rather on how the target readers access the TT and decide on its reality "whether believable, homogenous or relevant" (Baker 1992/2011). To this end, the translator needs to render the "exact contextual meaning of the [source text] ST [...] through the medium of a TL which is acceptable to the TL reader and easily understood by him" (Adab 1997: 9–10). Hall (2008: 23) writes:

> To achieve effective communication, the translator needs to take account of the cognitive and cultural environment of the targeted language community and its likely expectations of the transmitted text and make his/her translation as informative and accessible as possible.

With respect to readership, Sager (1993 cited in El-Farahaty 2015: 11) holds that legal texts can be classified into two main types, namely '*directive*' and '*informative*'. They are informative when they address all people, thus providing them with information. However, they are directive when they address specific group of people. Sager's classification of legal texts can be modelled here (Fig. 1.5).

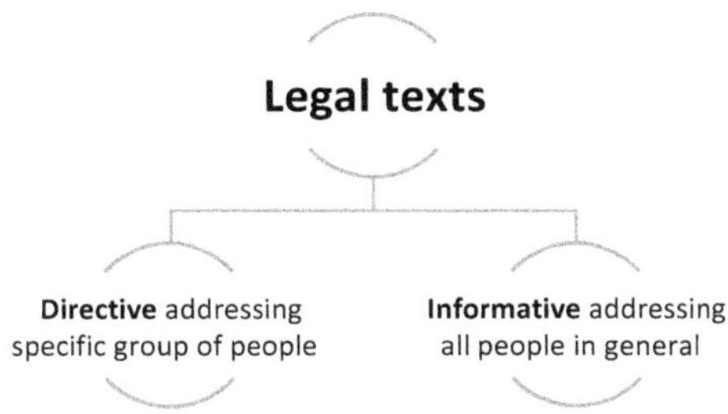

Fig. 1.5 Sager's classification of legal texts according to their readership

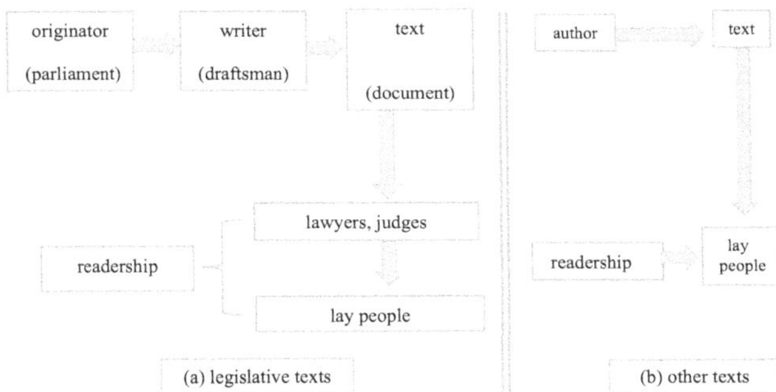

Fig. 1.6 Communicative purpose and readership

In legislative writing, the readership is completely different from other varieties of language as in legislative writing, "the document is meant for ordinary citizens; but the real readers are lawyers and judges, who are responsible for interpreting these provisions for ordinary citizens" (Bhatia 1993: 103). As a result, in legislative writing there are two types of readers: the document is meant for ordinary people, but the real readers are those people expert in law. The above diagram (Fig. 1.6) that shows the differences between legislative writing and other varieties of language can be considered.

Intra-system Differences

English is used in a great number of countries, thereby having many varieties, such as British English, American English, Australian English, Irish English, Scottish English, Welsh English, Canadian English, New Zealand English, South African English, Nigerian English, Singapore English and many other Englishes. The same holds true for Arabic; there are many varieties of Arabic.

This makes the task of the translator working between these two languages, i.e. Arabic and English, more challenging because s/he has to decide on the variety that should be opted for with the potential to live up to the target-language readers' expectations. To make what I have in mind clear, let us discuss the terminology relating to courts in these six countries only:

Iraq	---	محكمة البداءة	محكمة الأحوال الشّخصية		محكمة الاستئناف	محكمة التّمييز
Egypt	---	المحكمة الابتدائية	محكمة الأسرة	المحكمة الشّرعية	محكمة الاستئناف	محكمة النّقض
Morocco	---	المحكمة الابتدائية		المحكمة الشّرعية	محكمة الاستئناف	المحكمة العليا
Saudi Arabia	---	المحكمة الابتدائية		المحكمة الشّرعية		المحكمة العليا
Lebanon	----	محكمة الدرجة الأولى		المحكمة الشّرعية	محكمة الاستئناف	محكمة التّمييز
Jordan	محكمة الصّلح	محكمة البداية		المحكمة الشّرعية	محكمة الاستئناف	محكمة التّمييز

As can be observed, among these six countries only Jordan has محكمة الصّلح that can lend itself to '*Magistrate's Court*' in countries like England and Wales. What is called محكمة التّمييز '*Court of Cassation*' in Iraq, Lebanon and Jordan is called محكمة النّقض '*Court of Cassation*' in Egypt and المحكمة العليا '*Supreme Court*' in Morocco and Saudi Arabia. In translating '*Court of Cassation*' into Arabic, in the following text taken from *Wikipedia* there are two options that can be used by the translator, namely محكمة التّمييز and محكمة النّقض, depending on the judicial system and target language readers.

> A court of cassation is a high-instance court that exists in some judicial systems. Courts of cassation do not re-examine the facts of a case, they only interpret the relevant law.

> محكمة التّمييز/محكمة النّقض هي محكمة عليا موجودة في بعض الأنظمة القضائية، وهي لا تعيد النّظر في حيثيات القضية، بل يقتصر عملها على تفسير القانون ذي الصلة.

Why is it ذي *not* ذو *or* ذا?

Here, as one may observe, there is an example of divergence as the denotative meaning of the phrase '*Court of Cassation*' is wider and less specific when it is compared with محكمة التّمييز or محكمة النّقض. In the following sentence, the term '*dowry*' can be translated into مهر or صداق, again depending on the judicial system and readers.

Is there any difference between المهر *and* الصّداق *in Arabic? Discuss.*

> In the Arab culture, a woman's dowry is given to the bride before the wedding day.
>
> في الثّقافة العربية، تسلّمُ العروسُ المهر/الصّداق قبل يوم الزّفاف.

Re-translate this sentence by using تستلم *and* تُعطى.

Similarly, in translating the lexical item '*parliament*' into Arabic, the judicial system and readers should be given full consideration; otherwise, it can be translated into برلمان. By way of example, let us discuss the translation of this article taken from the UK Constitution, article 77.1 no 1:

Note that in English, there are three words, namely 'Arab', 'Arabic' *and* 'Arabian' *that usually lend themselves to one word, i.e.* عربيّ *or* عربيّة*. Therefore, when we translate from English into Arabic, there will be an example of convergence. What about the word* لجنة *here?*

> The Constitutional Commission shall establish from amongst its members who are members of Parliament a committee to be known as the Integrity Committee.
>
> تُنشئ اللجنة الدّستورية من بين أعضائها الذين هم أعضاء البرلمان لجنةً تُعرف بلجنة النّزاهة.

It is worth noting that the legislative bodies in the Arab world have different names, such as مجلس الأمة in Kuwait and Jordan, مجلس النّواب in Iraq, مجلس الشّورى in Egypt, Algeria, Oman, Qatar, and Saudi Arabia, مجلس المستشارين in Morocco and Tunisia and the like (for more details, see Husni and Newman 2015: 110–11). Below are some illustrative examples along with their translations:

Note that a disjunctive hamza همزة قطع *should be used in* إن.

يشترط في نائب الأمير الشروط المنصوص عليها في المادة 82 من هذا الدستور وان كان وزيرا أو عضوا في مجلس الأمة فلا يشترك في أعمال الوزارة أو المجلس مدة نيابته عن الأمير. The Deputy Amir has to satisfy the qualifications laid down in Article 82. If he is a Minister or a member of the National Assembly, he may not take part in the ministerial functions or in the work of the Assembly during the period he is acting as Deputy for the Amir. (the Kuwaiti Constitution, article 62).	مجلس الأمة ↓ the National Assembly
يتولى مجلس الشورى سلطة التشريع، ويقر الموازنة العامة للدولة، كما يمارس الرقابة على السلطة التنفيذية، وذلك على الوجه المبين في هذا الدستور. Al-Shoura Council shall assume the legislative authority, approve the general policy of the Government, the budget, and it shall exercise control over the executive authority as specified in this Constitution. (the Qatari Constitution, article 76)	مجلس الشّورى ↓ Al-Shoura Council

Note that in Arabic legal discourse على الوجه المبين *can be shortened to* كما مبيّن.

مجلس الشّورى
↓
Majlis Al Shura

يقوم مجلس العائلة الحاكمة، خلال ثلاثة أيام من شغور منصب السلطان، بتحديد من تنتقل إليه ولاية الحكم. فإذا لم يتفق مجلس العائلة الحاكمة على اختيار سلطان للبلاد قام مجلس الدفاع بتثبيت من أشار به السلطان في رسالته الى مجلس العائلة.

Can we say شغر *in place of* شغور*? If yes, which one do you prefer?*

The Royal Family Council shall, within three days of the throne falling vacant, determine the successor to the throne. If the Royal Family Council does not agree on a choice of a Sultan for the Country, the Defence Council together with the Chairman of Majlis Al Dawla, the Chairman of Majlis Al Shura, and the Chairman of the Supreme Court along with two of his most senior deputies, shall instate the person designated by His Majesty the Sultan in his letter to the Royal Family Council. (the Omani Constitution, article 6).

Here, the translator decided to add more than three lines. What is your opinion about this addition? Is it justified? Discuss.

مجلس النّواب
↓
The Council of Representatives

يتكون مجلس النواب من عدد من الاعضاء بنسبة مقعد واحد لكل مائة الف نسمة من نفوس العراق يمثلون الشعب العراقي باكمله، يتم انتخابهم بطريق الاقتراع العام السري المباشر، ويراعى تمثيل سائر مكونات الشعب فيه.

Note that a disjunctive hamza همزة قطع *should be used in words like* أعضاء*,* ألف*, and* أكمله*. What about* انتخاب*? Is it spelt correctly?*

Can we say مجلس الأسرة *here? If no, what is the difference between* أسرة *and* عائلة*?*

Can we say يحدد *in place of* يقوم بتحديد*?*

The Council of Representatives shall consist of a number of members, at a ratio of one seat per 100,000 Iraqi persons representing the entire Iraqi people. They shall be elected through a direct secret general ballot. The representation of all components of the people shall be upheld in it. (the Iraqi Constitution, article 49 no 1).

Here again a disjunctive hamza همزة قطع *should be used in words like* ألف*,* أعضاء *and* بأكمله*. What about* انتخابهم *and* الاقتراع*? Are they spelt correctly?*

مجلس الأمة
↓
Parliament

تناط السلطة التشريعية بمجلس الامة والملك ويتألف مجلس الامة من مجلسي الاعيان والنواب.

The Legislative Power shall be vested in the Parliament and the King. The Parliament shall consist of the Senate and the House of Representatives. (the Jordanian Constitution, article 25).

Here again a disjunctive hamza همزة قطع *should be used in words like* أمة *and* أعيان*.*

Discussion

1. How would you define legal translation?
2. Why is legal translation different from other types of translation? Discuss.
3. According to the communicative purpose, how would you classify legal texts?
4. According to the subject matter, how would you classify legal texts?
5. According to the reader, how would you classify legal texts?
6. In this chapter, legal texts are classified into many types by several scholars. Which classification do you prefer? And why?

7. What is the difference between Bhatia's classification and Cao's classification?
8. Why is the process of writing in legislative texts different from other types of writing? Discuss.

Assignment 1

The following hybrid text is taken from a newspaper titled اليوم السابع (December 7, 2021). Your task is to correct any spelling or grammatical mistakes, identify the text type of each paragraph by referring to one of the classifications discussed in this chapter and then translate the whole text into English:

Text type

تمكنت هيئة الرقابة الإدارية من ضبط عميد معهد للدراسات العليا، ومدير عام المشتريات بإحدى الجامعات، لتلقيهم مبالغ مالية على سبيل الرشوة من أحد المتعاملين مع الجامعة، وتناول البعض سؤال "ما هي جريمة الرشوة؟ وما هي عقوبتها في القانون؟"، والإجابة على هذا السؤال.

Note that in Arabic, we say الإجابة عن, not على.

هي متاجرة الموظف العام في أعمال وظيفته عن طريق الطلب، أو الأخذ أو قبوله لنفسه أو لغيره عطية من أجل القيام بعمل أو الامتناع عن عمل، يعد من أعمال وظيفته أو الاخلال بواجب من واجبات وظيفته.

Can we replace من أجل here with words like بغية, بقصد, بنية, بهدف, لكي, كي, etc.? Discuss.

عقوبة جريمة الرشوة:

عقوبة جريمة الرشوة تختلف من واقعة إلى أخرى، عما إذا كان الشخص المرتشي موظف عام، أو شخص عادي، ونص القانون على عقوبة الرشوة من المادة 103 حتى المادة 111 من قانون العقوبات.

Is it كان الشخص المرتشي موظف عام، أو شخص عادي or كان الشخص المرتشي موظفًا عامًا، أو شخصًا عاديًا? Discuss.

المادة 103

كل موظف عمومي طلب لنفسه أو لغيره أو قبل أو أخذ وعداً أو عطية لأداء عمل من أعمال وظيفته يعد مرتشياً ويعاقب بالسجن المؤبد وبغرامة لا تقل عن ألف جنيه ولا تزيد على ما أعطى أو وعد به.

Is there any difference between السّجن and الحبس? If no, can we say الحبس المؤبد or these words do not collocate well? Discuss.

Is it عما إذا كان or فيما إذا كان? Discuss.

Assignment 2

The following text titled '*Alimony*' is taken from '*Investopedia*' (www.investopedia.com). Your task is to

1. Identify the text type according to Trosborg's classification of legal texts.
2. Identify the text type according to Sager's classification of legal texts according to their readership.
3. Translate it into Arabic, paying extra attention to the differences between the interfacing languages/cultures.

Alimony

Alimony, also known as "spousal support" or "spousal maintenance", refers to the obligation of an individual to provide their spouse with financial support after a separation or divorce.

Traditionally, alimony was the sole obligation of a husband, but in modern times, wives can be responsible to pay support to their husbands, especially in cases where her income is considerably higher than his. To explore this concept, consider the following alimony definition.

What Is Alimony?

The concept of alimony dates back to the Babylonian Code of Hammurabi, from ancient Mesopotamia more than 1700 years BC.

This ancient law provided that a man must provide sustenance to a woman who has born his children, so that she can raise them. The history of alimony, and concept of spousal support, is mentioned in many codes and laws throughout history, and the modern concept of alimony came from English common law. Through the early history of alimony, English courts believed that, if a man and woman separated, he should continue to support her until the divorce is legally ended.

In nineteenth century, it became common place for a man to be ordered to pay his wife alimony if he was at fault for the divorce. If the women committed any acts that lead to the divorce, however, the courts considered her acts to be a forfeiture of the alimony. As time went on, the United States began seeing more no-fault divorces, which required changes to the alimony process. In the 1970s, the U.S. Supreme Court determined that ordering only men to pay alimony constituted gender bias. This decision resulted in more women being ordered to pay spousal support.

Factors Affecting Alimony

Each state has statutes, or guidelines, that determine the factors affecting alimony, and the amount of alimony that should be paid. Some states, such as Texas and Utah, have guidelines that are more explicit as to how much alimony should be ordered, and for how long it should be paid. For example, in Texas, alimony may be ordered for 5, 7, or 10 years, depending on the length of the marriage, and the amount that may be ordered is limited to 20 percent of the payee's income, or $5,000 per month, whichever is greater. Checking an online alimony calculator may give an individual an idea of how much alimony would be required in their case. In states such as California and New York, the factors affecting alimony, and guidelines for determining the amount and length of time, are very vague, giving the judge quite a bit of latitude.

In these cases, the judge considers several factors when determining the amount of support, including:

- Length of the marriage. Most states require the couple to have been married for a minimum amount of time.
- Time separated while still married. Some states do not recognize separation as a factor affecting alimony, so if a couple is married for 6 years and separated for 4 more years; it is considered a 10-year marriage. Other states consider the period of separation different from the actual marriage.
- Age of the parties. Many courts believe that if the parties are younger, they are more employable, and able to get on with their lives easier after a divorce. The older the couple is, the harder it might be to find or start a career.
- Income of both parties. The courts look at the income of both parties and adjust the alimony to enable the receiving spouse to live according to the means to which they have become accustomed.
- Future financial prospects. While alimony is calculated based on what the parties earn at the time of the divorce, in the event one spouse is likely to have a significant increase in the near future, it may affect the amount awarded.
- Health of both parties. Poor health constitutes more need, so if one party needs medical support, the other person may have to pay more alimony.

References

Adab, B. J. 1997. *Translation Strategies and Cross-Cultural Constraints: A Case Study of the Translation of Advertising Texts.* Unpublished doctoral dissertation. Aston: Aston University.

Alcaraz Varó, E. 2009. Isomorphism and Anisomorphism in the Translation of Legal Texts. In *Translation Issues in Language and Law*, ed. F. Olson, R.A. Lorz, and D. Stein, 182–192. London/New York: Palgrave Macmillan.

Almanna, A. 2014. *Translation Theories Exemplified from Cicero to Pierre Bourdieu.* München: Lincom Europa Academic Publishers.

Baker, M. 1992/2011. *In Other Words.* London/New York: Routledge.

Bhatia, V. K. 1982. *An Investigation into Formal and Functional Characteristics of Qualifications in Legislative Writing and its Application to English for Academic Legal Purposes.* Unpublished doctoral dissertation. Aston: Aston University.

Bhatia, V.K. 1993. *Analysing Genre—Language Use in Professional Settings*, Applied Linguistics and Language Study Series. London: Longman.

Cao, D. 2007. *Translating Law.* Clevedon: Multilingual Matters.

Crystal, D., and D. Davy. 1969. *Investigating English Style.* London: Longman.

Danet, B. 1980. Language in the Legal Process. *Law and Society Review* 14 (3): 447–564.

El-Farahaty, H. 2015. *Arabic-English-Arabic Legal Translation.* London/New York: Routledge.

Hall. M. F. 2008. *Discourse Analysis of Fictional Dialogue in Arabic to English Translation.* Unpublished doctoral dissertation. London: University of London.

Holmes, J. 1992/2013. *An Introduction to Sociolinguistics*, 4th edn. London/New York: Routledge.

Husni, R., and D. Newman. 2015. *Arabic-English-Arabic Translation.* London/New York: Routledge.

Kurzon, D. 1986. *It is Hereby Performed: Explorations in Legal Speech Acts.* Amsterdam/Philadelphia: John Benjamins Publishing Company.

Mellinkoff, D. 1963. *The Language of the Law.* Boston: Little Brown.

O'Barr, W.M. 1982. *Linguistic Evidence: Language, Power and Strategy in the Courtroom.* New York: Academic Press.

Sabra, M. M. A. 2003. ترجمة العقود *Translation of Contracts.* Cairo: Dār Al-Kutub Al-Qānūniyya.

Šarčević, S. 1997. *New Approach to Legal Translation.* London/Boston: Kluwer Law International.

Trosborg, A. 1997. *Rhetorical Strategies in Legal Language: Discourse Analysis of Statutes and Contracts.* Tübingen: Gunter Narr Verlag Tubingen.

CHAPTER 2

Global and Local Strategies

Translation Strategies

In translation studies, strategies (also known by some scholars as methods, procedures and techniques) have been investigated by a great number of scholars and theorists (cf. Vinay and Darbelnet 1958/1995; Nida 1964; Malone 1988; Newmark 1988; Baker 1992/2011; Chesterman 1993, 1997/2000; Almanna 2014, 2016 among others). Strategies are classified into *global strategies* (i.e. the general strategies adopted by the translator to deal with the whole text) and *local strategies* (i.e. the decisions taken by the translator when facing any problem while translating the text at hand, such as addition, omission, reordering, paraphrasing, etc.), as modelled in Fig. 2.1.

These factors are called 'translation brief'.

In this section, global strategies are discussed in a direct connection with legal texts. In order to be in a position to decide on the appropriateness of a particular global strategy and exclude others, translators need to consider a number of factors, such as the purpose of translation, intended readership, text type, generic convention and the like (for more details, see Almanna 2016: 39). As such, when the translator, having taken into account all these elements, adopts a global strategy where s/he tries to live up to the TL readers' expectations, thus ensuring issues such as acceptability, readability, naturalness, and so on, his/her translation is *reader-oriented*. In this type of translation, the

A. Almanna, *Legal Translation between English and Arabic*,
https://doi.org/10.1007/978-3-031-14838-5_2

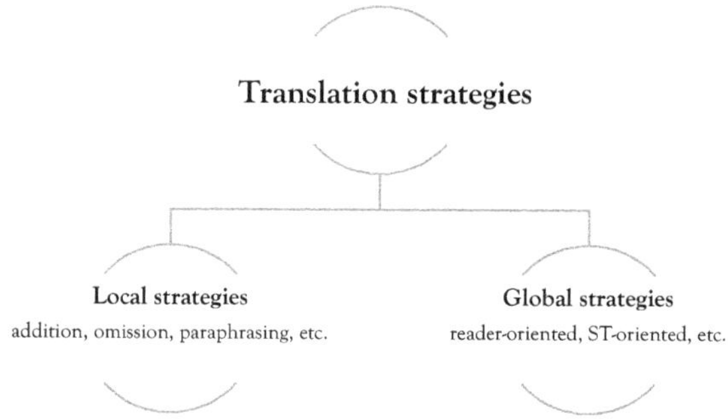

Fig. 2.1 Classification of translation strategies

relationship between the source text (ST) and target text (TT) is weak as the translator has more freedom while translating the text at hand. However, when the translator adopts a translation where s/he tries to produce a TT very close to the ST, thus safeguarding accuracy at the expense of acceptability, readability, idiomaticity, and the like, his/her translation is *ST-oriented*.

Do you agree? Discuss.

As shown in the first chapter, legal texts can be classified into many a type. Such a classification will be of great importance for translators to decide on the appropriateness of a particular global strategy and exclude others. A reader-oriented translation could be used when we translate, for example lawyers' speech with their clients in their offices, but it cannot be used to translate a legislative text. To make what I have in my mind clear, the following example extracted along with its translation from Hatim et al. (1995: 176–177; also discussed in Chap. 6 of this book) can be discussed:

Can we use يستحق *in place of* استحق*? Discuss by supporting your answer with authentic examples.*

إذا أُصيب المتعاقد بجرح أو مرض يمنعانه من أداء عمله بصورة مؤقتة استحقّ إجازة مرضية مدتها شهر واحد براتب كامل ويجوز تمديدها شهرين آخرين بنصف راتب وذلك عن كلّ سنة كاملة من سنوات الخدمة.

If the Contracted Party is stricken with an illness or an injury which temporarily prevents him from performing his work, he shall be entitled to sick leave of one month on full pay, which may be extended by a further two months on half pay, for each full year of service.

As can be seen, this text is taken from a contract; therefore, it belongs to *legislative texts* (according to

Bhatia's classification) and *private legal texts* (according to Cao's classification). Further, its language is not used in courtrooms by prosecutors, witnesses, lawyers, and judges, nor is it used by lay people when talking about law. Having taken into consideration the text type, purpose of communication, and readership, the translators decided to adopt a global strategy that would safeguard accuracy at the expense of acceptability, readability, authenticity, and idiomaticity that feed into naturalness.

To reinforce this point, the following example taken from Al-Aqaileh (2015: 205–211; also discussed in Chap. 6 of this book) can be considered:

Rewrite the first sentence by using the active form.

بشكل عام *can be replaced with* عمومًا.

بشكل عام، فإن الحق هو مصلحة معترف بها ومحمية من قبل قواعد القانون. محل الحق قد يكون شيئاً مادياً (ملموساً) مثل حق الملكية المقرر على قطعة من الأرض أو شيئاً غير مادي (غير ملموس) .... وبشكل عام فإن الحقوق القانونية يمكن أن تقسّم إلى حقوق كاملة وحقوق ناقصة، وحقوق إيجابية وحقوق سلبية، وحقوق عينية وحقوق شخصيّة، وحقوق عامة وحقوق خاصة.

'rights in personam' *can be replaced with* 'personal rights'. *What about* 'rights in rem'?

Generally speaking, a right is an interest recognized and protected by the rules of law. The object of the right may be a material thing, such as the right of ownership over a piece of land, or immaterial thing … In general, legal rights can be categorized into: perfect and imperfect rights; positive and negative rights; rights *in rem* and rights *in personam*; and public and private rights.

As one may notice, the above text is taken from a textbook that explains legal rights in general; therefore, it is an academic text (Bhatia's classification) and a legal scholarly text (Cao's classification). With this in mind, the translator can adopt a translation that strikes a balance between accuracy, on the one hand, and acceptability and readability, on the other. As it is not a legislative text whose function is to impose an obligation and prohibition, confer rights and give permission, and so on, but rather, it is just a legal scholarly text explaining a legal issue, the translator can for example

Can you think of more local strategies other than those suggested here?

- add a linking word, such as *further*, as in:
  Generally speaking, a right is an interest recognized and protected by the rules of law. Further, the object of the right may be …
- join two sentences together by using a relative pronoun, such as *whose*, as in:

Generally speaking, a right whose object of the right may be … is an interest recognized and protected by the rules of law.

- change a non-finite clause to a finite clause, as in: Generally speaking, a right is an interest which is recognized and protected by the rules of law.
- delete some words, as in: Generally speaking, a right is an interest recognized and protected by law. The object of the right may be material, such as the right of ownership over a piece of land, or immaterial….

Local Strategies

How would you define 'adequate translation'?

Local strategies, as hinted above, can be defined as the decisions taken by the translator when facing any problem while translating the text at hand, such as addition, omission, reordering, paraphrasing, etc. In translating between language A and language B, the local strategies opted for by the translators should mirror the global strategy adopted by them before embarking on the actual act of translating. If the global strategy is ST-oriented (see the previous section), then the local strategies should be in line with this global strategy adopted in order to produce an adequate translation. So much is the case with a reader-oriented translation. The local strategies should be in line with the global strategy adopted in order to produce an adequate translation. With this in mind, local strategies can also be divided into two main types, namely (1) ST-oriented and (2) reader-oriented mirroring the two types of global strategies, as shown in this Fig. 2.2:

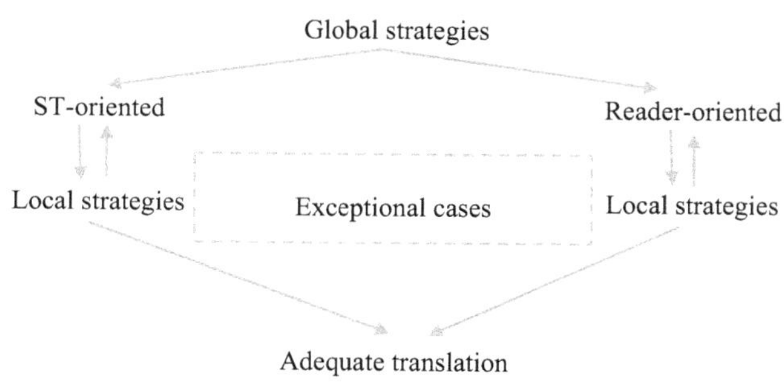

Fig. 2.2 The relationship between global strategies and local strategies

To make this point clear, the following example extracted from the Omani Constitution, article 44, 9, can be considered:

Is this a pure literal translation or not? If yes, what about 'and Muscat is its Capital' *that should be* 'and its Capital is Muscat'. *Discuss.*

سلطنة عمان دولة عربية إسلامية مستقلة ذات سيادة تامة عاصمتها مسقط.

The Sultanate of Oman is an Arab, Islamic, Independent State with full sovereignty and Muscat is its Capital.

In translating legislative texts, in particular constitutions, the most appropriate translation is the one, which is very close to the original text, i.e. ST-oriented. Here, in translating this article, the translator decided to opt for a literal translation without addition, omission, reordering, and the like, thereby producing a pure ST-oriented translation. However, it is worth mentioning that at times due to the differences between the interfacing languages/cultures the translators find themselves in a situation where they act against this 'golden rule'. To put it differently, they might add, delete, reorder, etc. while their global strategy is ST-oriented. To explain, the following example extracted from the United Nations Convention against Corruption can be considered:

Try to translate the same article literally without any syntactic structuring to discover by yourself whether the syntactic structuring opted for by the translator is justified or not.

Each State Party [Subject] shall furnish [verb] copies of its laws that give effect to this article and of any subsequent changes to such laws or a description thereof [Complex Direct Object] to the Secretary-General of the United Nations [Indirect Object] … (article 23, 2)

تزوّد [verb] كل دولة طرف [subject] الأمين العام للأمم المتحدة [indirect Object] بنسخ من قوانينها المنفذة لهذه المادة وبنسخ من أي تغييرات تدخل على تلك القوانين لاحقا أو بوصف لها [Complex Direct Object] ....

In this example, as one may observe, the translator decided to restructure the sentence syntactically by placing the indirect object, i.e. '*the Secretary-General of the United Nations*, before the direct object, i.e. *copies of its laws that give effect to this article and of any subsequent changes to such laws or a description thereof.* This local strategy, i.e. syntactic restructuring, is somehow justified as adhering to the original syntactic structure, thereby producing a pure ST-oriented translation, might affect issues, such as readability, acceptability, and authenticity that feed into naturalness.

Now, let us move on to touch on the common local strategies opted for by legal translators when translating between Arabic and English. They can be summarized as follows:

1. **Literal translation**

A literal translation can be defined as a translation in which the translator can transfer the original expression, phrase, clause, sentence, and so on into the target text literally without any change, apart from those required by the grammar of the target language. However, a literal translation in this book is classified into two main types, namely a 'pure literal translation' and 'semi literal translation'.

Pure Literal Translation

A pure literal translation, to make a start, is a type of translation commonly used by legal translators, particularly when translating legislative texts; it refers to that type of translation in which the translator translates very close to the original text without any addition, omission, merging, substitution, etc., apart from those required by the target language grammar, as hinted above. To explain, the following example extracted from the Jordanian Constitution, article 3, can be considered:

If we delete 'the City of' *to have only* 'Amman', *will it be a pure literal translation? Discuss.*

مدينة عمان عاصمة المملكة ويجوز نقلها إلى مكان آخر بقانون خاص.

> The City of Amman is the capital of the Kingdom, and it may be transferred to another place by a special law.

Here, as can be seen, the translator transferred the original expressions, phrases, and clauses literally without any change, apart from replacing *idafa*-structure with *of*-structure and inserting the verb '*to be*'.

Semi Literal Translation

A semi literal translation is a kind of a literal translation in which the translator, for a variety of different reasons, such as to avoid repetition, for a greater comprehensibility or better style, overtly intervenes into the text to modify some parts of the text at hand, but the overall translation is still literal. By way of illustration, let us consider this example quoted from an Employment Contract for an Unspecified Period and translated by Hatim et al. (1995: 170):

What about translating يتمتع *into* 'be entitled to'? *Will it be considered a semi literal translation?*

يتمتع الطرف الثاني، أثناء العقد، بكل الامتيازات والحقوق التي يقرها نظام العمل في المملكة العربية السعودية والتي تنطبق على جميع موظفي الطرف الأول.

> During the period of this contract, the Second Party shall enjoy all the privileges and rights recognized by the Labour Law and which apply to all employees of the First Party.

Here, as can be seen, the overall translation is literal. This article was translated in a way which is very close to the original article in terms of reflecting the denotative meanings of the words as well as the grammatical categories used in the original text. However, the translators decided to move the adverbial '*during the period of this contract*' from its place to be put before the subject. So, it is a literal translation with a syntactic restructuring (see syntactic structuring for more details).

2. **Borrowing**

Borrowing, as a local strategy that can be employed by the translator, refers to the process of transferring a lexical item from the source language to the target language for a variety of different reasons, such as a gap in the lexicon of the target language, to add an element of local colour, to mention but a few. In the following article, the word شورى derived from شاور, i.e. exchange opinions and views, in مجلس الشورى that can be translated functionally into '*advisory council*' or '*consultative council*' is transferred from Arabic to English without any further explanation.

How would you translate يتولاها *literally?*

السلطة التشريعية يتولاها مجلس الشورى على الوجه المبين في هذا الدستور.

The Legislative Authority shall be vested in Al-Shoura Council as prescribed in this Constitution.

In this regard, it is worth noting that there are a number of words that are originated in an Islamic cultural context, such as شريعة, جهاد, إمام, etc., but they are now established words in the English language and were long integrated into the English dictionary. As such, in case of using one of them by the translator, while translating from Arabic into English, there will be an example of old borrowings, as in the following example taken from the Qatari Constitution (article 1) where the word شريعة is used.

Is it رئيس *or* رئيسي*? If both are correct, which one is more Arabic?*

قطر دولة عربية ذات سيادة مستقلة. دينها الإسلام والشريعة الإسلامية مصدر رئيسي لتشريعاتها، ونظامها ديمقراطي، ولغتها الرسمية هي اللغة العربية. وشعب قطر جزء من الأمة العربية.

Qatar is an independent sovereign Arab State. Its religion is Islam and Shari'a law shall be a main source of its legislations. Its political system is democratic. The Arabic Language shall be its official language. The people of Qatar are a part of the Arab nation.

The word شريعة from شرّع '*legislate*', شرعي '*legal*', etc. is first transferred from Arabic to English, then grammatically transposed to be used as an adjective.

3. Substitution

The word عام *can be translated into* 'public' *or* 'general' *depending on the context. Here we have an example of divergence as the denotative meaning of the word* عام *in Arabic is wider and less specific. Find more examples of divergence.*

Substitution refers to the process of replacing certain structures or culture-specific terms, and the like with other structures or terms in the target language due to the differences between the interfacing languages/culture. To explain, in the following example taken from the Omani Constitution, article 11 n° 5, المفعول المطلق 'absolute object' تعويضه تعويضا was replaced with the verb '*compensated*'.

الملكية الخاصة مصونة، فلا يمنع أحد من التصّرف في ملكه إلا في حدود القانون، ولا ينزع عن أحد ملكه إلا بسبب المنفعة العامة في الأحوال المبينة في القانون، وبالكيفية المنصوص عليها فيه، وبشرط تعويضه عنه تعويضا عادلا. والميراث حق تحكمه الشريعة الإسلامية.

Private ownership is safeguarded and no one shall be prevented from disposing of his property except within the limits of the Law. No property shall be expropriated except for the public interest in cases stipulated by the

Law and in the manner specified therein, provided that the person dispossessed shall be fairly compensated. Inheritance is a right governed by Islamic Sharia.

Below is another example taken from the Qatari Constitution (article 10).

أقسم بالله العظيم أن أحترم النظام الأساسي للدولة والقوانين، وأن أرعى مصالح المواطنين وحرياتهم رعاية كاملة، وأن أحافظ على استقلال الوطن وسلامة أراضيه.

"I swear by Allah the Almighty to honour the Basic Statute of the State and the Laws and to fully safeguard the interests of the Citizens and their freedom and to preserve the independence of the Country and its territorial integrity".

As can be observed, the absolute object أرعى ... رعاية is replaced with the verb '*safeguard*'. However, in the following example extracted from the same constitution (article 52), مقيم إقامة مشروعة, which is a form of absolute object was substituted with the noun phrase 'a legal resident' in a relative clause '*who is a legal resident*' due to the differences between the interfacing languages.

Why is إقامة *a form of absolute object? Discuss*

يتمتع كل شخص مقيم في الدولة إقامة مشروعة بحماية لشخصه وماله، وفقاً لأحكام القانون.

Every person who is a legal resident of the State shall enjoy protection to his person and property in accordance with the provisions of the law.

In the following example taken from the Iraqi Constitution (article 85), فيه is substituted with '*therein*' in place of being rendered literally as '*in it*':

Can we delete the word سير *from the original text without changing the meaning?*

يضع مجلس الوزراء نظاما داخليا لتنظيم سير العمل فيه.

The Council of Ministers shall establish internal bylaws to organize the work therein.

The adverb '*promptly*' in the following article taken from the Constitution of the UK (5.2) can be substituted with على وجه السرعة or على الفور, thus leading to transposition as well as a unit shift.

In this text type, can we opt for بشكل سريع *as an equivalent to* 'promptly'*? Discuss.*

Anyone who is arrested shall, at the time of arrest, be informed in a language which they understand of the reasons for their arrest and shall be promptly informed of any charges against them.

يبلغ أي شخص يلقى القبض عليه، في لحظة إلقاء القبض وباللغة التي يفهمها، بأسباب إلقاء القبض، ويبلغ على الفور بالتهم الموجه ضده.

In a similar way, the preposition phrase بالإجماع used in this example taken from the Iraqi Constitution (article 138) was replaced with an adverb, i.e. 'unanimously':

In Arabic يتخذ قرارًا *is an example of unmarked collocation that lends itself to* 'to make a decision'. *However, the translator opted for* 'to issue a decision'. *Did s/he change the unmarked collocation to marked one? Further, what about* 'to take a decision'. *Discuss.*

رابعاً: يتخذ مجلس الرئاسة قراراته بالإجماع ويجوز لأي عضو أن ينيب أحد العضوين الآخرين مكانه.

Fourth: The Presidency Council shall issue its decisions unanimously and any member may delegate to one of the two other members to take his place.

In this example extracted from the Qatari Constitution (article 33), المفعول لأجله 'accusative of purpose' was substituted with a non-finite clause of purpose introduced by '*in order to*'.

تعمل الدولة على حماية البيئة وتوازنها الطبيعي، تحقيقاً للتنمية الشاملة والمستدامة لكل الأجيال.

The State shall preserve the environment and its natural balance in order to achieve comprehensive and sustainable development for all generations.

4. Expansion

Expansion results from a variety of different local strategies, such as addition, paraphrasing, unpacking and explicitation. Such expansion occurs due to, for example, the lexical item used in the original text is not lexicalized in the target language or culturally specific. At times, the translator while trying to meet the requirements of the genre or make the target text clear, adds, unpacks or paraphrases. At other times, the original social deixis makes references to gender or social classes, hence the importance of expansion.

Think of more types of expansion.

Unpacking

Unpacking, as a local strategy, is used when there is no established equivalent in the target language. For example, the word متعاقد is usually unpacked, i.e. its main components are analyzed by dint of making a pre-transferring adjustment, when translating into English. As such, متعاقد means الطرف/الدولة المتعاقد(ة) (pre-transferring adjustment), thus lending itself to a contracted party/state (unpacking). The following example quoted from Hatim et al. (1995: 176–7) can be considered:

What is the difference between الآتية *and* التّالية *in Arabic?*

المادة 4: تؤمن الوزارة للمتعاقد ولعائلته تذاكر السفر الجوي الآتية:

أ- من وطنه إلى المملكة في بداية مدة العقد مالم يكن مقيمًا بالمملكة عند تعينه.

ب- من المملكة إلى موطنه ذهابًا وإيابًا مرة كل سنة أثناء مدة العقد عندما يرخص له بإجازة عادية. [...]

Can we consider the translation of موطنه *into* 'his home country' *as an example of unpacking? Discuss*

Article 4

The Ministry shall provide the Contracted Party and his dependents with the following air tickets:

a. From his home country to the Kingdom at the beginning of the contract unless he is resident in the Kingdom at the time of his appointment;
b. Return tickets from the Kingdom to his home country once every year during the period of the contract and when he is permitted a normal leave; [...]

What is your opinion about translating عائلته *into* 'his dependents'?

In the following example extracted from Hatim et al. (1995: 82–3), the lexical items القاصر and المُعرّف need to be unpacked while translating into English.

في المجلس الشرعي المعقود لدي أنا ... قاضي ... الشرعي حضر ...
من ... وسكان ... وطلب تثبيت ولايته على القاصرتين ... بنات ابنه
المرحوم ... وبحضور المعرفين ... و ... كلاهما سكان ... اللذين أخبرا
بأمانته واستقامته وكفائته وأهليته لذلك فقط ثبت ولايته على القاصرين
المذكورين.

What is your opinion about translating لدي *into* 'in my presence'?

In the Legal Council convened in my presence, I ..., the Religious Judge of ..., have received Mr. ... from and resident in ... who applied for confirmation of his custody of the two legal minors ... and ..., daughters of his deceased son Mr ... in the presence of two identifying witnesses Mr. ... and Mr. ... both resident in ... and who informed me of his honesty, uprightness, eligibility and competence. I have accordingly confirmed his custody of the forementioned legal minors ...

A 'unit shift' occurs when a smaller unit is translated into a larger one, as in translating a word into a phrase, etc.; therefore, any example of expansion or reduction results in a 'unit shift'. Do you agree?

As can be seen, these two words القاصر and المُعرّف were translated into '*legal minors*' and '*identifying witnesses*' respectively, thus resulting in a unit shift.

In marriage contracts, words like زوج, زوجة, بالغ, عاقل, ثيب, and the like are often used. These words, for the sake of clarity and due to the differences between the interfacing languages, sometimes, depending on the context in which they are used, need to be unpacked. By way of illustration, let us consider this example taken from Hatim et al. (1995: 86–7) to see if they need to be unpacked or not.

Note that a conjunctive hamza همزة وصل*, not a disjunctive hamza* همزة قطع*, should be used in this example ; therefore, we should write* اسم *not* إسم*.*

الصنعة	الجنسية	العمر	مكان الإقامة	البلد	الإسم الكامل
					الزوج—الرجل—البالغ—العاقل—الأعزب
					الزوجة—البنت—بكر / ثيب—بالغة—عاقلة

Full name	*Town*	*Place of Residence*	*Age*	*Nationality*	*Profession*
The male spouse, a bachelor/ married man of legal age and of sound mind					
The female spouse, a virgin/ non-virgin of legal age and of sound mind					

Here, as one may observe, most of them were unpacked. الزوج, to begin with, was translated into '*the male spouse*'. The lexical item '*male*' added to reflect the gender is redundant as the word '*man*' can see to this. With this in mind, one may opt for a translation which is very close to the original text as in:

> The male spouse, of legal age, of sound mind, bachelor.
> The female spouse, virgin/non-virgin, of legal age, and of sound mind

Further, it is worth mentioning that in Arabic, there is a difference between بلد meaning '*country*' and بلدة '*town*', which is a scaled down version of مدينة '*city*'. As such, opting for '*town*' as an equivalent to بلد can be considered as a semantic shift. Alternatively, if this is the intended meaning of the word بلد in the country in which this contract is formed, then it can be considered as a contextual translation where the context is given a front seat here.

Paraphrase

Closely related to unpacking is paraphrase. So, when the translators, after analyzing the main components of the lexical item, phrase, etc., feel the intended meaning might not be reflected accurately by falling back on unpacking, they can go for paraphrasing, which is a kind of translation by illustration, i.e. using more words. By way of example, the following text extracted from Hatim et al. (1995: 98–9) can be considered:

Which one is more Arabic… قرر قائلاً إنني or…قرر قائلًا أنني ?

... قرر قائلاً إنني كنت قد طلقت زوجتي ومدخولتي الشرعية ... طلقة رجعية بموجب حجة الطلاق رقم ... تاريخ ... الصادرة عن محكمة ... الشرعية وحيث إنها مازالت في العدة الشرعية فأنني أرجعها إلى عصمتي وعقد نكاحي ...

He resolved, stating: I revocably divorced my wife with whom I had legally consumed the marriage … in accordance with Divorce Certificate No. … dated … issued by the Religious Court of …, and whereas she is still within the legally prescribed waiting period before remarrying, I return her to my matrimonial authority and to my contract of marriage.

Note that in Islamic court documents, the word حجة *is commonly used in place of* شهادة *or* وثيقة*, thus lending itself to* 'certificate'*, as in* حجة إرث 'Certificate of Legacy'*,* حجة ولاية 'Certificate of Custody'*,* حجة إبراء 'Certificate of Non-liability'*,* حجة إسلام 'Certificate of Conversion to Islam'*, etc.*

Here, in the translation of this text, the translator employed several local strategies, such as substitution, transposition, unpacking, and paraphrase. To explain, المفعول المطلق 'Cognate Object' in طلقت طلقة رجعية (also used in Arabic in this way طلقت تطليقًا رجعيًا) was substituted with '*I revocably divorced*'. In this substitution, to elaborate, we have an example of transposition where the adjective رجعية lends itself to an adverb '*revocably*'. As regards عصمتي, it was unpacked by virtue of analyzing its main components, thus being translated into '*my matrimonial authority*'. The noun phrases مدخولتي الشرعية and العدة الشرعية were paraphrased respectively into '*with whom I had legally consumed the marriage*' and '*the legally prescribed waiting period before remarrying*'.

It is worth noting that by dint of the grammatical forms and content specifications used in the original text, the action of divorcing his wife occurred before the merged process (i.e. mental process and verbal process) expressed by قرر قائلا. This can be grammaticalized by opting for the past perfect '*I had revocably divorced my wife*'; however, the translators decided not to do so.

To reinforce this point, the following example quoted from Hatim et al. (1995: 96–7) can be discussed:

What is your opinion about translating حضر *into 'I received'? Can we avoid such modulation? Discuss.*

في المجلس الشرعي المعقود لدي أنا ... قاضي ... الشرعي حضر المكلف شرعًا ... الولي/الوصي على القاصر ... بموجب حجة ... الصادرة من محكمة ... الشرعية رقم ... تاريخ ... وبعد التعريف عليه من قبل المكلفين شرعًا وهم ...

In the Legal Council convened in my presence, I ..., the Religious Judge of ..., received the legally capable ... guardian of the legal minor ... in accordance with the Certificate of ... issues by the Religious Court of ... No. ... dated ... and after his identification by the legally capable trustworthy and reliable informants ....

In the following example translated by Husni and Newman (2015: 145), the word عدول in شهود عدول was paraphrased:

إنه في يوم ... الموافق ...
بعون الله اجتمع كل من وبحضور الشهود العدول المبين أسمائهم بباطن هذا العقد ...

On this the ... day of ... A.H., corresponding to ...
With the help of God the Almighty, have appeared in the presence of witnesses of reputable background and sound character, whose names are stated in the present contract, the following: (p.147)

How would you translate 'competent witnesses' *into Arabic?*

Here, as can be seen, the translators, in place of opting for '*competent witnesses*', thus naturalizing the text, decided to paraphrase the word عدول, thereby expanding the text. A competent witness, to illustrate, refers to a witness who has the sufficient mental capacity to perceive, remember, and narrate what s/he saw or experienced, i.e. it has something to do with capacity, while what was suggested by the translators has something to do with the character and the positive qualities that it has.

Explicitation

Explicitation refers to the process of becoming explicit or causing something, which is implicitly expressed in the original text, to become explicit for greater compressibility, better style, or due to the differences between the interfacing languages. To explain, the following two examples taken from the Omani Constitution (article 2 and article 38) can be considered:

How would you translate لا جريمة ولا عقوبة إلا بنص*?*

لا جريمة ولا عقوبة إلا بناء على قانون، ولا عقاب إلا على الأفعال اللاحقة للعمل بالقانون الذي ينص عليها.

There shall be no crime except by virtue of a Law. There shall be no punishment, except for acts subsequent to the entry into force of the Law wherein such acts are stated.

In this example, لا النافية للجنس 'la of absolute negation' is used three times, namely لا جريمة, لا عقوبة and لا عقاب. In these structures, to elaborate, there is a noun deleted, i.e. موجود(ة), that needs to be brought back while translating into English, thus lending itself to '*there shall be no* …' in the above example.

Below is the second example

الحفاظ على الوحدة الوطنية وصيانة أسرار الدولة واجب على كل مواطن.

Re-translate this article by using 'shall' *in this way* 'Every citizen shall …'*. Then, comment on the local strategies opted for by you.*

Preserving the national unity and safeguarding the secrets of the State is a duty incumbent upon every Citizen.

In this equation sentence, there is an implicit word, i.e. مفروض '*imposed*', that can be invoked by virtue of the grammatical form and content specification used. This implicit word was translated as '*incumbent*'.

Addition

At times, the legal translators, while translating between Arabic and English, opt for adding certain elements for a variety of different reasons, such as to avoid confusion, reflect a semiotic dimension, meet the requirements of the genre, or for the purpose of greater comprehensibility. To explain, let us discuss this text taken along with its translation from Husni and Newman (2015: 145):

The word صداق *can be replaced with* مهر *in some other countries.*

طلب الطرف الأول من الطرف الثاني الارتباط بها على كتاب الله وسنة رسوله بقوله لها أريد الزواج منك على كتاب الله وسنة رسوله وعلى مذهب الإمام أبي حنيفة النعمان والصداق المسمّى بيننا ووافقته الطرف الثاني على ذلك بقولها له قبلت الزواج منك.

The groom hereby requests to enter into a bond with the bride, in accordance with the Holy Quran and the Sunna of the Prophet Muhammed, by saying, 'I wish to marry you, in accordance with the Holy Quran, the

Sunna of the Prophet Muhammed and the Hanafi School of Islamic Jurisprudence, and in exchange of the dowry fixed between us'. The bride hereby agrees to this by saying, 'I accept to marry you'.

In this example, as one may notice, the translators, opted for several local strategies, namely 'addition', 'specification', 'contextual translation', 'literal translation', and 'omission' (for more details, see Chap. 3 of this book where this example is discussed from a different perspective). As regards addition, they added the phrase '*Islamic Jurisprudence*' while translating the word مذهب into '*school*'. It is worth noting that the denotative meaning of the word '*school*' is wider and less specific when it is compared with مذهب that invokes in our mind a *religion*-frame. As such, for the sake of clarity and with the potential to reflect the *religion*-frame associated with the term مذهب, the translators decided to add the phrase '*Islamic Jurisprudence*', thus expanding the text.

5. Reduction

Reduction results from a variety of different local strategies, such as omission, convergence, condensing, and merging. Such reduction frequently occurs in translating from Arabic to English or *vice versa*. The main reason for such reduction is when the element is not important to the development of the text and omitting it does not harm the author's intention or alter the text-type focus but, on the contrary, retaining it in the TT might complicate the structure and strike the TL receptor as unusual. Other reasons for such reduction can be to avoid repetition, have a better style, maintain a desired level of naturalness, and the like.

Omission

Omission refers to the process of ignoring certain elements while translating from language A to language B. To explain, the following example taken from the Qatari Constitution (article 10) can be discussed:

ولي العهد *can be also translated into* 'Crown Prince', *as in* 'the Crown Prince of Spain'.

يؤدي ولي العهد عند تعيينه أمام الأمير اليمين التالية: "أقسم بالله العظيم أن أحترم الشريعة الإسلامية والدستور والقانون، وأن أصون استقلال البلاد وأحافظ على سلامة أقاليمها، وأن أذود عن حريات الشعب ومصالحه، وأن أكون مخلصا للوطن والأمير.

Is it 'the following of oath' *or* 'the following oath'?

The Heir Apparent, on his appointment, shall take the following of oath: "I swear by Almighty God to respect Shari'a law, the Constitution and the law, maintain the independence of the State and safeguard its territorial integrity, defend the freedom and interests of its people, and be loyal to the State and the Emir."

Here, as one may notice, in changing the noun أقاليم to an adjective '*territorial*' (transposition), translating سلامة into '*integrity*' (semantic shift), and modifying الشريعة الإسلامية '*Islamic Shari'a*' to 'Shari'a law' (transposition + semantic shift), the translator decided to ignore the phrase أمام الأمير (omission). Similarly, in the following example extracted from the Egyptian Constitution, certain elements were not translated into English:

Can we delete the lexical item جماهير *to say* ?نحن شعب مصر *Discuss.*

نحن جماهير شعب مصر تصميما ويقينا وإيمانا وإدراكا بكل مسئولياتنا الوطنية والقومية والدولية وعرفانا بحق الله ورسالاته وبحق الوطن والأمة وبحق المبدأ والمسئولية الإنسانية وباسم الله وبعون الله، نعلن في هذا اليوم الحادي عشر من شهر سبتمبر سنة 1971، أننا نقبل ونمنح لأنفسنا هذا الدستور، مؤكدين عزمنا الأكيد على الدفاع عنه وعلى حمايته وعلى تأكيد احترامه.

We, the people of Egypt, out of determination, confidence and faith in all national and international responsibilities, and in acknowledgement of God's right and His Heavenly Messages, and in the right of the country and nation, as well as of the principle and responsibility of mankind, and in the name of the Almighty and His assistance, declare on the 11th of September, 1971 that we accept, and grant, to ourselves this Constitution, affirming our determination to defend and protect it, and asserting our respect for it in letter and spirit.

How would you translate إدراكًا *and* يقينًا *to improve the quality of the translation suggested here?*

As can be seen, four accusatives of purpose were used in Arabic, namely تصميما, يقينا, إيمانا and إدراكا, but only three were translated. The accusative of purpose in إدراكا was left out, and يقينا was translated into '*confidence*', thus resulting in a semantic shift. In addition to that the lexical item أكيد in مؤكدين عزمنا الأكيد was left out and the phrase '*in letter and spirit*' was added.

Convergence

Find more examples of convergence.

Convergence, as opposite to divergence, has something to do with the denotative meaning of the word used. If the denotative meaning of the word used in the target text is wider and less specific, then we have a case of 'convergence'; otherwise, it is an example of 'divergence'. Convergence, to put it differently, occurs when two, or more than two, words, phrases, etc. used in the original text are converged into one word in the target text due to the differences between the interfacing languages. To explain, let us reconsider the previous example where the words الوطنية and القومية converged into one word, i.e. '*national*'. It is worth noting that the denotative meaning of the lexical item '*national*' is wider and less specific when it is compared with the original words وطني or قومي. Another example of convergence that results in reduction is the translation of '*solicitor*' and '*barrister*' into one word, i.e. محام in Arabic.

Condensing

Condensing occurs when the same idea expressed in the original text is made shorter by using fewer words; it is usually used to maintain a desired level of naturalness, have a better style, and the like. In this example extracted from the Omani Constitution, article 11, 3, the verb تقوم is used explicitly in تقوم على حفظها and implicitly in حسن استغلالها. In translating from Arabic to English, these structures might be condensed by first making a pre-transferring adjustment (تحفظها = تقوم على حفظها and تحسن استغلالها = تقوم على حسن استغلالها) and then translating them into English as '*preserve*' and '*utilize*'.

الثروات الطبيعية جميعها ومواردها كافة ملك للدولة، تقوم على حفظها وحسن استغلالها، بمراعاة مقتضيات أمن الدولة وصالح الاقتصاد الوطني. ...

جميع and كافة *were reduced to one word, i.e.* 'all'. *Can we consider this as an example of convergence? Discuss*

All natural wealth and resources thereof are the property of the State, which shall preserve and utilize them in the best manner taking into consideration the requirements of the security of the State and the interests of the national economy. ...

Similarly, in this example taken from the same constitution (article 6), we have two examples of condensing. يقوم بتحديد meaning يحدد (pre-transferring adjustment) was condensed to '*determine*' and من تنتقل إليه meaning الخلف (pre-transferring adjustment) was condensed to '*the successor*'.

يقوم مجلس العائلة الحاكمة، خلال ثلاثة أيام من شغور منصب السلطان، بتحديد من تنتقل إليه ولاية الحكم.

The Royal Family Council shall, within three days of the throne falling vacant, determine the successor to the throne.

To finish off this, let us consider this example taken from the Egyptian Constitution:

نحن جماهير شعب مصر؛ باسم الله وبعون الله نلتزم إلى غير ما حد، وبدون قيد أو شرط أن نبذل كل الجهود لنحقق ...

Which one is more Arabic باسم الله وبعون الله *or* باسم الله وعونه*? Discuss.*

We, the Egyptian people, in the name of God and by His assistance, pledge indefinitely and unconditionally to exert every effort to realize ...

Here, expressions such as إلى غير حد and بدون قيد أو شرط were condensed to '*indefinitely*' and '*unconditionally*' respectively.

Merging

What is the difference between 'convergence' and 'merging'? Discuss.

Merging occurs when two words semantically related are merged into one word as it might be difficult to maintain them in the target language without striking the target language's reader as unusual. Here, we talk about the translation of synonyms or near synonyms. As can be recognized, the semantically related words نشر and تعميم were merged into one word, i.e. '*spread*' in the translation of the Qatari Constitution, article 25:

What is the difference between نشر *and* تعميم*? Discuss.*

التعليم دعامة أساسية من دعائم تقدم المجتمع، تكفله الدولة وترعاه، وتسعى إلى نشره وتعميمه.

Education is one of the basic pillars of social progress. The state shall ensure, foster, and endeavor to spread it.

However, in a similar article taken from the Omani Constitution (article 13), the translator opted for maintaining such a semantic repetition when translating them into '*to disseminate and make accessible to all*'.

In these two examples, تقدم المجتمع *was translated differently. In your opinion, which one is more literal?*

التعليم ركن أساسي لتقدم المجتمع ترعاه الدولة وتسعى لنشره وتعميمه.

Education is a cornerstone for the progress of the Society which the State fosters and endeavours to disseminate and make accessible to all.

To reinforce this point, the words فنون and آداب in the following example taken from the Qatari Constitution, article 24, can be discussed:

In the Kuwaiti Constitution (article 14), the word آداب *was translated into* 'letters'*. What do you think of this translation?*

ترعى الدولة العلوم والآداب والفنون والتراث الثقافي الوطني، وتحافظ عليها وتساعد على نشرها، وتشجع البحث العلمي.

The State shall foster, preserve, and help disseminate sciences, arts, cultural and national heritage, and encourage scientific research.

Here, in addition to merging الآداب and الفنون into one word, i.e. '*arts*', the translator decided to opt for restructuring the components of the article for the sake of having a better style. To explain, in place of opting for compound sentences joined by the additive connector '*and*', the verbs, ترعى , تحافظ and تساعد على نشر were pieced together in a simple sentence '*The state shall foster, preserve, and help disseminate* ...'. As regards the words آداب وفنون, they can be translated into '*literature*' and '*(fine) arts*' respectively, as in the translation of this article taken from the Omani Constitution, article 13:

Which one is more Arabic ترعى وتحافظ الدولة *or* ترعى الدولة عليه وتحافظ عليه*?*

ترعى الدولة التراث وتحافظ عليه، وتشجع العلوم والفنون والآداب والبحوث العلمية وتساعد على نشرها.

The State shall foster and preserve the national heritage, encourage the sciences, arts, literature, scientific research and assist in their dissemination.

To make this point clear, let us discuss this formula usually used in marriage contracts (Hatim et al. 1995: 86–7):

The word وكيل *can be translated into* 'representative', 'agent' *or* 'attorney-in-fact'*, depending on the context. Can we consider this as an example of divergence? Discuss.*

قال وكيل الزوجة والدها مخاطبًا الزوج المذكور نفسه زوجتك وأنكحتك موكلتي ابنتي ... على مهر معجل قدره ... وتوابعه المذكورة ومهر مؤجل قدره ... فأجاب الزوج المذكور فورًا وأنا قبلت ورضيت بزواجها ونكاحها لنفسي على المهرين المذكورين وتوابعهما.

The representative for the female spouse (her father) said, addressing the aforementioned male spouse, "I have given my daughter ... to you in marriage for a dowry the down-payment of which is ..., the extras of which are mentioned above, and the deferred payment of which is …". The male spouse immediately replied, "I accepted your daughter in marriage and confirm the dowry's down-payment, deferred, and extras stipulated above.

Here, in this example, we have a case of semantic repetition made up of two synonymous words, namely زوّج and أنكح. The translators opted for merging the two synonymous words used in the source text into one phrase in the target text, i.e. '*to give her to you in marriage*'. The same holds true for the nouns زواج and نكاح derived from the aforementioned verbs when opting for merging them into one phrase, i.e. '*accepting your daughter in marriage*'. Another example of semantic repetition can be found in the use of the semantically related words قبلَ and رضى. These two words, to explain, are not fully synonymous; however, the translators opted for merging them into one word, which is '*to accept*'.

6. Shift

A shift can be defined here as any departure of literal translation in the process of moving from one language to another. A shift can be in the form of grammaticalization, lexicalization, semantic shift, transposition, or modulation.

Grammaticalization

What about 'unit shift'? Why is it excluded here? Discuss.

Grammaticalization refers to the process of translating a lexical item, phrase, etc. into a grammatical category, due to the differences between the interfacing languages. In this example taken from the preamble of the Egyptian Constitution, the emphasis placed on the whole period that began in the past and is seen as relevant to the moment of speaking is grammaticalized when opting for a combination of present tense and perfect progressive aspect.

The original text, by virtue of the evaluative word مجيدة*, is evaluative. Did the translator manage to reflect evaluativeness?*

نحن جماهير شعب مصر العامل على هذه الأرض المجيدة منذ فجر التاريخ والحضارة …

The verb 'to toil' *used in the target text means* 'to work extremely hard'. *In your opinion, is the translation accurate? Is it better to opt for* 'work'? *Discuss.*

We, the people of Egypt, who have been toiling on this great land since the dawn of history and the beginning of civilization …

As can be seen, by virtue of the grammatical form and content specification used in the original text, the emphasis is placed on (1) the whole period that began in the past (implicitly specified, i.e. فجر التاريخ والحضارة) and is seen as relevant to the moment of speaking and (2) the continuity of the act of working/toiling expressed by virtue of اسم الفاعل 'active participle'.

Lexicalization

By contrast, lexicalization, in this book, refers to the process of translating a grammatical category, such as a tense, aspect, mood, etc. into a lexical item or lexical items. To illustrate, the following example taken from the *Universal Declaration of Human Rights* can be considered:

> Whereas the peoples of the United Nations have in the Charter reaffirmed their faith in fundamental human rights, in the dignity and worth of the human person and in the equal rights of men and women and have determined to promote social progress and better standards of life in larger freedom, […].

> ولما كانت شعوب الأمم المتحدة قد أكدت في الميثاق من جديد إيمانها بحقوق الإنسان الأساسية وبكرامة الفرد وقدره وبما للرجال والنساء من حقوق متساوية وحزمت أمرها على أن تدفع بالرقي الاجتماعي قدماً وأن ترفع مستوى الحياة في جو من الحرية أفسح […]

What about وإذ أن شعوب العالم قد أكدت ... *? Will the translation be accurate? Discuss.*

Here, as one may observe, the combination of the present tense and perfect aspect '*have reaffirmed*' was lexicalized in Arabic into كانت+ قد + verb in the past. This is because Arabic, unlike English, does not have a grammatical category for aspect. The question that might rear its ugly head here is: Is the translation accurate? The answer is no. To explain, in the original text by the effect of the present perfect '*have reaffirmed*', the emphasis is placed on the whole period that started in the past (unspecified) and is seen as relevant to another point in the present. However, by virtue of كانت قد followed by a verb in the past أكدت, the emphasis is placed on the whole period that started in the past (unspecified) and is seen as relevant to another point in the past (unspecified), thereby resulting in a semantic shift. As regards the prefix '*re-*' attached to the complex word '*affirmed*' meaning again, it was accurately lexicalized into من جديد.

The verb يستفتي *was translated into* 'to seek public opinion'. *Can it be considered as an example of expansion? If yes, what do we call it?*

Semantic Shift

Semantic shift occurs when the meaning and/or function of a lexical item, phrase, etc. is modified by the translator while moving from one language to another. Although any type of semantic shift should be avoided while translating a legal document, in particular a legislative one, the translators at times find themselves in a situation where they have to opt for such a semantic shift. By way of illustration, the following example taken from the Qatari Constitution, article 6, can be considered:

Retranslate this article to have a pure literal translation

تحترم الدولة المواثيق والعهود الدولية، وتعمل على تنفيذ كافة الاتفاقيات والمواثيق والعهود الدولية التي تكون طرفا فيها.

The State shall respect the international charters and conventions, and strive to implement all international agreements, charters, and conventions it is party thereof.

Can we translate the verb يعمل *in this article into* 'to work'? *Discuss.*

Here, as one may notice, the overall translation is literal (see literal translation). However, it is literal with a minor semantic shift in the translation of تعمل على تنفيذ into '*strive to implement*'. It is a minor semantic shift that can be tolerated in such a text type as the verb '*to strive*' means to work, but by devoting serious effort or energy, thus lending itself in Arabic to يسعى. To avoid such a semantic shift, the translator can opt for '*shall implement*', thus shortening the structure. In this case, there will be an example of condensing (see reduction/condensing in this chapter).

Transposition

Transposition (also known as a 'class shift') refers to the process of changing the word-level categories through translation, as in translating a verb into a noun, a noun into an adjective, and the like. By way of explanation, the following example extracted from the Omani Constitution (article 16) can be considered:

What is the difference between إبعاد المواطن *and* نفيه?

لا يجوز إبعاد المواطنين أو نفيهم أو منعهم من العودة إلى السلطنة.

It is not permissible to deport, exile, or prevent Citizens from returning to the Sultanate.

Here, as can be observed, the prohibition expressed by لا يجوز was translated into '*it is not permissible*', thus resulting in some examples of transposition. The nouns نفي, إبعاد and منع were rendered into the verbs '*deport*', '*exile*', and '*prevent*'. It is worth mentioning that لا يجوز is usually translated into '*may not*' or '*shall not*' which also requires, in addition to changing those nouns to verbs, modulation, i.e. opting for the passive, as in

> Citizens may not be deported, exiled, or prevented from returning to the Sultanate.

To reinforce this point, below are two examples taken from the Qatari Constitution (articles 49 and 70):

وفقاً can be replaced with على وفق. Which one is more Arabic?

The expression المعمول بها can be replaced with المُطبقة in Arabic legal discourse.

> التعليم حق لكل مواطن وتسعى الدولة لتحقيق إلزامية ومجانية التعليم العام، وفقاً للنظم والقوانين المعمول بها في الدولة.

> All citizens have the right to education; and the State shall endeavor to make general education compulsory and free of charge in accordance with the applicable laws and regulations of the State.

In translating تسعى الدولة لتحقيق إلزامية ومجانية التعليم العام, there are some examples of transposition where the noun تحقيق was translated into an analytic causative expressed by '*to make*', the nouns إلزامية and مجانية were translated into the adjectives '*compulsory*' and '*free*'. Further, there is an example of reordering in dealing with وفقاً للنظم والقوانين المعمول بها في الدولة '*in accordance with the applicable laws and regulations of the State*' where the lexical item '*laws*' is put before '*regulations*'.

The word مراسيم is منصوبة 'accusative', but it is used without تنوين 'nunation' here. Why?

> يجوز للأمير في الأحوال الاستثنائية التي تتطلب اتخاذ تدابير عاجلة لا تحتمل التأخير، ويقتضي اتخاذها إصدار قوانين، ولم يكن مجلس الشورى منعقداً، أن يصدر في شأنها مراسيم لها قوة القانون.

> The Emir may, in the event of exceptional cases that require measures of utmost urgency which necessitate the issue of special laws and in case that Al-Shoura Council is not in session, issue pertinent decrees that have the power of law.

Here, the semantic repetition expressed by عاجلة لا تحتمل التأخير was translated into '*utmost urgency*'. The noun phrase, '*utmost urgency*', as one may notice, transposed the Arabic عاجلة لا تحتمل التأخير.

Modulation

Modulation occurs when the point of emphasis, the viewpoint, style, transitivity process, etc. is changed while translating from language A to language B, as shown in the following example extracted from the Qatari Constitution, article 2:

> عاصمة الدولة الدوحة. ويجوز أن يستبدل بها مكان آخر بقانون. وتمارس الدولة سيادتها على إقليمها، ولا يجوز لها أن تتنازل عن سيادتها أو أن تتخلى عن أي جزء من إقليمها.
>
> The capital of the State is Doha City; and it may be transferred to any other place by a law. The State shall exercise its sovereignty on its territory and it may not relinquish its sovereignty neither may it cede any part of its territory.

Here, as one may observe, the sentence ويجوز أن يستبدل بها مكان آخر بقانون was translated into '*and it may be transferred to any other place by a law*' that is ويجوز أن تُنقل إلى مكان آخر بقانون. Here, we have an example of modulation as the verb يستبدل '*to replace*' is changed to '*to transfer*'.

In the following example, for the sake of naturalness such issues as readability, acceptability, and well-formedness are given full consideration, thus resulting in an example of modulation where the equation sentence وهم متساوون في الحقوق والواجبات العامة was materialized by opting for the verb '*to share*'.

> المواطنون جميعهم سواسية أمام القانون، وهم متساوون في الحقوق والواجبات العامة، ولا تمييز بينهم في ذلك بسبب الجنس أو الأصل أو اللون أو اللغة أو الدين أو المذهب أو الموطن أو المركز الاجتماعي.
>
> All Citizens are equal before the Law and share the same public rights and duties. There shall be no discrimination amongst them on the ground of gender, origin, colour, language, religion, sect, domicile, or social status. (the Omani Constitution, article 17)

In this example بسبب *was translated into* 'on the ground of'. *Can you suggest another translation?*

Here, in this example the active form يبين فيه أسباب الحل where the implicit pronoun conjugated in the verb يبين refers back to the Emir was translated into passive, thus hiding the actor. This is an example of modulation that can easily be avoided by opting for a translation of the following kind '*in which he shall state the reasons for the dissolution*'.

للأمير أن يحل مجلس الشورى بمرسوم يبين فيه أسباب الحل، على أنه لا يجوز حل المجلس لذات الأسباب مرة أخرى، وإذا حل المجلس وجب إجراء انتخابات المجلس الجديد في موعد لا يتجاوز ستة أشهر من تاريخ الحل.

على أنه that can be replaced with شريطة أن, بشرط, على شرط, and the like was translated into 'however'. What do you think of this?

The Emir may dissolve the Council by a decree in which the reasons for the dissolution shall be stated; however, the Council shall not be dissolved twice for the same reasons. Where the Council is dissolved, the elections of the new Council shall take place within a period not exceeding six months as of the date of dissolution. (the Qatari Constitution, article 104)

In this sentence سقط حقه في... frequently used in Arabic legal discourse, the emphasis is placed on '*his right*' while in the target text, the emphasis is placed on the person when the translator opted for '*he shall forfeit his right*' roughly meaning مُلزَمٌ بالتّنازل عن حقه.

Note that a conjunctive hamza همزة وصل should be used in انقطاع and a disjunctive hamza همزة قطع should be used in إدانة.

أ- إذا انتهت خدمة المتعاقد بسبب الإنقطاع عن العمل سقط حقه في تذاكر العودة المستحقة له ولعائلته.
ب- إذا انتهت خدمة المتعاقد بسبب الإنقطاع أو فصله بقرار من مجلس المحاكمة أو ادانته جنائيًا سقط حقه في التعويض عن مدة الإجازة وفي مكافأة نهاية الخدمة.

a. If the service of the Contracted Party is terminated due to absence from work, he shall forfeit his right to the return tickets due to him and his dependents.
b. If the service of the Contracted Party is terminated due to absence from work, dismissal due to a court council decision or criminal conviction, he shall forfeit his right to the compensation for the period of leave and to the end-of-service payment. (Hatim et al. 1995: 180–1)

7. Syntactic restructuring

It occurs when the translator restructures the components of the sentence/clause syntactically due to the difference between the interfacing languages or to live up to the target language readers' expectations. To explain, the following example extracted from the United Nations Convention against Corruption can be considered:

> For the purposes of implementing this Convention, it shall not be necessary, except as otherwise stated herein, for the offences set forth in it to result in damage or harm to state property. (article 3, 2)
>
> لأغراض تنفيذ هذه الاتفاقية، ليس ضروريا أن تكون الجرائم المبينة فيها قد ألحقت ضررا أو أذى بأملاك الدولة، باستثناء ما تنص عليه خلافا لذلك.

In this example, as can be seen, the translator, to ensure readability and acceptability, opted for a syntactic restructuring when dealing with '*except as otherwise stated herein*'. This local strategy is justified. However, s/he decided to translate '*it shall not be necessary … for the offences set forth in it to result in damage or harm to state property*' into ليس ضروريا أن تكون الجرائم المبينة فيها قد ألحقت ضررا أو أذى بأملاك الدولة. As can be seen, by virtue of the particle قد followed by the verb ألحقت in the past, the emphasis is placed on the completion of the action, i.e. past-oriented while it is future-oriented, i.e. it is part of irreality, in the original text. This local strategy, i.e. changing the aspectual reference of the action, is unjustified. To produce an adequate translation without modifying the meaning, one can opt for

> ليس ضروريا/ليس من الضروري أن تلحق هذه الجرائم المبينة فيها ضررًا أو أذى بأملاك الدولة.

So, local strategies can be ST-oriented or reader-oriented depending on the global strategy adopted earlier by the translator after having taken into consideration the translation brief, i.e. the text type, readership, genre, purpose of translation, and the like. Further, those local strategies opted for by translators can be justified or unjustified.

8. Structural calquing

Structural calquing (also known as 'Structural calque') refers to the avoidance of the existing structures that are usually used by native speakers and, instead, opting for a new construction, which is very close to the structure used in the original text. To explain, let us consider this example taken from the USA Constitution (cited in Husni and Newman 2015: 107):

> We the People of the United States, in order to form a more perfect Union, establish Justice, insure domestic Tranquillity, provide for the common defence, promote

the general Welfare, and secure the Blessings of Liberty to ourselves and our Posterity, do ordain and establish this Constitution for the United states of America.

Note that من أجل *can be replaced with* بغية *here.*

نحن شعب الولايات المتحدة، نرسي ونؤسس هذا الدستور للولايات المتحدة الأمريكية، من أجل تشكيل اتحادٍ مثالي، وتحقيق العدالة، وضمان الاستقرار الداخلي، وتوفير سبل الدفاع المشترك، وتعزيز الرفاهية الشاملة، وتأمين نعمة الحرية لأنفسنا ولأجيالنا القادمة.(p. 143)

In this example, the translators opted for نرسي ونؤسس هذا الدستور للولايات المتحدة الأمريكية in place of نرسي هذا الدستور للولايات المتحدة الأمريكية ونؤسسه which is a fine style in Arabic, more natural and commonly used by native speakers in other text types. To reinforce this point, let us consider this example extracted from the Act to constitute the Commonwealth Australia and translated into Arabic by Husni and Newman (2015: 144):

What do you think of translating 'may' *into* يمكن *in a legal discourse? Can it be replaced by* يجوز *here? If yes, which one is better? Discuss.*

And such law may be repealed as to any State by the Parliament of the Commonwealth, or as to any colony not being a State by the Parliament thereof.

يمكن الغاء أي من هذه القوانين في أي من الولايات من قبل برلمان الكومنولث، أو فيما يخص أي مستعمرة من غير الولايات من جانب البرلمان الخاص بها.

Here, the passive forms in the above examples were maintained, thus resulting in what is called the 'forced passive voice' typically expressed in Arabic by من قبل, من طرف or من جانب. As can be seen, in the translation of this example, the translators used two forms of this forced passive voice, namely من قبل and من جانب. These are examples of structural calquing, which is acceptable in this text type; however, it can be avoided if we adopt a reader-oriented translation, as in

يجوز لبرلمان الكومنولث إلغاء أي من هذه القوانين في أي من الولايات ...

9. Between-line translation

A between-line translation is a type of translation in which the translator overtly intervenes to read between the lines to understand what is really meant by a word, phrase, clause, etc. and then transfers what s/he understands to the target text even though it is not said openly in the original text. This can be in the form of a 'contextual translation', 'specification', and the like. Legal translators, in dealing with legislative texts, should avoid this type of translation as much as possible, particularly when alternatives are available. In the following example quoted from Husni and Newman (2015: 145), the phrases الطرف الأول and الطرف الثاني were translated into '*groom*' and '*pride*' respectively:

Here, طلب which is in the past was translated into a verb in the simple present. What is your opinion of this? Can we consider this as an example of 'tense shift'?

> طلب الطرف الأول من الطرف الثاني الارتباط بها على كتاب الله وسنة رسوله بقوله لها أريد الزواج منك على كتاب الله وسنة رسوله وعلى مذهب الإمام أبي حنيفة النعمان والصداق المسمّى بيننا ووافقته الطرف الثاني على ذلك بقولها له قبلت الزواج منك.
>
> The groom hereby requests to enter into a bond with the bride, in accordance with the Holy Quran and the Sunna of the Prophet Muhammed, by saying, 'I wish to marry you, in accordance with the Holy Quran, the Sunna of the Prophet Muhammed and the Hanafi School of Islamic Jurisprudence, and in exchange of the dowry fixed between us'. The bride hereby agrees to this by saying, 'I accept to marry you'.

In this example, as one may notice, the translators opted for several local strategies, namely 'specification', 'contextual translation', 'literal translation', 'addition', and 'omission'. Here, suffice it to say something about 'specification' and 'contextual translation'. For the sake of clarity, as can be observed, the religious terms كتاب الله '*the God's book*' and سنة رسوله '*His Messenger's Sunna*' were translated into '*the Holy Quran*' and '*Sunna of the Prophet Muhammed*' respectively. As God has more than one book and messengers, the translators decided to make it clear which book and which messenger by naming the book '*The Holy Quran*' and the messenger '*Muhammed*'. These are examples of 'specification'.

With respect to الطرف الأول and الطرف الثاني that can lend themselves to '*the first party*' and '*the second party*' respectively, they were translated into '*groom*' العريس and '*bride*' العروسة. This is an example of a contextual translation where the context in which these two terms are used is given full consideration by the translators when letting the text speak. This procedure, i.e. 'letting the text speak' تنطيقُ النّص resulting in a contextual translation, can be used to remove any state of confusion, but the question that might rear its ugly head here is: Is there any ambiguity with the use of '*the first party*' and '*the second party*'? The answer is 'no'. Actually, opting for the terms '*groom*' and '*bride*' changed the formality of the text.

10. Naturalizing

Naturalizing is a local strategy sometimes adopted by legal translators to live up to the target language readers' expectations or when dealing with culture-specific terms. In this case, issues such as readability, acceptability, authenticity, idiomaticity, and well-formedness are given serious consideration by the translators with the potential to make the target text fluent and natural as if it has not been translated from another language. To make this point clear, the following text extracted from the Commonwealth of Australia Constitution Act (9th July 1900) can be discussed:

> WHEREAS the people of New South Wales, Victoria, South Australia, Queensland, and Tasmania, humbly relying on the blessing of Almighty God, have agreed to unite in one indissoluble Federal Commonwealth under the Crown of the United Kingdom of Great Britain and Ireland, and under the Constitution hereby established:

This part was translated into Arabic by Husni and Newman (2015: 143) as

What do you think of the use of وافق شعوب*? Can we say* وافقت شعوب*? If yes, which one is better? Discuss.*

> لقد وافق شعوب كل من الولايات التالية، نيو ساوث ويلز وفيكتوريا وجنوب استراليا وكوينزلاند وتسمانيا، بعون الله سبحانه وتعالى وتوفيقه، على أن يتحدوا في كومنولث (اتحاد) فيدرالي واحد، لا ينفصل، تحت حكم/رعاية (تاج) المملكة المتحدة لبريطانيا العظمى وايرلندا، وبموجب هذا الدستور قرروا ما يلي:

Here, as can be observed, the translators tried their hand to live up to the target language readers' expectations; therefore, they naturalized the expression '*humbly relying on the blessing of Almighty God*' when opting for بعون الله سبحانه وتعالى وتوفيقه. To further naturalize their translation, they began their own translation with لقد وافق instead of translating '*whereas*' into لما. Added to this, they restructured the text to sound more Arabic by adding, for example كل من الولايات التالية and ما يلي. Further, they opted for a semantic repetition واحد، لا ينفصل in dealing with the adjective '*indissoluble*' meaning unable to be destroyed or lasting.

11. **Idiomatic translation**

Closely related to 'naturalizing' is 'idiomatic translation'. Idiomatic translation occurs when translating (non-)idiomatic expressions idiomatically, i.e. concentrating on the form rather than the idea. To explain, let us reconsider the following example taken from the USA Constitution (cited in Husni and Newman 2015: 107):

> We the People of the United States, in order to form a more perfect Union, establish Justice, insure domestic Tranquillity, provide for the common defence, promote the general Welfare, and secure the Blessings of Liberty to ourselves and our Posterity, do ordain and establish this Constitution for the United states of America.

It is من أجل *or* لأجل*? Which one is more Arabic?*

> نحن شعب الولايات المتحدة، نرسي ونؤسس هذا الدستور للولايات المتحدة الأمريكية، من أجل تشكيل اتحادٍ مثالي، وتحقيق العدالة، وضمان الاستقرار الداخلي، وتوفير سبل الدفاع المشترك، وتعزيز الرفاهية الشاملة، وتأمين نعمة الحرية لأنفسنا ولأجيالنا القادمة. (p. 143)

Here, as one may observe, the translators opted for several unmarked collocations, such as تحقيق العدالة, ضمان الاستقرار, توفير سبل الدفاع المشترك, تعزيز الرفاهية and تأمين نعمة. These can be considered idiomatic expressions as they collocate well in Arabic.

12. **Ideational translation**

Ideational translation occurs when translating (non-) idiomatic expressions ideationally, i.e. concentrating on the idea rather than the form, as in the translation of the idiomatic expression أمانة في عنق كل مواطن extracted from the Omani Constitution (article 14 n° 1):

> السلام هدف الدولة، وسلامة الوطن أمانة في عنق كل مواطن. ويتولى مجلس الدفاع النظر في الموضوعات المتعلقة بالمحافظة على سلامة السلطنة والدفاع عنها.

> Peace is the objective of the State, and the safety of the Nation is a duty incumbent on every Citizen. The Defence Council shall undertake the consideration of the matters related to preserving the safety of the Sultanate and the defence thereof.

What can be recognized here is that the translator reduced the idiomatic expression أمانة في عنق كل مواطن to its sense when opting for '*a duty incumbent on every Citizen*' roughly meaning واجب مفروض على كلّ مواطن.

Assignment 1

Adopt a global strategy to translate the following text taken from the Constitution of the UK into Arabic. Then, comment on your local strategies.

---

5. **Right to liberty and security**

5.1.1 1. Everyone has the right to liberty and security of person.

2. No one shall be deprived of their liberty except, on reasonable grounds and in accordance with fair procedures established by law, in the following cases—
   a. the lawful detention of a person after conviction by a competent court;
   b. the lawful arrest or detention of a person for noncompliance with the lawful order of a court or in order to secure the fulfilment of any obligation prescribed by law;
   c. the lawful arrest or detention of a person effected for the purpose of bringing them before the competent legal authority on reasonable suspicion of having committed an offence or when it is reasonably considered necessary to prevent their committing an offence or fleeing after having done so;
   d. the lawful detention of persons for the prevention of the spreading of infectious diseases constituting a serious threat to public health, or of persons suffering from mental disorder where necessary for the prevention of harm to themselves or others;
   e. the lawful arrest or detention of a person to prevent their effecting an unauthorized entry into the United Kingdom or of a person against whom action is being taken with a view to deportation or extradition.

5.2 Anyone who is arrested shall, at the time of arrest, be informed in a language which they understand of the reasons for their arrest and shall be promptly informed of any charges against them.

5.3 1. It shall not be the general rule that persons awaiting trial shall be detained in custody.

2. Anyone arrested or detained on a criminal charge shall be brought promptly before a judge or other officer authorized by law to exercise judicial power and is entitled to trial within a reasonable time or to release pending trial.

3. Release may be subject to guarantees to appear for trial or at any other stage of the judicial proceedings.

Assignment 2

Identify the type of the local strategy highlighted for you in bold in the following examples.

Source text	أنا ... مأذون عقد زواج في ... قد أجريت هذا العقد على الوجه المفصل أعلاه بعد التحقق من استكمال الشروط وعدم الموانع.
Target text	I, ..., **the registrar authorised to perform marriages** in ..., having ascertained that **the conditions have been fully met**, and that **eligibility is established**, have executed this contract in the manner detailed above. (Hatim et al. 1995: 86–7)
Type	
Type	
Type	

Source text	للملكية العامة حرمة، لا يجوز المساس بها، وحمايتها واجب وفقًا للقانون
Target text	Public property is inviolable and may not be infringed upon. It is the duty **of every citizen** to **protect** it in accordance with the law. (the Egyptian Constitution, article 34)
Type	
Type	

Source text	العدل والحرية والمساواة دعامات المجتمع، والتعاون والتراحم صلة وثقى بين المواطنين.
Target text	Justice, Liberty, and Equality are the pillars of society; co-operation and **mutual help** are **the firmest bonds** between citizens. (the Kuwaiti Constitution, article 7)
Type	
Type	

Source text	تختص حكومة الإقليم بكل ما تتطلبه إدارة الإقليم، وبوجه خاص إنشاء وتنظيم قوى الأمن الداخلي للإقليم كالشرطة والأمن وحرس الإقليم.
Target text	The regional government shall **be responsible for** all the **administrative** requirements of the region, **particularly** the establishment and organization of the internal security forces for the region such as police, security forces, and guards of the region. (the Iraqi Constitution, article 121, n° 5)
Type	
Type	
Type	

Source text	الملكية الخاصة مصونة، فلا يمنع أحد من التصرّف في ملكه إلا في حدود القانون، ولا ينزع عن أحد ملكه إلا بسبب المنفعة العامة في الأحوال المبينة في القانون، وبالكيفية المنصوص عليها فيه، وبشرط تعويضه عنه تعويضا عادلا. والميراث حق تحكمه الشريعة الإسلامية.
Target text	Private ownership is safeguarded and no one shall be prevented from disposing of his property **except within the limits of the Law**. No property shall be expropriated except for the public interest in cases stipulated by the Law and in the manner specified **therein**, provided that the person dispossessed shall be **fairly** compensated. Inheritance is a right **governed** by Islamic Sharia. (the Omani Constitution, article 11 n° 5)
Type	
Type	
Type	
Type	

Source text	الجنسية ينظمها القانون، ولا يجوز اسقاطها أو سحبها إلا في حدود القانون.
Target text	Nationality **is regulated** by the Law and **it is not permissible** to **denaturalise** or revoke it except within the limits of the Law. (the Omani Constitution, article 15)
Type	
Type	
Type	

Source text	لا يفرض التشغيل الالزامي على أحد غير أنه يجوز بمقتضى القانون فرض شغل أو خدمة على اي شخص:
Target text	Compulsory labour shall not be imposed on any person, but pursuant to law, **work or service may be imposed** on any person: (the Jordanian Constitution, article 13)
Type	

References

Al-Aqaileh, Z. M. 2015. المصطلحات القانونية باللغة الإنجليزية مع ترجمة كاملة إلى اللغة العربية *'Legal Terms in English fully Translated into Arabic'*. Jordan: Dār Al-Thaqāfa for Publication & Distribution

Almanna, A. 2014. *Translation Theories Exemplified from Cicero to Pierre Bourdieu*. München: Lincom Europa Academic Publishers.

———. 2016. *The Routledge Course in Translation Annotation: Arabic-English-Arabic*. London/New York: Routledge.

Baker, M. 1992/2011. *In Other Words*. London/New York: Routledge.

Chesterman, A. 1993. From 'is' to 'ought': Laws, Norms and Strategies in Translation Studies. *Target* 5: 1–20.

Chesterman, A. 1997/2000. *Memes of Translation: The Spread of Ideas in Translation Theory*. Amsterdam/Philadelphia: John Benjamins.

Hatim, B., A. Shunnaq, and R. Buckley. 1995. *The Legal Translator at Work: A Practical Guide*. Jordan: Dār al-Hilāl for Translating and Publishing.

Husni, R., and D. Newman. 2015. *Arabic-English-Arabic Translation*. London/New York: Routledge.

Malone, J.L. 1988. *The Science of Linguistics in the Art of Translation*. Albany: State University of New York Press.

Newmark, P. 1988. *A Textbook of Translation*. New York/London/Toronto/Sydney/Tokyo: Prentice Hall.

Nida, E. 1964. *Towards a Science of Translation, with Special Reference to Principles and Procedures Involved in Bible Translating*. Leiden: E. J. Brill.

Vinay, J. P., and J. Darbelnet. 1958/1995. *Stylistique comparée du français et de l'anglais. Méthode de traduction*. Paris: Didier (trans. and ed.) J. C. Sager & M. J. Hamel, *Comparative Stylistics of French and English: A Methodology for Translation*. Amsterdam/Philadelphia: John Benjamins.

CHAPTER 3

Lexical Features

In this chapter, the main lexical features that distinguish legal texts from other text types are given full consideration. Legal texts as stated in the previous chapter can be classified into legislative texts, judicial texts, academic texts, private legal texts, and the like (see Cao's (2007) classification as an example). Some of these texts are characterized by the use of (1) archaic words and expressions, (2) doublets and triplets, (3) Latin and French terms, and the like. In what follows, these lexical features are introduced and exemplified in both languages in a direct link to the actual act of translating between Arabic and English.

Lexical Features of English Legal Discourse

Archaicisms and Lawyerisms

One of the main characteristics of legal language in general and legislative texts in particular is the use of archaic words and expressions to add a formal nature to the language in which they occur (cf. Alcaraz Varó and Hughes 2014: 5). In this regard, Tiersma (1999: 95) holds that legal language "often strives toward great formality, it naturally gravitates towards archaic language". As such, one may argue that there is a strong relationship between 'formality' and the older English.

A. Almanna, *Legal Translation between English and Arabic*,
https://doi.org/10.1007/978-3-031-14838-5_3

Crystal and Davy (1969: 207/8) indicate that the reason for the use of such archaic words and expressions is just a matter of tradition and they provide us with an interesting example: '*witnesseth*' ending with the suffix '*-eth*', which is used in old English to refer to a third person singular. Using such an archaic suffix '*-eth*' despite the fact that there is a modern suffix '*-s/es*' that can be used instead, indicates that it is really just a matter of tradition, on the one hand, and to add a touch of formality to the language in which they occur, on the other.

Some of these archaic words and expressions used by lawyers are called lawyerisms. Examples of lawyerisms include words and expressions, such as

Find more examples.

- *pursuant to* (under, in accordance with)
- *in pursuance of* (in accordance with)
- *prior to* (before)
- *anterior to* (before)
- *subsequent to* (after)
- *vel non* (or not, or the lack of it).
- *inasmuch as* (because)
- *forthwith* (immediately)
- *to wit* (for example, namely, that is to say)
- *abutting* (next to)

Think of their equivalents in Arabic.

Veretina-Chiriac (2012: 53; also discussed in Awe and Fanokun 2018: 6) is of the view that archaisms are typical examples of legalisms and lawyerisms—when they are used, they inject the language with formality. In this connection, Awe and Fanokun (2018) rightly comment that although lawyerisms or legalisms make the document concise and precise, they lead to comprehension problems for lay people.

Do you agree with Awe and Fanokum? Discuss.

Words like *herein, hereof, hereafter, thereon, therewith, whereof,* etc. are rarely used in other varieties of English anymore, but they are still heavily used in legal language, in particular legislative texts. By way of clarification, let us consider this example:

> The Landlord **hereby** may enter the dwelling without Tenant's consent in case of emergency. (adapted from Sabra 2003: 29)

'hereby' *refers to the document in which it is used, thus lending itself to* بموجب هذا العقد, بموجب هذه الاتفاقية*, etc.*

Below are some illustrative examples extracted from the United Nations Convention against Corruption (www.trans-lex.org):

Example 1 (article 3, 2):

For the purposes of implementing this Convention, it shall not be necessary, except as otherwise stated **herein**, for the offences set forth in it to result in damage or harm to state property.

Is there any difference between الأذى and الضّرر? And what is the difference between الضّرر and الضِّرار, as in لا ضرر ولا ضِرار?

لأغراض تنفيذ هذه الاتفاقية، ليس ضروريا أن تكون الجرائم المبينة **فيها** قد ألحقت ضررا أو أذى بأملاك الدولة، باستثناء ما تنص عليه خلافا لذلك.

Example 2 (article 23, 2):

Each State Party shall furnish copies of its laws that give effect to this article and of any subsequent changes to such laws or a description **thereof** to the Secretary-General of the United Nations …

تزوّد كل دولة طرف الأمين العام للأمم المتحدة بنسخ من قوانينها المنفذة لهذه المادة وبنسخ من أي تغييرات تدخل على تلك القوانين لاحقا أو بوصف **لها**...

Example 3 (article 44, 9):

States Parties shall, subject to their domestic law, endeavour to expedite extradition procedures and to simplify evidentiary requirements relating **thereto** in respect of any offence to which this article applies.

Can we replace تسعى with تعمل? If yes, which one in stronger in Arabic?

تسعى الدول الأطراف، رهنا بقوانينها الداخلية، إلى التعجيل بإجراءات التسليم وتبسيط ما يتصل **بها** من متطلبات إثباتية فيما يخص أي جرم تنطبق عليه هذه المادة.

Following are more examples extracted from the Omani Constitution along with their translations into English:

Example 4 (article 14, 1):

السلام هدف الدولة، وسلامة الوطن أمانة في عنق كل مواطن. ويتولى مجلس الدفاع النظر في الموضوعات المتعلقة بالمحافظة على سلامة السلطنة والدفاع عنها.

Note that ينزَع عن can be replaced with ينتزع عن or ينتزع من, as in انتزع الشّيء من كذا أو عن كذا meaning أخذَهُ بالقوة أي عنوة.

Peace is the objective of the State, and the safety of the Nation is a duty incumbent on every Citizen. The Defence Council shall undertake the consideration of the matters related to preserving the safety of the Sultanate and the defence **thereof**.

Example 5 (article 11, 5):

Which one is better إلا لسبب المنفعة العامة or إلا لمنفعةٍ عامةٍ?

الملكية الخاصة مصونة، فلا يمنع أحد من التصّرف في ملكه إلا في حدود القانون، ولا ينزع عن أحد ملكه إلا بسبب المنفعة العامة في الأحوال المبينة في القانون، وبالكيفية المنصوص عليها فيه، وبشرط تعويضه عنه تعويضا عادلا. والميراث حق تحكمه الشريعة الإسلامية.

Private ownership is safeguarded and no one shall be prevented from disposing of his property except within the limits of the Law. No property shall be expropriated except for the public interest in cases stipulated by the Law and in the manner specified **therein**, provided that the person dispossessed shall be fairly compensated. Inheritance is a right governed by Islamic Sharia.

The lexical item صالح, *which is in the singular form lends itself to* 'interests', *which is in the plural form. Is there any example of shift here?*

Example 6 (article 11, 3):

الثروات الطبيعية جميعها ومواردها كافة ملك للدولة، **تقوم** على حفظها وحسن استغلالها، بمراعاة مقتضيات أمن الدولة وصالح الاقتصاد الوطني...

All natural wealth and resources **thereof** are the property of the State, which shall preserve and utilise them in the best manner taking into consideration the requirements of the security of the State and the interests of the national economy …

In Arabic, we can say الثروات الطبيعية جميعها ... جميعُ or ملك للدولة الثروات الطبيعية ... ملك للدولة. *In your opinion, which one is frequently used in Arabic legal discourse?*

Example 7 (article 21):

لا جريمة ولا عقوبة إلا بناء على قانون، ولا عقاب إلا على الأفعال اللاحقة للعمل بالقانون الذي ينص عليها.

There shall be no crime except by virtue of a Law. There shall be no punishment, except for acts subsequent to the entry into force of the Law **wherein** such acts are stated.

In Arabic, we can also say لا جريمة ولا عقوبة إلا بنص or بقانون.

Example 8 (article 51):

يتولى نواب رئيس الوزراء والوزراء الإشراف على شؤون وحداتهم ويقومون بتنفيذ السياسة العامة للحكومة فيها. كما يرسمون اتجاهات الوحدة ويتابعون تنفيذها.

The Deputies to the Prime Minister and the Ministers shall supervise the affairs of their units, implement the general policy of the Government therein, draw the guidelines of the unit and follow up the implementation **thereof**.

Note that يتولى الإشراف على *and* يقومون بتنفيذ *were reduced to* 'supervise' *and* 'implement' *respectively. Now, back translate the text to see if you will have* يشرف *and* ينفذون *or* يتولى الإشراف *and* يقومون بتنفيذ?

Doublets and Triplets

In addition to using archaic expressions, there is a tendency to use more than one lexical item to stand for one referent. Danet (1985: 280; also discussed in El-Farahaty

2015: 25) holds that these doublets and triplets are "frozen expressions which are irreversible; they are formal syntactic features rather than lexical ones". Typical examples of this include

!	*made and entered into*	أُبرم ودخل حيّز التنفيذ أو تحرر	!
!	*under and in accordance with*	بموجب (أو بمقتضى) وتمشيًا مع	!
!	*goods and chattels*	البضائع والسّلع	!
!	*true and correct*	حقيقي وصحيح	!
!	*null and void*	لاغ وباطل	!
!	*acknowledge and confess*	يقرّ ويعترف	!
!	*safe and sound*	مأمون وسليم	!
!	*unless and until*	مالم وإلى أن	!
!	*save and except*	فيما عدا وباستثناء	!
!	*fraud and deceit*	غش وخداع	!
!	*shun and avoid*	يتجنب ويتحاشى	!
!	*act and deed*	عمل وفعل	!
!	*shall be and remain*	يكون ويظل	!
!	*each and every*	كلّ	!
!	*free and clear of*	خال من	!
!	*made and signed*	تحرر (أو: أُبرم)	!
!	*deem and consider*	يعدّ ويعتبر	!
!	*keep and maintain*	يبقي ويحافظ على	!
!	*part and parcel*	جزء لا يتجزأ	!
!	*terms and conditions*	شروط (وأحكام)	!
!	*requisite and necessary*	ضروري ولازم	!
!	*bind and obligate*	يلزم	!
!	*rules and regulations*	القواعد والتعليمات (أو: القواعد واللوائح)	!
!	*aid and abet*	يساعد ويحرّض	!
!	*honour and reputation*	شرف وسمعة	!
!	*will and testament*	وصيّة	!

In law, there is a difference between الإقرار and الاعتراف.

Williard (in Sabra 2003) points out that the use of these doublets and triplets results from both the draftsmen's desire to write in an elegant style and the tradition that is followed in writing legal documents. Following are some examples taken from Sabra (2003) to make this point clear:

لا يجوز **تعديل** هذا الاتفاق بشكل جوهري أو ثانوي أو **تغييره** أو **تحويره** مالم يتم الاتفاق على ذلك كتابيًا ويوقع من الطرف الذي سيتحمل مصاريف ذلك.

What do you think of this translation in terms of accuracy?

This Agreement may not be **altered**, **amended**, **changed** or **modified** unless the same shall be agreed in writing and signed by the party to be charged. (p. 35)

يتعهّد المستأجر بإزالة كل **الأتربة والمخلفات والقمامة وغيرها من الفضلات** من الوحدة السكنية بطريقة **نظيفة ومأمونة**.

Note that the lexical item 'tenant' *can be replaced with* 'lessee'.

Tenant shall dispose from the dwelling unit all **ashes**, **rubbish**, **garbage**, and **other waste** in a **clean** and **safe** manner.

أبرمت هذه الاتفاقية **ودخلت حيّز التنفيذ** بتاريخ ... **بين كل من الطرف الأول والطرف الثاني**... .

Note that 'the party of the first part' *means* 'the first party', *thus lending itself to* الطرف الأول.

This agreement **made and entered into** this day of … **by and between, the party of the first part**, and, **the party of the second part** …

Latin and French Terms

Another feature of legal English, in particular legislative writing, is the use of certain terms borrowed from Latin and French. To make this point clear, the following Latin terms can be given full consideration:

To be familiar with these Latin terms, listen to this video https://www.youtube.com/watch?v=SdSJFYYIcPM

Try to translate them into Arabic.

- *ab initio* meaning from the beginning
- *actus reus* meaning a guilt act
- *mens rea* meaning a guilt mind
- *ad hominem* meaning at the person
- *affidavit* meaning under oath or sworn facts
- *amicus curiae* meaning a friend of court
- *bona fida* meaning in good faith
- *de minimis* referring to trivial matters
- *dictum* referring to a part of a legal opinion
- *in camera* referring to something conducted in secret
- *in personam* meaning personal
- *in rem* referring to real property (rights)
- *corpus delicti* referring to the place of the crime
- *corpus juris* meaning the body of the law
- *malum in se* meaning wrong in itself
- *malum prohibitum* meaning prohibited wrong
- *per curiam* meaning through the court
- *per incuriam* referring to a judgment given without reference to precedent
- *pari passu* meaning on equal footing
- *prima facie* referring to meeting all the necessary elements of a cause of an action
- *pro tempore* referring to a judge appointed on a temporary basis
- *respondeat superior* referring to the employer's liability for the torts committed by their employees

- *subpoena* meaning under penalty
- *stare decisis* meaning to stand by things decided
- *scienter* meaning knowingly, intentionally and willfully
- *res judicata* meaning matter judged
- *de facto* meaning in fact
- *de futuro* meaning with respect to future
- *de jure* meaning according to law
- *de lege lata* meaning of the law as it is
- *culpa lata* meaning gross negligence
- *culpa levis* meaning ordinary negligence
- *culpa levissima* meaning slight negligence
- *ad hoc* meaning for this (purposes)
- *dolus* referring to a fraudulent conduct
- *in mora* meaning in delay or in default

It is worth noting that some of these terms borrowed, in particular those borrowed from French, are used in other varieties of English these days. Examples of these terms include *purchase*, *court*, *evidence*, *jury*, *judge*, *fiancé*, *entrepreneur*, and the like (for more details, see Mellinkoff 1963: 58 and Beveridge 2002: 59).

Lexical Features of Arabic Legal Discourse

Arabic legal discourse, in particular legislative writing, is characterized by the use of religious terms, culture-specific terms and semantic repetition. To make a start, let us reconsider this text taken along with its translation from Husni and Newman (2015: 145):

طلب الطرف الأول من الطرف الثاني الارتباط بها على كتاب الله وسنة رسوله بقوله لها أريد الزواج منك على كتاب الله وسنة رسوله وعلى مذهب الإمام أبي حنيفة النعمان والصداق المسمّى بيننا ووافقته الطرف الثاني على ذلك بقولها له قبلت الزواج منك.

The groom hereby requests to enter into a bond with the bride, in accordance with the Holy Quran and the Sunna of the Prophet Muhammed, by saying, 'I wish to marry you, in accordance with the Holy Quran, the Sunna of the Prophet Muhammed and the Hanafi School of Islamic Jurisprudence, and in exchange of the dowry fixed between us'. The bride hereby agrees to this by saying, 'I accept to marry you'.

In this example, as one may notice, the translators opted for several local strategies, namely 'specification', 'contextual translation', 'literal translation', 'addition' and 'omission', as explained below:

Specification: here, as one may notice, for the sake of clarity the religious terms كتاب الله '*the God's book*' and سنة رسوله '*His Messenger's Sunna*' were translated into '*the Holy Quran*' and '*Sunna of the Prophet Muhammed*' respectively. As God has more than one book and messengers, the translators decided to make it clear which book and which messenger by naming the book '*The Holy Quran*' and the messenger '*Muhammed*'. These are examples of 'specification'.

Contextual translation: الطرف الأول and الطرف الثاني that can lend themselves to '*the first party*' and '*the second party*' respectively were translated into '*groom*' العريس and '*bride*' العروسة. This is an example of a contextual translation where the context in which these two terms are used is given full consideration by the translators when letting the text speak. This procedure, i.e. 'letting the text speak' تنطيقُ النَّصِ, can be used to remove any state of confusion, but the question that might rear its ugly head here is: Is there any ambiguity with the use of '*the first party*' and '*the second party*'? The answer is 'no', but opting for the terms '*groom*' and '*bride*' changed the formality of the text.

Literal translation: the lexical item ارتباط from the verb ارتبط, which is characterized by dyadic personation type, i.e. it requires two participants, can be replaced with زواج, thus lending itself to '*marriage*' in place of '*bond*', but the translators decided to be very close to the source text, thereby translating it literally as '*bond*'. This requires them to add the phrasal verb '*to enter into*'.

Addition and omission: the religious term مذهب, as can be seen, was translated into '*school*'. It is worth noting that the denotative meaning of the word '*school*' is wider and less specific when it is compared with مذهب that invokes in our mind a *religion*-frame. As such, for the sake of clarity and an attempt to reflect the *religion*-frame associated with the term مذهب, the translators decided to add the phrase '*Islamic Jurisprudence*'. On the other hand, for the sake of readability, acceptability, idiomaticity, authenticity, and well-formedness that feed into naturalness, they decided not to opt for the literal translation of أبو حنيفة النعمان '*Abu Hanifa Al-Nu'man*', but rather, they decided to use it as an adjective in a noun phrase.

In the following example extracted from Hatim et al. (1995: 90–1), the religious phrase سبحانه وتعالى usually used in Arabic after the word الله '*Allah*' to emphasize the distance and show inferiority as a sign of respect was translated into '*Almighty*', thus reflecting Allah's superiority to the speaker.

> أنني عن عقيدة راسخة وإيمان بالله **سبحانه وتعالى** أرغب اعتناق الدين الإسلامي الحنيف وأشهد أن لا إله ألا الله وأن محمدًا عبده ورسوله...

> On the basis of a firmly established conviction and a belief in **Almighty** God I wish to embrace the religion of true Islam and I bear witness that there is no god but God and that Muhammed is His servant and His prophet …

Arabic, in general, shows a preference for "semantic repetition" in which, at least, two synonyms, or near synonyms, are used in the same clause/sentence (Dickins and Watson 1999: 541–53; Dickins et al. 2002: 59; Almanna 2016: 103). It is worth mentioning that semantic repetition is of two kinds

1. semantic repetition made up of words or phrases that are synonymous up to a good degree as it is difficult for lay people to figure out the differences in meaning between them, as in

   القيمة and الثّمن, السّعر
   الاحتراز and الحيطة, الحذر
   المهر and الصّداق
   الخير and البِرّ
   الميراث and الإرث
   الاعتراف and الإقرار
   الأذى and الضّرر
   التّحاشي and التّجنب
   النّصيب and الحظ
   الجود and السّخاء and so on.

2. semantic repetition made up of semantically related words or phrases, but there is a clear difference in meaning between them, as in الجّسم and البدن; الخلق and التّكرار; الإعادة and الاستفهام; السّؤال and المُحتاج; الفقير and الإنفاق; الإعطاء and الاختلاق; العجلة and السّرعة, and the like.

To translate such semantic repetition from Arabic into English, the translator may opt for one of four techniques as suggested by Dickins et al. (2002: 60–1). They are

1. *merging*, that is, merging the two synonymous words used in the source text into one word in the target text.
2. *grammatical transposition*, that is, changing the part of speech of one of the synonymous words used in the source text, such as changing a noun into an adjective, a verb into an adverb, and so on.
3. *semantic distancing*, that is, translating the two synonymous words used in the source text into two words, but their meanings are slightly different in the target language.
4. *maintenance*, that is, maintaining the same form of semantic repetition along with the synonyms used.

To make this point clear, let us consider this example taken from Hatim et al. (1995: 94–5):

The lexical item المعقود *here can be replaced with* المُنعقِد.

في المجلس الشرعي المعقود لدي أنا ... قاضي ... الشرعي **عيّنت ونصّبت** المكلف شرعًا ... قيمًا شرعيّا على أموال المفقود الغائب ... وليس له بيع الأموال المنقولة وغير المنقولة أو رهنها أو قبض أي مبلغ من المال أكثر من خمسة وعشرين دينارًا إلا بإذن المحكمة الشرعية [...]

Note that وليس له *can be replaced with* ولا يحق له.

In the Legal Council convened in my presence, I …, the Religious Judge of …, have **appointed and installed** the legally capable Mr. … as a legal steward of the property of the missing person … he may neither sell nor mortgage the moveable or the immovable property, nor obtain any sum of money exceeding twenty-five dinars except by permission from the Religious Court.

Here, as one may see, the semantically related words, namely عيّن and نصّب were translated into '*to appoint*' and '*to install*'. This is an example of maintenance. It is worth mentioning that one of the meanings of the verb '*to install*' is to induct into an office, rank, or position, as in '*We will have a ceremony tomorrow to install the new governor*'.

Now, let us discuss this formula usually used in marriage contracts (Hatim et al. 1995: 86–7):

Is the mode of narration in the Arabic text direct or indirect?

قال وكيل الزوجة والدها مخاطبًا الزوج المذكور نفسه **زوجتك وأنكحتك** موكلتي ابنتي ... على مهر معجل قدره ... وتوابعه المذكورة ومهر مؤجل قدره ... فأجاب الزوج المذكور فورًا وأنا **قبلت ورضيت بزواجها ونكاحها** لنفسي على المهرين المذكورين وتوابعهما.

> The representative for the female spouse (her father) said, addressing the aforementioned male spouse, "I **have given my daughter … to you in marriage** for a dowry the down-payment of which is …, the extras of which are mentioned above, and the deferred payment of which is …". The male spouse immediately replied, "I **accepted your daughter in marriage** and confirm the dowry's down-payment, deferred, and extras stipulated above".

Here, we have an example of semantic repetition made up of two synonymous words, namely زوّج and أنكح. The translators opted for merging the two synonymous words used in the source text into one phrase in the target text, i.e. '*to give her to you in marriage*'. The same holds true for the nouns زواج and نكاح derived from the aforementioned verbs when opting for merging them into one phrase, i.e. '*accepting your daughter in marriage*'. Another example of semantic repetition can be found in the use of the semantically related words قبلَ and رضى. These two words, to explain, are not fully synonymous; however, the translators opted for merging them into one word, which is '*to accept*'.

To finish off this section, let us consider the translation of this article taken from the Omani Constitution, article 13 n° 3:

In Arabic, we can say ترعى وتحافظ الدولة على التّراث؟ *This style is called* أسلوب التّنازع. *What do you prefer* ترعى الدولة التّراث وتحافظ عليه *or* ترعى وتحافظ الدولة على التّراث؟

> ترعى الدولة التراث وتحافظ عليه، وتشجع العلوم والفنون والآداب والبحوث العلمية وتساعد على نشرها.

> The State shall foster and preserve the national heritage, encourage the sciences, arts, literature, scientific research and assist in their dissemination.

Here, as can be observed, two semantically related words are used, namely ترعى and تحافظ على. This is an example of 'semantic repetition' which is made up of two verbs, but they are not fully synonymous as there is a difference in meaning between them. To explain, يرعى, i.e. to care for, is different from يحافظ على, i.e. to keep safe from harm or injury. Having taken this difference in meaning between them into account, the translator opted for '*foster*' and '*preserve*' respectively, thereby maintaining the same form of semantic repetition along with the synonyms used.

Exercise 1

Translate the following sentences into Arabic, paying extra attention to the Latin words highlighted for you.

Note that the lexical item 'object' *here lends itself to* محل (العقد)*, and* محل *has nothing to do with* مكان *in such a context, but rather it refers to* موضوع التعاقد *whether it is lawful or not, etc.*

1. In the event the object of the contract is unlawful, the contract should be declared void *ab initio*.
2. We shouldn't deal with problems on an *ad hoc* basis.
3. They have never married, but they consider their thirty-year relationship to be a *de facto* marriage.
4. There is *prima facie* evidence that he was involved in committing a theft crime.
5. His offer to buy your farm was a *bona fide* offer.
6. It is *malum prohibitum* and, therefore, does not demand *mens rea*.
7. Legal rights can be classified into *in rem* rights and *in personam* rights.
8. Once the creditor falls into *mora*, the debtor is liable only for *dolus* or *culpa lata*.

Exercise 2

Go through the meanings of the following archaic adverbials adapted along with their meanings from Haigh (2004/2009: 35–8) to translate the English sentences into Arabic.

- **Hereinbefore** meaning previously in this document or matter

This tenancy agreement is made up between the landlord (hereinbefore referred to as the first party) and the tenant (hereinbefore referred to as the second party).

- **Hereinafter** meaning later referred to in this matter or document

This contract is conducted between the seller (hereinafter referred to as the first party) and the buyer (hereinafter referred to as the second party).

- **Herefrom** meaning from this place or point

The goods shall be collected herefrom.

- **Herewith** meaning with this letter or document

I enclose herewith the plan.

- **Thereafter** meaning after that time

The products shall be transported to The Grange. Thereafter, they shall be stored in a warehouse.

- **Therein** meaning in that place, document or respect

The parties hereto shall refer to the contract dated 1 May 1999. It is agreed therein that…

- **Thereof** meaning of the thing just mentioned

Reference is made in paragraph 2 to the contract dated 1 July 2018. The parties thereof agreed that…

Note that 'therefor' *is different from* 'therefore'.

- **Therefor** meaning for that

The machine shall be delivered on 2 April 2019. The Company agrees to pay therefor the sum of $100,000.

- **Thereupon** meaning immediately or shortly after that

Delivery shall take place on 10 October 2017. Thereupon, the machine shall be stored in the Company's warehouse.

- **Whereat** meaning at which

The seller attempted to charge extra interest on late payment, whereat the buyer objected.

- **Wherefore** meaning as a result of which

The seller breached the contract, wherefore the buyer suffered damage.

- **Whereupon** meaning immediately after which

The sum of $10,000 shall be paid by the buyer to the seller on 6 April 2010, whereupon the buyer's liability to the seller shall be discharged.

- **Wherein** meaning in which

The contract dated 1 May 1999, wherein it is stated that the sum of $1,000 shall be paid by the tenant to the landlord on 1 June 2012.

Exercise 3

The following examples are extracted from Sabra (2003) along with their translations. Translate the archaic words highlighted for you:

The Contractor shall not assign the Contract or any part **thereof**, or benefit or interest **therein** or **thereunder**, without the prior consent of the Employer. (p. 19)

يتعهّد المقاول بعدم التنازل عن العقد او أيّ جزء ... أو أي ميزة أو مصلحة ... أو ... بدون موافقة مسبقة من صاحب العمل.

Both parties **hereby** agree as follows: (p. 30)

اتّفق الطرفان ... على ما يلي:

The Contractor shall be deemed to have inspected the Work Site and the surroundings **thereof** and to have read all available information in connection **therewith**. (p.30)

يعتبر المقاول قد عاين موقع العمل والبيئة المحيطة ... وإطّلع على كلّ المعلومات المُتاحة المتعلّقة....

Assignment 1

The following contract is taken from '*Alexcham*' (www.alexcham.org). Your task is to

1. discuss the strategic decisions that you have to take before embarking on translating the text,
2. translate it into English, paying extra attention to the technical terms used, and
3. comment on at least two local strategies opted for by you while translating the text.

عقد بيع سيّارة

الطرف الأول:______________________________

الطرف الثاني:______________________________

بما أن الطرف الأول (المشار إليه فيما بعد "البائع") يملك السيّارة الخصوصي نوع __________ لون __________ رقم __________ ، رقم محركها __________ ، ورقم الشاصي __________ ، موديل سنة __________ ،

وبما أن الطرف الثاني (المشار إليه فيما بعد "المشتري") يرغب بشرائها،

فقد تمّ الاتفاق بما يلي:

1. يتنازل الطرف الأول إلى الطرف الثاني بموجب هذا العقد عن ملكية السيارة المذكورة أوصافها أعلاه نظير مبلغ قدره __________
2. يلتزم الطرف الأول بأنه المالك الشرعي للسيّارة ولا يشاركه في ملكيتها أي شخص آخر.
3. يقرّ الطرف الثاني بأنه عاين السيّارة معاينة تامة نافية للجهالة، وقام بفحصها لدى محلّ مختصّ وقَبِلَ بِشرائِها على وضعِها الحالي.
4. يقرّ البائع على أنه تسلّم المبلغ المُشار إليه أعلاه كاملًا من المشتري ولم يتبقَ له بذمةِ المشتري أيّ مستحقات.

Note that the lexical item نظير *here can be replaced with* مقابل.

Note that قام بفحصها *can be reduced to* فحصها.

Is there any difference between تسلّم *and* استلم*? If yes, which one do you prefer?*

Why is it طرف ثان *not* ثاني*?*

طرف أول/بائع:	طرف ثان/مشتري:
توقيع:	توقيع:
شاهد أول	شاهد ثان
توقيع:	توقيع:

Some notes

- The connector بما أن (also بما إن) can be rendered into '*whereas*'.
- The verb يملك in such a context can be rendered into '*to own*'.

- The technical words شاصي, محرّك, and موديل can be rendered into '*chassis*', '*engine*', and '*model*' respectively.
- The verb عاين can be rendered into '*to examine*'.
- The phrase معاينة تامة نافية للجهالة can be translated into the adverb '*fully*' or '*fully and carefully*', as in '*the car was fully and carefully examined by the buyer*'.

Assignment 2

The following articles taken from the Omani Constitution (articles 15, 16, 17, 18, 19, 20, 25 and 38) along with their professional translations. Your task is to

1. identify any example of semantic repetition,
2. name the local strategy used to translate it, and
3. suggest your own translation if you are not quite happy with any part.

Here, in place of opting for a verbal sentence ينظّم القانون الجنسيةَ *where more emphasis is placed on* القانون, *the language user opted for* أسلوب الاشتغال *in a nominal sentence to lay more emphasis on* الجنسية.

الجنسية ينظمها القانون، ولا يجوز اسقاطها أو سحبها إلا في حدود القانون.

Nationality is regulated by the Law and it is not permissible to denaturalize or revoke it except within the limits of the Law.

Note that a disjunctive hamza همزة قطع, *not a conjunctive hamza* همزة وصل, *should be used in this example; therefore, we should write* إبْعاد *not* ابعاد.

لا يجوز ابعاد المواطنين أو نفيهم أو منعهم من العودة إلى السلطنة.

It is not permissible to deport, exile, or prevent Citizens from returning to the Sultanate.

المواطنون جميعهم سواسية أمام القانون، وهم متساوون في الحقوق والواجبات العامة، ولا تمييز بينهم في ذلك بسبب الجنس أو الأصل أو اللون أو اللغة أو الدين أو المذهب أو الموطن أو المركز الاجتماعي.

All Citizens are equal before the Law and share the same public rights and duties. There shall be no discrimination amongst them on the ground of gender, origin, colour, language, religion, sect, domicile, or social status.

Here, we can say الحرية الشخصية يكفلها القانون *in lieu of* الحرية الشخصية مكفولة وفقًا للقانون.

الحرية الشخصية مكفولة وفقًا للقانون. ولا يجوز القبض على إنسان أو تفتيشه أو حجزه أو حبسه أو تحديد إقامته أو تقييد حريته في الإقامة أو التنقل إلا وفق أحكام القانون.

Learn the differences among 'to arrest', 'to detain' *and* 'to imprison'.

Personal freedom is guaranteed according to the Law, and it is not permissible to arrest a person, search, detain, imprison, subject to residence detention, or restrict his freedom of residency or movement except in accordance with the provisions of the Law.

لا يجوز الحجز أو الحبس في غير الأماكن المخصصة لذلك في قوانين السجون المشمولة بالرعاية الصحية والاجتماعية.

It is not permissible to detain or imprison in places other than those designated for such purpose under the laws of prisons, where health and social care are provided.

What is the difference between لا يعرض *and* لا يتعرّض*? Discuss.*

Can we say المسيئة للكرامة *in place of* الحاطة للكرامة*?*

In من يفعل ذلك *we have two examples of grammatical cohesion. Could you identify their types?*

Comment on the translation of كما يبطل كل قول أو اعتراف يثبت صدوره تحت وطأة التعذيب *in terms of accuracy.*

لا يعرض أي إنسان للتعذيب المادي أو المعنوي أو للإغراء، أو للمعاملة الحاطة بالكرامة. ويحدد القانون عقاب من يفعل ذلك. كما يبطل كل قول أو اعتراف يثبت صدوره تحت وطأة التعذيب أو بالإغراء أو لتلك المعاملة أو التهديد بأي منهما.

No person shall be subjected to physical or psychological torture, inducement, or demeaning treatment. The Law stipulates punishment of whomever commits such acts. Any statement or confession proven to have been obtained under torture, inducement, demeaning treatment, or the threat of any of these acts, shall be deemed void.

التقاضي حق مصون ومكفول للناس كافة.

Litigation is a protected right and it is guaranteed to all people.

The subject of the English sentence is 'Preserving the national unity and safeguarding the secrets of the state', *which is plural, but the verb is* 'is'? *What is your opinion?*

الحفاظ على الوحدة الوطنية وصيانة أسرار الدولة واجب على كلّ مواطن.

Preserving the national unity and safeguarding the secrets of the State is a duty incumbent upon every Citizen.

Assignment 3

The following marriage contract along with its translation is taken from Almanna and Almanna (2008: 181–2). Your task is to

1. identify the main lexical features of the Arabic text,
2. identify any examples of textual restructuring, and
3. comment on the translation in terms of accuracy (e.g. addition, omission, etc.) and naturalness (e.g. readability, acceptability, idiomaticity, authenticity, and well-formedness).

Target text	**Source text**
Marriage Record No.: ... Civil Registry Office: ... Date: ...	سجل الزواج رقم: ... مكتب سجل مدني: ... التاريخ: ...
Marriage Contract	**عقد زواج**
On ..., month..., year... A.H., corresponding to ..., month..., year... A.D., at ... o'clock, in my presence, I, ..., the marriage registrar of the subdistrict ... belonging to the court of ...for personal status, this Marriage Contract has been concluded and entered into BY AND BETWEEN: ...,	في يوم ... من شهر ... سنة ... هجرية، الموافق ... سنة ميلادية، الساعة ... بحضوري أنا ... مأذون ناحية ... التابعة ... لمحكمة الأحوال الشخصية، صدر عقد الزواج التالي:
holding the ... nationality, working as a..., born on..., in..., residing in/at..., holding the Identity Card no..., issued on ... by..., whose mother's name is ...	تزوج ...، يحمل الجنسية ...، مهنته ...، وتاريخ ميلاده ...، ومحل ميلاده ...، ومحل إقامته ...، يحمل بطاقة رقم ...، تاريخ ...، صادرة من ...، اسم والدته ...
AND ..., holding ... nationality, working as a ..., born on ..., in ..., residing in/at ..., holding Identity Card No. ..., issued on ... by, whose mother's name is ...,	من ...، تحمل الجنسية ...، مهنتها ...، وتاريخ ميلادها ...، ومحل ميلادها ...، ومحل إقامتها ...، تحمل بطاقة رقم ...، تاريخ ...، صادرة من ...، اسم والدتها ...
FOR a dowry of ..., the down-payment of which is ..., and the deferred payment of which is ...	على صداق قدره ...، الحال منه ...، والمؤجل منه ...

Which one is more Arabic صادرة من *or* صادرة عن?

The lexical items صداق *and* حال *here can be replaced with* مهر *and* مُعجّل *respectively.*

The two parties hereto are married in accordance with the Holy Quran and the Sunna of the Prophet Mohammed, following an offer from the male spouse and an acceptance from the female spouse. This Contract has been executed after having been ascertained that eligibility is established and the two contracting parties hereto are of legal age for marriage, as witnessed by:	زواجًا شرعيًا على كتاب الله وسنة رسول الله (صل الله عليه وسلم) بإيجاب صادر عن الزوج وقبول صادر عن الزوجة، وذلك بعد التحقق من خلو الطرفين من كلِّ مانع شرعيّ ونظامي والتحقق من أن الزوجين قد بلغا السن القانونية، وذلك بشهادة كلّ من:
Name and signature of the first witness …	اسم الشاهد الأول وتوقيعه: …
Name and signature of the second witness …	اسم الشاهد الثاني وتوقيعه: …
Signature of the registrar …	توقيع المأذون

References

Alcaraz Varó, E. & Hughes, B. 2014. *Legal Translation Explained*. London/New York: Routledge. Fist published in 2002.

Almanna, A. 2016. *Semantics for Translation Students. Arabic-English-Arabic*. Oxford: Peter Lang.

Almanna, A., and Almanna, F. 2008. الترجمة: تاريخها، نظرياتها، تطبيقاتها *Translation: History, Theory & Practice*. London: Sayyab Books Ltd.

Awe, B.I., and P.S. Fanokun. 2018. Archaisms in Legal Contracts- A Corpus-based Analysis. *European Journal of English Language and Literature Studies* 6 (4): 5–20.

Beveridge, B.J. 2002. Legal English, How it Developed and Why it is not Appropriate for International Commercial Contracts. In *The Development of Legal Language*, ed. H.E.S. Mattila, 55–79. Helsinki: Kauppakaari.

Cao, D. 2007. *Translating Law*. Clevedon: Multilingual Matters.

Crystal, D., and D. Davy. 1969. *Investigating English Style*. London: Longman.

Danet, B. 1985. Legal Discourse. In *Handbook of Discourse Analysis*, ed. T. van Dijk, vol. 1, 273–291. London: Academic Press.

Dickins, J., and J.C.E. Watson. 1999. *Standard Arabic: An Advanced Course*. Cambridge: Cambridge University Press.

Dickins, J., S. Hervey, and I. Higgins. 2002. *Thinking Arabic Translation*. London/New York: Routledge.
El-Farahaty, H. 2015. *Arabic-English-Arabic Legal Translation*. London/New York: Routledge.
Haigh, R. 2004/2009. Legal English (2nd edition). London/New York: Routledge/Cavendish.
Hatim, B., A. Shunnaq, and R. Buckley. 1995. *The Legal Translator at Work: A Practical Guide*. Jordan: Dār al-Hilāl for Translating and Publishing.
Husni, R., and D. Newman. 2015. *Arabic-English-Arabic Translation*. London/New York: Routledge.
Mellinkoff, D. 1963. *The Language of the Law*. Boston: Little Brown.
Sabra, M. M. A. 2003. ترجمة العقود *Translation of Contracts*. Cairo: Dār Al-Kutub Al-Qānūniyya.
Tiersma, P.M. 1999. *Legal Language*. Chicago: University of Chicago Press.
Veretina-Chiriac, I. 2012. Characteristics and Features of Legal English Vocabulary. Accessed January 18, 2018. studiamsu.eu/wp-content/uploads/20.-p.103-107.pdf

CHAPTER 4

Syntactic Features

One way of describing legal language is to point out the linguistic features of the legal language at different levels: lexical, syntactical and discoursal, etc. Crystal and Davy (1969), Bhatia (1993), Tiersma (1999) and many others have worked along these lines. In this chapter, an attempt is made to outline the main syntactic features of legal language.

Syntax is the study of the structure of sentences. Syntacticians describe how words are put together to form phrases, clauses and sentences. For example, '*I bought a book two days ago*' is embedded as a relative clause in the sentence, '*The book that I bought two days ago is quite valuable or interesting*'.

In legal English, "syntactic features are probably more distinctive of legal English than are lexical ones, and certainly account for more of the difficulties of lay persons in comprehending it" (Danet 1985: 281). She identifies eleven of such features: 'nominalization', 'complex prepositional phrases', 'sentence length and complexity', 'unique determiners', 'impersonality', 'negatives', 'passive constructions', 'whiz deletion', 'conditionals', 'binomial expressions' and 'parallel structures'. Some of these syntactic features are discussed in detail in this chapter.

A. Almanna, *Legal Translation between English and Arabic*, https://doi.org/10.1007/978-3-031-14838-5_4

Sentence Length and Complexity

Legislative texts are characterized by the abundant use of long and complex sentences (cf. Crystal and Davy 1969: 200–201; Danet 1985: 281; Bhatia 1993: 111; Farghal and Shunnq 1992: 204; Rylance 1994: 18; Alcaraz Varó and Hughes 2014: 18–19; Janulevičienė and Rackevičienė 2011: 143 among others). A legislative English sentence can stretch over a number of lines, thus forming one whole paragraph. The length and complexity of these legislative sentences result from the use of both coordinating and subordinating clauses as well as reduced and embedded clauses with heavy use of modifications, prepositional phrases, long noun phrases and the like (Stanojević 2011: 72). In this regard, Janulevičienė and Rackevičienė (2011: 134) rightly comment: "The complexity of long sentences in written legal English is often enhanced by yet another grammatical trait, namely, several embeddings of different syntactical nature".

By way of explanation, let us consider the following example quoted from Hatim et al. (1995: 176–177):

إذا تخلّف المتعاقد عن التقدم لمباشرة مهام وظيفته وفقاً لتعليمات الوزارة ودون عذر مشروع خلال شهر من تاريخ توقيعه على العقد جاز للوزارة إلغاء العقد ويعتبر عندئذ كأن لم يكن وتخطر الوزارة المتعاقد بذلك كتابياً وتسقط كافة حقوقه قبلها.

The verb 'to assume', *which means here to take or begin to have power or responsibility, is different from* 'to resume' *which means to begin to do or pursue an activity, etc. again after a pause or interruption.*

If the Contracted Party fails to assume the duties of his post in accordance with the Ministry's instructions and without a legitimate excuse within one month of his signing the contract, the Ministry may cancel the contract which will then become null and void. In this event the Ministry shall notify the Contracted Party of this in writing and he shall have no claims regarding the Ministry.

This example clearly explains that "embeddings serve the striving for stating the whole legal principle in a single sentence". Being motivated by the desire to include all possibly arising circumstances, the draftsman uses a number of embeddings, thus creating "vagueness for a layperson reader, but is highly valued for accuracy and precision by legal professionals" (Janulevičienė and Rackevičienė 2011: 144).

Following is another example quoted from Hatim et al. (1995: 178–179):

إذا لم يرغب أيّ من طرفي العقد تجديده وجب عليه إخطار الطرف الآخر بذلك كتابة قبل اِنتهاء مدة العقد بشهرين على الأقل وإلا تجدد العقد لمثل مدته بقوة النظام.

What about the use of 'shall' *instead of* 'must'?

What about 'If neither party wishes to…'?

What about the use of '… has aversion to …'?

If one of the two parties does not wish to renew the contract this party must notify the other party of this in writing at least two months prior to the expiry of the contract, otherwise the contract shall by force of law be renewed for a similar period.

Complex Prepositional Phrases

One of the striking features in legal English in general and in legislative writing in particular is the use of, what Quirk et al. (1985: 302; also discussed in Bhatia 1993: 107; Danet 1985: 282; Almanna 2005: 55) refer to as, a 'complex prepositional phrase' instead of a simple preposition. For Bhatia (1993: 107) complex prepositional phrases are used in place of simple prepositions to avoid ambiguity that might be derived from the use of the simple ones. Similarity, in this text type, priority is given to clarity, precision, and all-inclusiveness at the expense of naturalness (for more details, see Almanna 2005: 55). Below are some examples:

Find more examples.

Complex prepositional phrases		*Simple prepositions*
! *in consideration of*	instead of	*for*
! *for the purpose of*	instead of	*for*
! *in accordance with*	instead of	*according to*
! *in the course of*	instead of	*during*
! *with the exception of*	instead of	*except*
! *in respect of*	instead of	*concerning*
! *with regard to*	instead of	*regarding*
! *in pursuance of*	instead of	*pursuant to*
! *by virtue of*	instead of	*by*
! *by the effect of*	instead of	*by*
! *by (the) dint of*	instead of	*by*

In addition to their high frequency in legal texts, the complex prepositional phrases "are often misplaced" (Danet 1985: 282)—they are usually placed between the subject and predicate of a sentence. To explain, let us consider the following example quoted from an agreement between the State of Kuwait and the Republic of Austria for the Encouragement and Reciprocal Protection of Investment (article 2):

> Each Contracting State shall in its territory and in accordance with its applicable laws and regulations encourage and admit investment and associated activities by investors of the other Contracting State …

Here, المُطبقة *can be replaced with* المعمول بها.

> تقوم كل من الدولتين المتعاقدتين وفقا لقوانينها ونظمها المطبقة بتشجيع وقبول الاستثمارات والأنشطة المرتبطة في أقليمها والتي يقوم بها مستثمرون تابعون للدولة المتعاقدة الأخرى.

Following is another example quoted from Hatim et al. (1995: 186–187):

> عند انتهاء مدة الإجارة وإذا لم يجدد العقد كما هو مذكور بهذا البند فعلى المستأجر أن يأخذ وصلاً خطياً من المؤجّر يتضمن استلامه للمأجور وتوابعه سالماً، وبحال اخلائه للمأجور بانتهاء المدة وإشعار المؤجر بذلك قبل ثلاثة أشهر من انتهاء هذه الاجارة أو بانتهاء السنة التي تجدد العقد بها بحكم هذا البند بدون استحصاله على وصل فللمؤجر إن وجد عيباً في المأجور أو تلفاً في التوابع او خللاً كليّا او جزئياً فيه أو فيها أن يقوم بتصليحه ويعود بما ينفقه هذا السبيل على المستأجر وهو مصدّق في قوله من جهة وجود العيب والتلف والخلل وبمقدار ما أنفق ولا تطلب منه بينة وقوله مصدّق بلا يمين.

Is the clause 'In the event of the lessee vacating the rented property …' *finite or non-finite? Can we delete the subject* 'the lessee'? *Discuss.*

> At the expiry of the period of lease, and in the event that the contract is not renewed as referred to in this clause, the lessee must obtain a written receipt from the lessor stating that the lessor has received intact the rented property and its accessories. In the event of the lessee vacating the rented property at the expiry of the period of lease and having notified the lessor of this three months prior to the expiry of this lease he/she may repair this and claim the costs from the lessee. The lessor is deemed to be trustworthy in his account of the fault, the harm or the damage, and the costs of repairing these, and does not have to provide any evidence as he is to be trusted without recourse to any oath.

Having perused a number of legal documents, we have found that the following prepositional phrases are quite often used:

Is it اختيار *or* إختيار*? Why?*

Is it بناءً على *or* بناءاً على*? Why?*

at
at a ratio of بمعدل
at the choice of باختيار
at the rate of بمعدل
at the request of بناء على طلب
at the service of في خدمة
at the expense of على حساب

for
for a period of لفترة
for the commencement of في بداية
for the purpose(s) of لأغراض
for the sake of من أجل
for the benefit of لفائدة

in
in accordance with طبقاً لـ
in conformity with وفقاً لـ
in agreement with تماشياً مع/تمشياً مع/مجاراة لـ/تناغماً مع
in connection with فيما يتعلّق بـ/فيما يخصّ/فيما يختص بـ/بشأن/بخصوص
in connexion with فيما يتعلّق بـ/فيما يخصّ/فيما يختص بـ/بشأن/بخصوص
in consideration of بقيمة
in consultation with بالتشاور مع
in cooperation with بالتعاون مع
in favour of لصالح
in lieu of بدلا من/بدلا عن
in line with تماشياً مع/تمشياً مع/مجاراة لـ/تناغماً مع
in need of بحاجة إلى
in place of بدلا من/بدلا عن
in preparation of تمهيداً لـ، تحضيراً لـ
in pursuance of عملًا بـ/بناء على
in relation with فيما يتعلّق بـ/فيما يخصّ/فيما يختص بـ/بشأن/بخصوص
in respect of فيما يتعلّق بـ/فيما يخصّ/فيما يختص بـ/بشأن/بخصوص
in terms of من حيث
in the course of أثناء
in the determination of للفصل بـ
in the exercise of في ممارسة
in the field of في مجال/في حقل
in the light of في ضوء
in the name of باسم/نيابة عن
in the presence of بحضور
in view of نظراً لـ
in violation of يخلّ بـ
in the absence of بغياب
in exchange for مقابل
in compensation for تعويضًا عن
in the determination of في تحديد، تحديدًا لـ

Is there any difference between بدلًا من *and* بدلاً عن*? If no, which one is more Arabic?*

on
on behalf of نيابة عن
on the basis of على أساس/بناء على

on the grounds of	بحجة، على أساس
on the pretext of	بذريعة
with	
with a view to	بغية أن
with emphasis on	تأكيداً على/مع التشديد على
with regard to	فيما يتعلّق بـ/فيما يخصّ/فيما يختص بـ/بشأن/ بخصوص
with respect to (also: *in respect of*)	فيما يتعلّق بـ/فيما يخصّ/فيما يختص بـ/بشأن/ بخصوص
with the aim of	بهدف
with the approval of	بموافقة
with the assistance of	بمساعدة/بمعاونة/بعون
with the consent of	برضا
with the exception of	باستثناء
with the exclusion of	باستثناء
with the grade of	بدرجة
with (the) intend of	بنيّة/بقصد
with the intention of	بنيّة/بقصد
with the object of	بهدف
with the support of	بمساندة/مساندة لـ
with the potential to	بهدف/بغية/مع إمكانية
under	
under the (safe) custody of	بحيازة (آمنة)
under the patronage of	تحت رعاية
under the vision of	تحت رؤية

Is it استثناء *or* إستثناء*? Why?*

Find more examples in this book and other sources.

Moreover, legislative writing sometimes includes both types, i.e. complex prepositional phrase and a simple preposition, joined by some syntactic devices, such as '*and*' or '*or*', for instance:

How would you translate them into Arabic?

- *In consideration of and for*
- *Under and in accordance with*
- *By virtue of and by*

Nominalization

Nominalization refers to the act of changing another part of speech, such as an adjective, verb, etc., into a noun by adding certain suffixes, such as *–tion*, *–ment*, *–dom*, *–ance*, and so on. A morphological tree can be drawn for the first example to make the point clear:

!	*accept*	→	*acceptance*
!	*legalize*	→	*legalization*
!	*authorize*	→	*authorization*
!	*found*	→	*foundation*
!	*pay*	→	*payment*
!	*inform*	→	*information*
!	*provide*	→	*provision*
!	*free*	→	*freedom*

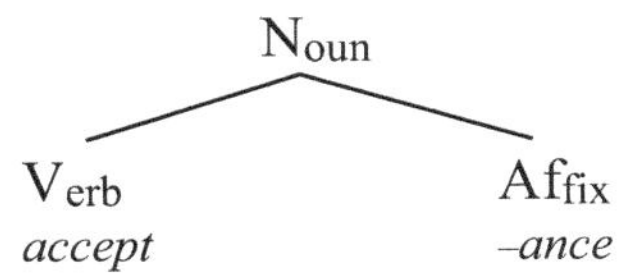

Nominalization is frequently used in legislative writing in order for law to "be stated as broadly as possible" (Tiersma 1999: 78). By way of explanation, let us consider this example extracted from the Preamble to the Human Rights Charter:

> Whereas recognition of the inherent dignity and of the equal and inalienable rights of all members of the human family is the foundation of freedom, justice, and peace in the world,...
>
> لمّا كان الاعتراف بالكرامة المتأصلة في جميع أعضاء الأسرة البشرية وبحقوقهم المتساوية الثابتة هو أساس الحرية والعدل والسلام في العالم، ...

Here, as can be observed, by the effect of nominalization opted for by the draftsman, the senser in the process of sensing expressed by the noun 'recognition = اعتراف' is obscured with the potential to include as many people as possible, thereby impersonalizing the clause.

Non-finite Clauses

Closely related to nominalization is the issue of non-finite clauses. To understand non-finite clauses, let us first distinguish between finite verbs and non-finite verbs. In some languages, such as English, the forms of finite verbs indicate tense, person, and number and non-finite verbs do not indicate tense, person, and number. In English, for example, a verb has three non-finite forms, viz.

1. Infinitive: *I have moved to another city* *to find a job*. (to find = non-finite verb)

To change this simple sentence to a complex one, i.e. to change the non-finite clause '*to find a job*' to a finite clause, one can opt for '*so that*' or '*in order that*' in place of '*to*', as in:

I have moved to another city *so that I can find a job*.

2. Past participle: *The question asked by you was very difficult.* (asked = non-finite verb)

In this simple sentence, there are two processes, namely process of being expressed by the verb '*to be*' in the past and process of saying expressed by the verb '*to ask*' in the past. Syntactically speaking, this simple sentence can be divided into two main parts:

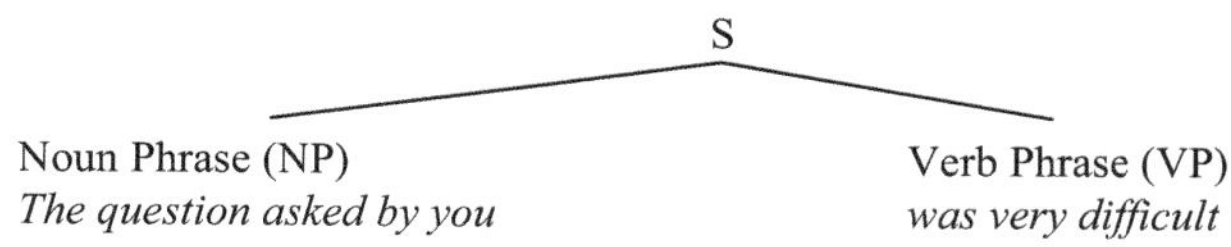

As can be noticed, the NP in the above sentence is complex as it contains another clause, which is non-finite. To change it to a finite clause, one needs a relative pronoun, such as '*which*' as in '*the question which was asked by you*'. When we translate such a structure into Arabic, the relative pronoun deleted in English is often brought back, as in السؤال الذي سألته (أو طرحته) كان صعبًا جدًا, i.e. '*The question that you asked was very difficult*'.

3. Gerund: *Having cleaned my flat*, *I went out.* (having = non-finite verb)

In this simple sentence, there are two material processes expressed by the verbs '*to clean*' and '*to go*'. It is worth mentioning that the first material process expressed by the verb '*to clean*' occurred before the second material process expressed by the verb '*to go*', thus indicating a time lapse. Further, in this sentence '*having cleaned my flat*' is a non-finite clause whereas '*I went out*' is finite. Now, to change this simple sentence to a complex one, i.e. to change the non-finite clause '*having cleaned my flat*' to a finite clause, one needs to bring back the subject '*I*' that fills a verb-specific semantic role of cleaner and inject the verb '*to clean*' with certain grammatical categories, such as tense (past), aspect (perfect), voice (active), and the like. This requires a linking word, such as '*after*', as in:

> *After I had cleaned my flat, I went out.* (After I had cleaned my flat = finite clause)

It is worth noting that these non-finite clauses cannot stand alone as they are dependent clauses serving as a subject or complement to a verb, preposition, noun, etc.

Whiz Deletion

It refers to the deletion of the relative pronoun, such as *who*, *which*, or *that*, and a form of the verb *to be* (cf. Dámová 2007: 20). When the relative pronoun along with verb *to be* is left out, the relative clause is called 'a reduced clause' or a non-finite clause as explained above. To make this point clear, let us consider the following example quoted from a treaty between the State of Bahrain and the government of the United States of America (article 9):

> For the purposes of this Treaty, an investment dispute is a dispute between a Party and a national or company of the other Party [~~which is~~] arising out of or [~~which is~~] relating to an investment authorization, an investment agreement or an alleged breach of any right [~~which is~~] conferred, created, or recognized by this Treaty with respect to a covered investment.

> لغايات هذه الاتفاقية النزاع الاستثماري هو نزاع بين طرف متعاقد ومواطن أو شركة من الطرف المتعاقد الآخر ناشيء عن أو يتعلّق بتفويض استثمار أو اتفاقية استثمار أو الإدعاء بانتهاك أي حق ممنوح أو ناشيء أو معترف به بموجب هذه الاتفاقية فيما يتعلّق باستثمار مشمول.

Is it ناشيء *or* ناشئ?

Is it إدعاء *or* ادعاء?

Following is another example adapted from Sabra (2003: 124):

> يدعو صاحب العمل المبيّن اسمه في استمارة بيانات التعليمات الخاصة بمقدمي العطاءات إلى التقديم بعطاءات المحددة في هذه المستندات والمشار إليها باسم "الأعمال"

> The Employer [~~which is~~] named in the ITB Data Sheet invites bids for the construction of the works, as [~~it is~~] defined in these documents, [~~which are~~] referred to as 'the Works'.

Passive Constructions

Passive forms are overused by legal writers because of its useful indirectness and formality. It comes in handy when the author strategically prefers not to mention the agent of the action, or when the text can apply to more than one possible agent (Tiersma 1999: 74–77). The following two examples quoted from *the Universal Declaration of Human Rights* (articles 1 and 2) illustrate this point:

> All human beings are born free and equal in dignity and rights. They are endowed with reason and conscience and should act towards one another in a spirit of brotherhood.

> يولد جميع الناس أحراراً متساوين في الكرامة والحقوق، وقد وهبوا عقلاً وضميراً وعليهم أن يعامل بعضهم بعضاً بروح الإخاء.

Note that 'be entitled to' *here can be replaced with* 'have the right to'.

> Everyone is entitled to all the rights and freedoms set forth in this Declaration, without distinction of any kind, such as race, colour, sex, language, religion, political or other opinion, national, or social origin, property, birth or other status.

Is it دون أي تمييز *or* من دون/بدون أي تمييز؟

> لكل إنسان حق التمتع بكافة الحقوق والحريات الواردة في هذا الإعلان، دون أي تمييز، كالتمييز بسبب العنصر أو اللون أو الجنس أو اللغة أو الدين أو الرأي السياسي أو أي رأي آخر، أو الأصل الوطني أو الاجتماعي أو الثروة أو الميلاد أو أي وضع آخر، دون أية تفرقة بين الرجال والنساء.

Conditionals

Conditionals are indicated by such syntactic indicators as

- If إذا
- In case في حال، في حالة
- In the event في حال، في حالة
- Should إذا
- Subject to بشرط، شريطة، على شرط

- Provided (that) بشرط، شريطة، على شرط
- Providing (that) بشرط، شريطة، على شرط
- On condition (that) بشرط، شريطة، على شرط
- So long as طالما
- As long as طالما
- Whereas لمّا
- Wherever كلّما

Conditionals are used for different reasons, for example, to specify who is included in a certain term, in particular when there are more people concerned. Let us discuss the following example quoted from Hatim et al. (1995: 176–177):

(على ألا *also*) على أن لا *means* شريطة أن *or* بشرط, *thus lending itself to* 'provided that', 'providing', *etc.*

يستحق المتعاقد إجازة عادية براتب كامل مقدارها خمسة وأربعين يوماً عن كل سنة كاملة من سنوات الخدمة. وتعتبر العطلة الصيفية بالنسبة إلى المدرّسين بمثابة الإجازة العادية ويجوز للوزارة تكليفهم أثناء الإجازة بمهام تتعلّق بعملهم <u>على أن لا</u> يقلّ ما يتمتع به المدرّس من إجازة عن خمسة وأربعين يوماً سنوياً.

The Contracted Party shall be entitled to a fully paid normal leave of forty-five days for each full year of service. The summer leave regarding teachers shall be considered as normal leave. During the leave the Ministry may charge them with duties related to their work <u>provided that</u> the leave enjoyed by the teacher is not less than forty-five days annually.

Following is an example adapted from Sabra (2003: 38–9):

Can we say يدفع المشتري *in place of* يتعيّن على المشتري أن يدفع? *Discuss.*

يتعيّن على المشتري أن يدفع فائدة بنسبة 5% على جميع الأقساط التي يتخلّف عن سدادها. <u>وفي حالة</u> عدم معالجة الانتهاك في غضون 30 يوماً من تاريخ الإستحقاق، يحق للبائع أن ينهي هذه الإتفاقية. يحق للمالك <u>بشرط</u> موافقة المستأجر دخول الوحدة السكنية لمعاينة العقار على إنه يجوز للمالك دخول السكن بدون موافقة المستأجر <u>في حالة</u> الطوارئ.

The Buyer shall pay 5% interest on all the installments for which the payments are in default. <u>In the event that</u> the default is not cured within 30 days from the due date, then the Seller shall have the right to determine this Agreement. Landlord shall have the right, <u>subject to</u> Tenant's consent, to enter the dwelling unit to inspect the premises provided that landlord may enter the dwelling unit without tenant's consent <u>in case of</u> emergency.

Unique Determiners

In legislative writing, in place of using demonstrative pronouns, words such as *such* and *said* are frequently used to simply mean *this*, *these*, *the*, *the particular*, *the one that is being concerned and no other*, and so forth. Let us consider these examples quoted from Sabra (2003: 39):

يوافق الطرف الثاني بموجب هذا العقد على شراء العقار المذكور بالمبلغ المذكور وهو ...

The said party of the second part hereby agrees to purchase said premises at said consideration of…

Is it أية تكاليفِ *or* أية تكاليفَ؟ *Discuss.*

في حالة تحمّل المقاول أيّة تكاليف أخرى ... يضع صاحب العمل هذه التكاليف في الِاعتبار.

If the Contractor incurs any further costs …, then the Employer shall take such costs into consideration.

Syntactic Features of Arabic Legal Discourse

Like English legal discourse, Arabic legal discourse is characterized by the use of 'nominalization', 'sentence length and complexity', 'impersonality', 'passivization', 'conditionals', and 'binomial expressions' as shown in the examples above.

In addition to these, Arabic legal language is also characterized by gender-biased terms. Gender, following Scott (1986: 1054) and Castro (2010: 106), can be defined as a "combination of socio-cultural roles" that are filled by social agents in a systematic and structural way based on their sex. Therefore, to overcome gender discrimination, social agents need to make every possible effort to change those practices that involve gender discrimination in a particular society. Linguistic discrimination, as an example of gender discrimination, reflects, in one way or another, what is going on in a particular society. So, if there is a kind of discrimination in a given society, this discrimination is reflected in the language used by those people practising discrimination.

Over the last four decades, a great number of studies on linguistic representation have been conducted in different languages (see for example Hellinger and

Bussmann 2001; Castro 2010; among others). They conclude that women and men are represented differently in these languages: more emphasis is placed on men, thus foregrounding them in the scene and making them visible. In this regard, Castro (2010: 107) holds that "language is sexist and androcentric, that it renders women invisible and that it stereotypes gender roles, in a way that is presented as natural, normal, and common sensical". Building on this, an androcentric translation can be defined as a type of translation where more emphasis is placed on men by the effect of certain grammatical forms and/or content specifications, thus foregrounding them in a given scene.

How would you define 'androcentric translation'?

In the following example extracted form Hatim et al. (1995: 186–187), the lexical item المستأجر that linguistically refers to male lessee, refers to both as reading or hearing the lexical item المستأجر in such a text/context invokes in our minds both sexes.

عند انتهاء مدة الإجارة وإذا لم يجدد العقد كما هو مذكور بهذا البند فعلى المستأجر أن يأخذ وصلاً خطياً من المؤجّر يتضمن استلامه للمأجور وتوابعه سالماً ...

Which one is more Arabic يتضمن استلامه *or* يتضمن تسلّمه*?*

At the expiry of the period of lease, and in the event that the contract is not renewed as referred to in this clause, the lessee must obtain a written receipt from the lessor stating that the lessor has received intact the rented property and its accessories.

Being fully aware of such a difference between the interfacing languages, the translators opted for the lexical item '*lessee*' that refers to both as the sex of the referent is not made explicit in the target language.

Another technique that can be used by translators is called 'neutralization' by Castro (2010). Neutralization refers to the act of removing any form or marker assigned to each gender in the source language. By way of example, let us discuss this example written for the purposes of this course:

ذهبتِ السّيدةُ أمس إلى مركزِ الشّرطةِ لتشتكي ضد أحد رجالِ الشّرطةِ.

Translation 1: The lady went yesterday to the police office to complain against one of the policemen.

Translation 2: The lady went yesterday to the police office to complain against one of the police officers.

Here, as one may observe, in translation 2, we have an example of neutralization where the neutral lexical item '*officer*' is used; therefore, the sex of the referent is not made explicit in the target text, thus resulting in a 'non-sexist translation'. This technique should be avoided as much as possible when dealing with legislative texts where accuracy is given a front seat.

More recently, we have seen, for example, the use of both words عزيزي and عزيزتي as equivalent to '*dear*' in an official letter sent to students in place of using the word عزيزي الطالب to stand for '*dear student*'. Not only does this specification, i.e. specifying both sexes without taking into account the nature of the language, require the verb conjugation, but also influences Arabic in terms of readability, authenticity, and idiomaticity that feed into naturalness, as shown in this example:

عزيزتي الطالبة، عزيزي الطالب،
كما تعلم، كانت المدارس مغلقةً لبعض الوقت بسبب فيروس كورونا ويتم الآن إعادة فتحها تدريجياً مرة أخرى. هذه الفترة كانت ولا تزال تمثل تحديًا كبيرًا لنا جميعًا. كطالب، لديك أيضًا مهام إضافية تتمثل بمتابعة التعلم والدراسة .... بمساعدة نصائحنا، نودّ أن نقدم لك الدعم اللازم حتى تتمكن/تتمكني من الاستمرار في الدراسة والتعلم وعدم تفويت الكثير من المواد التعليمية دون أن تضع نفسك تحت ضغط إضافي.

(<https://media.essen.de/media/wwwessende/aemter/40/KKBN_-_Schuelerbrief_arabisch.pdf>)

Here, as one may notice, the language user managed to conjugate the verb تتمكن or تتمكني, but s/he could not carry on dealing with the rest of words in this short passage, thereby failing to deal with the following examples:

كما تعلم/تعلمين or كما تعلمـ(ين)	كما تعلم
كطالب/طالبة or كطالبـ(ـة)	كطالب
تضع/تضعي or تضعـ(ي)	تضع

Below is another example taken from the Omani Constitution, article 35:

يحق لكل عماني وعمانية الترشح لعضوية مجلس الشورى والمشاركة في انتخاب أعضائه وفقًا للشروط المعتمدة للترشح أو لممارسة حق الانتخاب.

> Every Omani man or woman has the right to be a member in the Shura Council or vote for a member.

Accusative of Purpose المفعول لأجله

Accusative of purpose المفعول لأجله is an accusative Masdar, such as تقديرًا, اكرامًا, احترامًا, انتقامًا, طلبًا, خوفًا, خشيةً, أملاً, طمعًا, رغبة, تلبيةً, إنكارًا, اعترافًا, شوقًا, عونًا, رحمةً, شفقةً, إكبارًا, تعظيمًا, etc. used to specify the purpose, motive, or reason behind an action, as in

> وضعتُ أموالي في المصرف قبل أيام [why] خشيةَ أن يسرقها اللصوص.

As can be seen, خشيةَ أن يسرقها اللصوص is used to specify the purpose for putting the money in the bank. Here, there is an implicit process of sensing expressed by the accusative of purpose خشية. It is worth noting that with such a structure, i.e. the accusative of purpose, the actor in وضعتُ أموالي and senser in خشيةَ refer to the same referent. Further, there is no time lapse between the action and its reason, purpose, or motive. With this in mind, the above sentence can be translated into

> I put my money in the bank some days ago [why] for fear that the thieves might steal it.

To reinforce this point, let us consider the following example:

Can we say لرغبتها في إكمال دراستها؟ *If yes, is it still an accusative of purpose? Discuss.*

> سافرتْ [actor/traveller] إلى المملكة المُتّحدة [why] رغبةً [senser] في إكمال دراستها.

In the above example where the actor/traveller and senser refer to the same referent, i.e. هي '*she*', رغبة في إكمال دراستها is used to specify the reason behind travelling to the UK. Further, there is no time lapse between her desire to complete her studies and travelling to the UK. In translating the accusative of purpose into English, it is usually replaced with a purpose clause (be it finite or non-finite) introduced by '*to*', '*in order to*', '*with a view to*', '*so that*', '*in order that*', '*for fear that*', '*for fear of*', etc., depending on the context. As such, the above sentence can be translated into:

> She has travelled to the UK in order to complete her studies.

In Arabic legal discourse, the accusative of purpose is frequently used, as in the following example extracted from the Qatari Constitution (article 33). The accusative of purpose, as one may notice, was substituted with a non-finite clause of purpose introduced by '*in order to*'.

تعمل الدولة على حماية البيئة وتوازنها الطبيعي، تحقيقاً للتنمية الشاملة والمستدامة لكل الأجيال.

Use 'with a view to' *in place of* 'in order to'.

The State shall preserve the environment and its natural balance in order to achieve comprehensive and sustainable development for all generations.

Absolute Object المفعول المطلق

The absolute object (also known as 'absolute accusative' or 'cognate accusative') is a verb's object used after the verb; it is etymologically related to the verb, that is, it is derived from the same root, as in:

بكتِ الطّالبةُ بُكاءً مُرًّا البارحة. (بكتْ ... بكاءً)
ضَحِكَ الرّجلُ ضحكةً قصيرةً وقالَ ... (ضَحِكَ ... ضحكةً)

The absolute object is not only acceptable in Arabic, but it is a fine style and used fairly frequently for:

1. Emphasis, as in ضرب الرّجلُ الصّبيَ ضربًا,
2. Explanation of the type, as in أعملُ عملًا نافعًا,
3. Telling a number, as in دقتِ السّاعةُ دقتين.

As far as translation is concerned, it is usually reduced to a verb or phrasal verb. As regards the adjective, it lends itself to an adverb, thus resulting in transposition/class shift, as in the translations of the above sentences:

The student cried bitterly last night. (an adverb of manner)
The man let out a short laugh and said … (a phrasal verb collocating with the noun)

In Arabic legal discourse, the absolute object is frequently used. To explain, in the following example taken from the Omani Constitution, article 11 n° 5, the absolute object تعويضه تعويضا was replaced with the verb '*compensated*'.

الملكية الخاصة مصونة، فلا يمنع أحد من التصرّف في ملكه إلا في حدود القانون، ولا ينزع عن أحد ملكه إلا بسبب المنفعة العامة في الأحوال المبينة في القانون، وبالكيفية المنصوص عليها فيه، وبشرط تعويضه عنه تعويضا عادلا. والميراث حق تحكمه الشريعة الإسلامية.

Private ownership is safeguarded and no one shall be prevented from disposing of his property except within the limits of the Law. No property shall be expropriated except for the public interest in cases stipulated by the Law and in the manner specified therein, provided that the person dispossessed shall be fairly compensated. Inheritance is a right governed by Islamic Sharia.

Below is another example taken from the Qatari Constitution (article 10).

أقسم بالله العظيم أن أحترم النظام الأساسي للدولة والقوانين، وأن أرعى مصالح المواطنين وحرياتهم رعاية كاملة، وأن أحافظ على استقلال الوطن وسلامة أراضيه.

"I swear by Allah the Almighty to honour the Basic Statute of the State and the Laws and to fully safeguard the interests of the Citizens and their freedom and to preserve the independence of the Country and its territorial integrity".

As can be observed, the absolute object أرعى ... رعاية lends itself to '*fully safeguard*'. However, in the following example extracted from the same constitution (article 52), مقيم إقامة مشروعة, which is a form of absolute object was substituted with the noun phrase '*a legal resident*' in a relative clause '*who is a legal resident*' due to the differences between the interfacing languages.

يتمتع كل شخص مقيم في الدولة إقامة مشروعة بحماية لشخصه وماله، وفقاً لأحكام القانون.

Every person who is a legal resident of the State shall enjoy protection to his person and property in accordance with the provisions of the law.

Exercise 1

The following text is written and translated for the purpose of this course. Your task is to identify any complex prepositional phrase and replace it with a simple one if possible:

بما أنني أنا مالك الأموال غير المنقولة بموجب سندات التسجيل المرفقة قد إتّفقت على بيع حصصي المبيّنة أعلاه بثمن وقدره ... إلى المشترين المدرجة أسماؤهم وحصصهم أدناه، فإنني أرجو اتمام معاملة البيع حسب ما هو مبيّن أعلاه.

Whereas I am the owner of the immovable properties in accordance with the enclosed registration certificates and have agreed to sell my above-mentioned shares in consideration of and for ... to the buyers whose names and shares listed below, I request the completion of the selling transaction in accordance with the above-mentioned details.

Exercise 2

Translate the following sentences written for the purpose of this course into Arabic. Then, change the following underling clauses to non-finite clauses.

1. <u>After the contractor's tender is accepted</u>, the contractor shall submit a work programme.
2. <u>The man who was arrested by the police yesterday</u> was found guilty.
3. In the absence of any brothers or nephews, the throne shall pass to the uncles and their descendants according to the order <u>which is prescribed in paragraph (b) above</u>.

Exercise 3

The following texts are extracted from Hatim et al. (1995: 176–177). Change any sentence in the active form to passive:

تؤمن الوزارة للمتعاقد ولعائلته تذاكر السفر الجوي الآتية:
- من موطنه إلى المملكة في بداية مدة العقد مالم يكن مقيما بالمملكة عند تعيينه.
- من المملكة إلى موطنه ذهاباً وإياباً مرّة كلّ سنة أثناء مدة العقد عندما يُرخّص له بإجازة عادية.

The Ministry shall provide the Contracted Party and his dependents with the following air tickets:

- From his home country to the Kingdom at the beginning of the contract unless he is resident in the Kingdom at the time of his appointment.
- Return tickets from the Kingdom to his home country once every year during the period of the contract and when he is permitted a normal leave.

Is it ثلاثةِ رواتبِ *or* ثلاثة رواتبَ? *Discuss.*

Is it a 'three months salary' *or* 'three-month salary'?

تدفع الوزارة إلى المتعاقد بدلَ سكنٍ مقداره ثلاثة رواتب ويدفع هذا البدل دفعة واحدة سنويًا ومقدمًا في بداية مدة العقد ...

The Ministry shall pay the Contracted Party a housing allowance equivalent to three months salary. This allowance shall be paid in a lump sum annually and in advance at the commencement of the contract ...

يتعهد المقاول بعدم شراء منتجات أو خدمات بدون موافقة المالك المُسبقة.

The Contractor shall not purchase products or services without prior approval from the owner.

Assignment 1

The following text is taken from the UK Constitution. Your task is to

1. list the most common syntactic features,
2. discuss the strategic decisions that you have to take before embarking on translating the text into Arabic,
3. translate the text into Arabic, and
4. comment on at least three local strategies opted for by you while translating the text.

17. Freedom from expulsion from United Kingdom

17.1

No British National shall be expelled from the United Kingdom or deprived of the right to enter the United Kingdom.

17.2

1. Other persons may be expelled from the United Kingdom only in pursuance of a decision reached in accordance with law.
2. Any such persons who have been lawfully admitted to the United Kingdom shall be allowed, prior to expulsion,
   1. to submit reasons against expulsion; and
   2. have their cases reviewed by, and be represented for the purpose before, the competent authority or a person or persons especially designated by the competent authority.

17.3

This Article does not prevent the extradition of persons, through established legal procedures, for the purpose of standing trial for a criminal offence or serving a sentence lawfully imposed on them in another jurisdiction.

18. Right of asylum

18.1

Every person has the right to seek and be granted asylum in the United Kingdom in accordance with the law of the United Kingdom and international conventions, if they are being pursued for political offences.

18.2

In no case may an alien be deported or returned to a country, regardless of whether or not it is their country of origin, if in that country their right to life or personal freedom is in danger of being violated because of their race, nationality, religion, social status, or political opinions.

19. Equality

19.1

Everyone has the right to recognition as a person before the law.

19.2

All persons are entitled without any discrimination to the equal protection of the law.

19.3

The equal protection of the law and the enjoyment of the rights and freedoms set out in this Bill of Rights shall be secured without discrimination on any ground such as sex, race, colour, language, religion, political or other opinion, national or social origin, association with a national minority, property, birth, homosexuality, disability, age, or other status.

Assignment 2

The following text is adapted from the Iraqi Personal Status Law No. 188 of 1959. Your task is to

1. correct any spelling or grammatical mistakes, if any,
2. list the most common syntactic features used in the text,
3. discuss the strategic decisions that you have to take before embarking on translating the text into English,
4. translate the text into English, and
5. comment on at least four local strategies opted for by you while translating the text.

بعد الإطلاع على الدستور المؤقت وبناء على ما عرضه وزير العدل ووافق عليه مجلس الوزراء.
صدر القانون الآتي :
المادة الأولى:

1. تسري النصوص التشريعية في هذا القانون على جميع المسائل التي تتناولها هذه النصوص في لفظها أو في فحواها.
2. إذا لم يوجد نص تشريعي يمكن تطبيقه فيحكم بمقتضى مبادئ الشريعة الإسلامية الأكثر ملاءمة لنصوص هذا القانون.
3. تسترشد المحاكم في كل ذلك بالأحكام التي أقرها القضاء والفقه الإسلامي في العراق وفي البلاد الإسلامية الأخرى التي تتقارب قوانينها من القوانين العراقية.

المادة الثانية:

1. تسري أحكام هذا القانون على العراقيين إلا من أستثني منهم بقانون خاص.
2. تطبق أحكام المواد 19 و20 و21 و22 و23 و24 من القانون المدني في حالة تنازع القوانين من حيث المكان.

المادة الثالثة:

1. الزواج عقد بين رجل وإمرأة تحل له شرعاً غايته إنشاء رابطة الحياة المشتركة والنسل.
2. إذا تحقق إنعقاد الزوجية لزم الطرفين أحكامها المترتبة عليه حين إنعقاده.
3. الوعد بالزواج وقراءة الفاتحة والخطبة لا تعتبر عقداً.
4. لا يجوز الزواج بأكثر من واحدة إلا بإذن القاضي ويشترط لإعطاء الإذن تحقق الشرطين التاليين:

أ. أن تكون للزوج كفاية مالية لإعالة أكثر من زوجة واحدة.
ب. أن تكون هناك مصلحة مشروعة.

5. إذا خيف عدم العدل بين الزوجات فلا يجوز التعدد ويترك تقدير ذلك للقاضي.
6. كل من أجرى عقداً بالزواج باكثر من واحدة خلافاً لما ذكر في الفقرتين 4 و5 يعاقب بالحبس مدة لا تزيد على سنة أو بالغرامة بما لا يزيد على مائة دينار أو بهما.
7. إستثناء من أحكام الفقرتين 4 و5 من هذه المادة يجوز الزواج بأكثر من واحدة إذا كان المراد الزواج بها أرملة.

المادة الرابعة:

ينعقد الزواج بإيجاب -يفيده لغة أو عرفاً- من أحد العاقدين وقبول من الآخر ويقوم الوكيل مقامه.

Is there any difference between توفّر and توافر? If yes, which one do you prefer in such a context? Discuss.

المادة الخامسة:

تتحقق الأهلية في عقد الزواج بتوافر الشروط القانونية والشرعية في العاقدين أو من يقوم مقامهما.

المادة السادسة:

1. -لا ينعقد عقد الزواج إذا فقد شرطاً من شروط الإنعقاد أو الصحة المبينة فيما يلي:
   أ. إتحاد مجلس الإيجاب والقبول.
   ب. سماع كل من العاقدين كلام الآخر واستيعابهما بأنه المقصود منه عقد الزواج.
   ت. موافقة القبول للإيجاب.
   ث. شهادة شاهدين متمتعين بالأهلية القانونية على عقد الزواج.
   ج. أن يكون العقد غير معلق على شرط أو حادثة غير محققة.
2. ينعقد الزواج بالكتابة من الغائب لمن يريد أن يتزوجها بشرط أن تقرأ الكتاب أو تقرؤه على الشاهدين وتسمعهما عبارته ونشهدهما على أنها قبلت الزواج منه.
3. الشروط المشروعة التي تشترط ضمن عقد الزواج معتبرة يجب الإيفاء بها.
4. للزوجة طلب فسخ العقد عند عدم إيفاء الزوج بما اشترط ضمن عقد الزواج.

Note that العقد غير المعلّق *can be replaced with* العقد غير المشروط *in Arabic legal discourse.*

Assignment 3

The following text is taken from the Kuwaiti Constitution (articles 60–65). Your task is to list

1. the most common syntactic features used in the text,
2. any type of shift occurred through the process of translation,
3. any syntactic structuring opted for by the translator, and
4. any examples of expansion or reduction through the process of translation.

Is there any difference between الآتية *and* التّالية*? If yes, which one is correct here?*

يؤدي الأمير قبل ممارسة صلاحياته في جلسة خاصة لمجلس الأمة اليمين الآتية:
(أقسم بالله العظيم أن احترم الدستور وقوانين الدولة، وأذود عن حريات الشعب ومصالحه وأمواله وأصون استقلال الوطن وسلامة أراضيه)

Before assuming his powers, the Amir takes the following oath at a special sitting of the National Assembly: "I swear by Almighty God to respect the Constitution and the laws of the State, to defend the liberties, interests, and properties of the people, and to safeguard the independence and territorial integrity of the Country".

يعين الأمير، في حالة تغيبه خارج الإمارة وتعذر نيابة ولي العهد عنه نائبا يمارس صلاحياته مدة غيابه وذلك بأمر أميري. ويجوز أن يتضمن هذا الأمر تنظيما خاصا لممارسة هذه الصالحيات نيابة عنه أو تحديدا لنطاقها.

In the event of his absence outside the Country and the inability of the Heir Apparent to act as Deputy for him, the Amir shall appoint, by an Amiri Order, a Deputy who shall exercise his powers during his absence. The said Amiri Order may include a specified arrangement for the exercise of the said powers on behalf of the Amir, or a limitation of their scope.

يشترط في نائب الأمير الشروط المنصوص عليها في المادة 82 من هذا الدستور وان كان وزيرا أو عضوا في مجلس الأمة فلا يشترك في أعمال الوزارة أو المجلس مدة نيابته عن الأمير.

The Deputy Amir has to satisfy the qualifications laid down in Article 82. If he is a Minister or a member of the National Assembly, he may not take part in the ministerial functions or in the work of the Assembly during the period he is acting as Deputy for the Amir.

يؤدي نائب الأمير قبل مباشرة صلاحياته في جلسة خاصة لمجلس الأمة اليمين المنصوص عليها في المادة 61 مشفوعة بعبارة "وأن أكون مخلصا للأمير". وفي حالة عدم انعقاد المجلس يكون أداء اليمين المذكور أمام الأمير.

Before assuming his powers the Deputy Amir, at a special sitting of the National Assembly, takes the oath mentioned in Article 60 with the following phrase added thereto: "and be loyal to the Amir".

In case the National Assembly is not in session, the Oath shall be taken before the Amir.

تسري بالنسبة لنائب الأمير الأحكام المنصوص عليها في المادة 131 من هذا الدستور.

The provisions of Article 131 apply to the Deputy Amir.

للأمير حق اقتراح القوانين وحق التصديق عليها وإصدارها. ويكون الإصدار خلال ثلاثين يوما من تاريخ رفعها إليه من مجلس الأمة وتخفض هذه المدة إلى سبعة أيام في حالة الاستعجال ويكون تقرير صفة الاستعجال بقرار من مجلس الأمة بأغلبية الأعضاء الذين يتألف منهم. ولا تحسب أيام العطلة الرسمية من مدة الإصدار. ويعتبر القانون مصدقا عليه ويصدر إذا مضت المدة المقررة للإصدار دون أن يطلب رئيس الدولة إعادة نظره.

The Amir has the right to initiate, sanction, and promulgate laws. Promulgation of laws takes place within thirty days from the date of their submission by the National Assembly to the Amir. This period is reduced to seven days in case of urgency. Such urgency is decided upon by a majority vote of the members constituting the National Assembly. Official holidays are not counted in computing the promulgation. If the period of promulgation expires without the Head of State demanding reconsideration, the bill is considered as having been sanctioned and is promulgated.

Assignment 4

Determine whether the underlined verbs in the following agreement between the government of Ireland and the government of the United Kingdom of Great Britain and Northern Ireland are finite or non-finite. Then, translate it into Arabic:

The British and Irish Governments:
Welcoming the strong commitment to the Agreement reached on 10th April 1998 by themselves and other participants in the multi-party talks and set out in Annex 1 to this Agreement (hereinafter "the Multi-Party Agreement");
Considering that the Multi-Party Agreement offers an opportunity for a new beginning in relationships within Northern Ireland, within the island of Ireland and between the peoples of these islands;
Wishing to develop still further the unique relationship between their peoples and the close co-operation between their countries as friendly neighbours and as partners in the European Union;
Reaffirming their total commitment to the principles of democracy and non-violence which have been fundamental to the multi-party talks;
Reaffirming their commitment to the principles of partnership, equality and mutual respect and to the protection of civil, political, social, economic, and cultural rights in their respective jurisdictions;
HAVE AGREED as follows …

Some notes

- In the above text, '*welcoming*', '*considering*' and '*wishing to*' lend themselves to إذ ترحبان, وإذ ترغبان and وإذ تأخذان بنظر الاعتبار respectively.
- Similarly, '*reaffirming*' in '*reaffirming their total commitment*' can be translated as وإذ تؤكدان من جديد التزامهما التام

References

Alcaraz Varó, E. & Hughes, B. 2014. *Legal Translation Explained*. London/New York: Routledge. Fist published in 2002.

Almanna, A. 2005. *Aspects of Cohesion in Translating Legislative Texts from Arabic into English*. Unpublished master thesis. London: University of Westminster.

Bhatia, V.K. 1993. *Analysing Genre—Language Use in Professional Settings*, Applied Linguistics and Language Study Series. London: Longman.

Castro, O. 2010. Non sexist-Translation and/in Social Change: Gender Issues in Translation. In *Compromiso socialy traducción/Interpretación translation/Interpreting and Social Activism*, ed. J. Boéri and C. Maier. Granada (ES): ECOS.

Crystal, D., and D. Davy. 1969. *Investigating English Style*. London: Longman.

Dámová, P. 2007. *The Language of Law-A Stylistic Analysis with a Focus on Lexical (Binomial) Expressions*. Unpublished doctoral dissertation. Brno: Masaryk University.

Danet, B. 1985. Legal Discourse. In *Handbook of Discourse Analysis*, ed. T. van Dijk, vol. 1, 273–291. London: Academic Press.

Farghal, M., and A. Shunnaq. 1992. Major Problems in Students' Translations of English Legal Texts into Arabic. *Babel* 38 (4): 203–210.

Hatim, B., A. Shunnaq, and R. Buckley. 1995. *The Legal Translator at Work: A Practical Guide*. Jordan: Dār al-Hilāl for Translating and Publishing.

Hellinger, M., and H. Bussmann, eds. 2001. *Gender Across Languages: The Linguistic Representation of Women and Men*. Vol. 1. John Benjamins Publishing.

Janulevičienė, V., and S. Rackevičienė. 2011. Translation Strategies of English Legal Terms in the Bilingual Lithuanian and Norwegian Law Dictionaries. *Socialinių mokslų studijos/Societal Studies* 3 (3): 1073–1093.

Quirk, R., Greenbaum, S., Leech, G., & Svartvik, J. 1985. A *Comprehensive Grammar of the English Language*. Harlow: Addison Wesley Longman.

Rylance, P. 1994. *Legal writing and Drafting*. London: Blackstone Press Limited.

Sabra, M. M. A. 2003. ترجمة العقود *Translation of Contracts*. Cairo: Dār Al-Kutub Al-Qānūniyya.

Scott, J.W. 1986. Gender: A Useful Category of Historical Analysis. *The American Historical Review* 91 (5): 1053–1075.

Stanojević, M. 2011. Legal English – Changing Perspective. *Facta Universitatis, Series Linguistics and Literature* 9 (1): 65–75.

Tiersma, P.M. 1999. *Legal Language*. Chicago: University of Chicago Press.

CHAPTER 5

Modality

Is there any difference between 'modality' and 'modal verbs' or they refer to the same thing?

Modality refers to the language user's attitudes, opinions or moods towards what happens, towards what exists in the outside world, towards the truth of an utterance or towards the event described by that utterance. Modality in language falls into two main categories (Halliday 1970; Lyons 1977; Perkins 1983; Huddleston 1984; Farghal and Shunnaq 1999; Jarjour 2006; Almanna 2016a, 2018, among others):

1. deontic modality

The term 'deontic' comes from Greek where the word 'deon' means 'duty', 'necessity', 'obligation', etc. It is normally used to affect the situation; it is obligation/necessity-oriented. In other words, it describes how things ought to be. However, some scholars (cf. Downing and Locke 1992; Farghal and Shunnaq 1999; Jarjour 2006) state that deontic modality is also concerned with the concept of 'permission', as shown in these two examples:

How would you translate these two sentences into Arabic?

You [have to] visit your family. (obligation/necessity)
You [may] go. (permission)

Here, in these two sentences, as one may notice, the relationship between the speaker and the addressee expressed by the pronoun '*you*' is not dynamically neutral, but rather it is characterized by having a force

A. Almanna, *Legal Translation between English and Arabic*,
https://doi.org/10.1007/978-3-031-14838-5_5

dynamic value. To explain, the speaker, in these two sentences, is characterized by being-able-to-do (authority) while the addressee is characterized by being-able-not-to-do (powerlessness). As such, deontic modality has something to do with force dynamics.

2. epistemic modality

The word 'epistemic' comes from Greek where the word 'epistemikos' means 'to understand' or 'to have knowledge'. Epistemic modality is concerned with the degree of the language user's commitment to the truth of the proposition (cf. Downing and Locke 1992; Farghal and Shunnaq 1999; Jarjour 2006; Almanna 2016a, 2018 among others).

How would you translate this sentence into Arabic?

He's studied well; he ^{should} pass the exam. ('*should*' here refers to expectation)

Further, there are two sub-types of modality in language. These are 'dynamic modality' and 'root modality' (cf. Jarjour 2006; Almanna 2016b, 2018).

3. dynamic modality

The dynamic modality centres on the concept of 'ability'. So, it has nothing to do with the language user's opinion, attitude or mood.

Can we have more than one translation here?

He ^{can} speak English fluently. ('*can*' refers to ability)

Here, the speaker is describing a factual situation about the doer of the action, i.e. the actor/speaker. So, the modal verb '*can*' in this sentence can be replaced with the modalized phrase '*be able to*'.

4. root modality

The root modality is characterized by ambiguity as it combines 'dynamic modality' and 'deontic modality'.

One can translate this sentence into .يستطيع توم أن يذهب إلى الحفلة *Can we consider* يستطيع *here as an example of 'root modality'? Discuss.*

Tom ^{can} go to the party. — permission / ability

Here, the bi-valent modal verb '*can*' can be replaced with the modalized phrase '*be able to*' as in '*Tom is able to go to the party*', i.e. 'dynamic modality' or can be understood as '*Tom is permitted to go to the party*', i.e. 'deontic modality' (for more details, see Almanna 2016a: 93–99).

Arabic, for its turn, although it does not have a closet, well-defined class of modals to express such notions as obligation, necessity, lack of necessity, prohibition, possibility, advisability, ability, permission, request, expectation, etc., still has the potential resources to express the speaker/writer's attitude, opinion or mood towards what happens or what exists in the outside world (Almanna 2016a: 95). In this chapter, modality in Arabic is classified into four groups:

Can you find more examples?

1. Modalized particles	ســ، سوف، لعل، قد ...
2. Modalized verbs	يحق، يستحق، يجوز، يفترض، يجب، يتعيّن، ينبغي، يتوجّب، يُرجّح، يُستحسن، يُحتمل، يستطيع، يفضّل، يُحبّذ، يُستبعد...
3. Modalized prepositions	على، لـ ...
4. Modalized prepositional phrases	من المُرجّح، من المُمكن، من الجائز، من المفروض، من الواجب، من المحتمل، من المستبعد، من المفضل، من المحبّذ، من المُستحسن، من المُتعيّن، بمقدوره ...

As far as legislative texts are concerned, a fifth group can be added, i.e. the use of simple present as it can impose action obligations that become valid once they are declared, thus reflecting the illocutionary force of an order. This simple present legally used in Arabic usually lends itself to '*shall*' in English. Consider the following example quoted from the Law of Income Tax on Companies of 1981 (article 1) along with its official translation (emphasis added):

Can we say على أنحاء سلطنة عمان كافة? *If yes, what is the difference?*

1. يُسمّى هذا القانون ضريبة الدخل على الشركات لعام 1981.
2. يسري مفعول هذا القانون على كافة أنحاء سلطنة عمان ...

1. This Law shall be called The Law of Income Tax on Companies of 1981.
2. This Law shall be effective in all parts of the Sultanate of Oman ...

Try to find another translation to يسري مفعول.

To reinforce this point, the following two examples taken from the Omani Constitution (articles 8 and 9) can be considered:

Note that حتى يتم *here means* إلى أن يتم.

تستمر الحكومة في تسيير أعمالها كالمعتاد حتى يتم اختيار السلطان ويقوم بممارسة صلاحياته.

The Government shall continue to perform its functions as usual until the Sultan is chosen and exercises his authority.

What is the difference between 'government' *and* 'governance'?

يقوم الحكم في السلطنة على أساس العدل والشورى والمساواة. وللمواطنين— وفقًا لهذا النظام الأساسي والشروط والأوضاع التي يبينها القانون—حق المشاركة في الشؤون العامة.

The word عام *or* عامة *can be translated into* 'public' *or* 'general'. *Can we consider its translation here into* 'public' *as an example of 'divergence'?*

The Governance in the Sultanate shall be based upon justice, Shura, and equality. The Citizens, pursuant to this Basic Statute and the conditions and provisions prescribed by the Law, shall have the right to participate in public affairs.

Translating Modality: A Cognitive Approach

Building on linguistic and psycholinguistic perspectives, Bell (1991: 20) states that the translation process mainly happens within 'memory' in the sense that the transformation process involves two main phases, namely:

1. semantic, syntactic, and pragmatic "analysis of one language specific text (the source language text…) into a universal (nonlanguage-specific) semantic representation"; and
2. the synthesis of that semantic representation into the second language-specific text (the target language text)" (Bell 1991: 20; emphasis his).

Bell's approach accounts for translation in terms of information processing and requires both short-term and long-term memories for the decoding of the original text input and the encoding of the target text output (for more details, see Bell 1991: 43–76). Bell's approach takes a V-shaped movement; it follows a top down/ bottom-up structure as follows:

1. it starts with the visual recognition of the lexical items of the source text,
2. then it undergoes syntactic parsing in combination with mechanisms of lexical search processed by a frequent structure analyzer,
3. this is followed by semantic and pragmatic processing to generate a semantic representation supported by an idea organizer and a planner.

Once the decision to translate is taken at the level of semantic representation, the input is reprocessed by synthesizers distributed in pragmatic, semantic, and lexico-grammatical levels to be encoded in a new writing system, thus producing a target text.

By way of illustration, let us consider the following example quoted from the Law of Income Tax imposed on Companies in the Sultanate of Oman 1981 along with its official translation:

للمدير من وقت لآخر بعد الحصول على موافقة الوزير أن يفوض عنه أي موظف معين لتنفيذ أغراض هذا القانون في ممارسة صلاحيات محددة موكول تنفيذها إلى المدير أصلا بموجب هذا القانون ...

The Director shall from time to time, having obtained the agreement of the Minister, appoint any designated officer to carry out the objects of this Law in the exercise of defined powers of the carrying out of defined tasks the execution of which was originally entrusted to the Director by virtue of this Law ….

1. Visual recognition
2. Identifying the modalized verb, expression, etc. used → لـ
3. Identifying the function of modality in the ST (the modalized preposition لـ in Arabic is used here to indicate a permissive discretionary act. It can be replaced with modalized verbs, such as يجوز, يحق depending on the context)
4. Mechanism of lexical research → '*may*'
5. Encoding the draft semantically, pragmatically, lexicogrammatically and stylistically in the target text as in:

Official translation

The Director shall from time to time, having obtained the agreement of the Minister, appoint any designated officer to carry out the objects of this Law in the exercise of defined powers of the carrying out of defined tasks the execution of which was originally entrusted to the Director by virtue of this Law ….

Comment

Taking into account the context and co-text, one would not hesitate to conclude that the modalized preposition لـ is permissive, expressing duties, rather than obligations or commands. When the modalized preposition لـ is paraphrased, its intended meaning, i.e. له الحق '*to have the right to*' or يحق له '*to be entitled to*', will be identified easily (for more details on paraphrasing modal verbs, see Abdel-Fattah 2005: 44). Despite that, the translator opted for the use of the modal verb '*shall*'.

In English, the modal verb '*shall*' is normally used to express futurity or in the interrogative forms to express suggestion. However, in legal texts, particularly in legislative texts, it is often used to express obligation, command and in the negative forms to express prohibition. As stated earlier, modal verbs are characterized by ambiguity, contextuality and indeterminacy; therefore, they should be approached carefully.

Suggested translation

> The Director may from time to time, having obtained the agreement of the Minister, appoint any designated officer to carry out the objects of this Law in the exercise of defined powers of the carrying out of defined tasks the execution of which was originally entrusted to the Director by virtue of this Law ….

Legal Modality

In legislative texts, an obligation is imposed, duty is set forth, responsibility is assigned, and prohibition is performed by dint of certain grammatical forms and/or content specifications. In English, for example, modal verbs, such '*shall*', '*may*', etc. are frequently used to this end. In Arabic, modalized verbs (e.g. يجب), modalized particles (e.g. لـ), modalized prepositions (e.g. على), and modalized phrases (e.g. من الواجب) can be used for the same token.

Obligations

Obligations, to begin with, are classified by Farghal (2019: 166) into three main types, viz. 'action obligations', 'duty obligations', and 'conditional obligations'.

1. Action obligations

Here, there is an implicit يجب أن *before these verbs in simple present as* يجب أن ينشر, يجب أن يعمل به, يجب أن يصدر, يجب أن يبصم *and* يجب أن ينفذ.

Arabic and English show divergence in imposing action legal obligations. To explain, while in Arabic the present tense is used, in English '*shall*' is frequently employed. By way of example, let us consider the following example quoted from the Egyptian General Sales Tax Law no 11 of the year 1991 (article 5; emphasis added):

ينشر هذا القانون في الجريدة الرسمية **ويعمل** به من اليوم التالي لتاريخ نشره **ويصدر** وزير المالية اللائحة التنفيذية لهذا القانون خلال شهر من هذا التاريخ. **يبصم** هذا القانون بخاتم الدولة **وينفذ** كقانون من قوانينها ...

This Law **shall** be published in the Official Gazette and **shall** come into force as of the next day of publication. The Minister of Finance **shall**, within one month of enforcement, issue the executive regulations hereof. This Law **shall** receive the seal of the State and **shall** come into force as one of the State Laws ...

In Arabic, the word اقتصادي *can be translated into* 'economic' *or* 'economical' *depending on the context. So, we need to learn the difference between them.*

Here, as can be observed, in Arabic the action obligations are expressed by simple present ينشر, يعمل, يصدر, يبصم, and ينفذ. These obligations imposed by virtue of this simple present lend themselves, as one may notice, to the modal verb '*shall*' plus verb 1. To reinforce this point, the following example quoted from the Libyan Commercial Law, Book One (in Practicing Economic Activities, Chapter One, General Provisions, article 2; emphasis added) can be given serious consideration:

The conditional clause على أن تطبيق هذه الأحكام... *was translated into* 'provided that such provisions shall be applied'. *Here, as can be seen, the modal verb* 'shall' *was employed in a conditional clause. Is it correct? Discuss.*

تطبق على الأنشطة الاقتصادية أحكام القانون المدني، فيما لم يرد بشأنه نص في هذا القانون. على أن تطبيق هذه الأحكام لا يكون إلا بمقدار اتفاقها مع المبادئ العامة في هذا القانون.

The provisions of the Civil Law **shall** be applied to the economic activities which are not provided for in this Law, provided that such provisions **shall** be applied in as much as their correspondence with General Principles in this law.

The action obligation in Arabic is expressed by simple present تطبق على الأنشطة الاقتصادية أحكام القانون المدني. This lends itself to '*The provisions of the Civil Law shall be applied to the economic activities*'. In the following example extracted from the Omani Constitution, article 91 (emphasis added), the modalized verb يجب is used to express the action obligation:

يجب أن تتطابق القوانين والإجراءات التي لها قوة القانون مع أحكام النظام الأساسي للدولة.

Laws and procedures which have the force of law **shall** conform to the provisions of the Basic Statute of the State.

As one may observe, يجب أن تتطابق... that can be shortened to تتطابق without affecting the intended meaning lends itself to '*shall conform to* ...'.

2. Duty obligations

Duties can be assigned by virtue of certain grammatical forms or content specifications. In Arabic, for instance, the modalized preposition على is frequently used to this end. However, this does not exclude other lexical items, such as the noun واجب, i.e. duty, or verbs such as يتعيّن, يجب, يتوجّب, etc. that can be followed by على. In English, '*shall*' is frequently used, as explained in this example taken from the Jordanian Constitution (article 61 no 2; emphasis added):

Can we say على رئيس المحكمة الدستورية وأعضائها؟ *If yes, what do we call this style?*

على رئيس وأعضاء المحكمة الدستورية قبل مباشرتهم أعمالهم أن يقسموا أمام الملك يمينا هذا نصه "أقسم بالله العظيم أن أكون مخلصا للملك والوطن، وأن أحافظ على الدستور وأن أخدم الأمة وأقوم بالواجبات الموكولة إليّ بأمانة."

The President and Members of the Constitutional Court **shall** prior to assuming their functions take -before the King—an oath the text of which is: "I swear by Almighty God to be loyal to the King and the country, to uphold the Constitution, to serve the Nation, and to honestly perform the duties entrusted to me".

In this example, the modalized preposition على is employed in Arabic to assign duties. This deontic preposition على can be preceded by modalized verbs, such as يتوجّب, يجب, and يتعيّن, as in this example extracted from Pacific Settlement of Disputes (United Nations Charter, Chapter VI, article 33 no 1; emphasis added):

Note that in Arabic the preposition على *should be changed to* لـ *when it is preceded by* ينبغي, *as in ...* ينبغي لأطراف أي نزاع

يجب على أطراف أي نزاع من شأن استمراره أن يعرض حفظ السلم والأمن الدولي للخطر أن يلتمسوا حله بادئ ذي بدء بطريق المفاوضة والتحقيق والوساطة والتوفيق والتحكيم والتسوية القضائية، أو أن يلجأوا إلى الوكالات والتنظيمات الإقليمية أو غيرها من الوسائل السلمية التي يقع عليها اختيارها.

> The parties to any dispute, the continuance of which is likely to endanger the maintenance of international peace and security, shall, first of all, seek a solution by negotiation, enquiry, mediation, conciliation, arbitration, judicial settlement, resort to regional agencies or arrangements, or other peaceful means of their own choice.

In this example, as one may notice, the verb يجب can be removed without changing the duties assigned. يجب على altogether lends itself in English to '*shall*'. In the following example taken from the Charter of the United Nations, Chapter VII, article 44, a duty is assigned by the effect of '*shall*'. As one may notice, it is translated into ينبغي لـ. It is worth noting that ينبغي لـ can be replaced by the modalized preposition على or modalized verbs, such as يجب or يتوجب without affecting the quality of translation.

> When the Security Council has decided to use force it shall, before calling upon a Member not represented on it to provide armed forces in fulfillment of the obligations assumed under Article 43, invite that Member, if the Member so desires, to participate in the decisions of the Security Council concerning the employment of contingents of that Member's armed forces.

> إذا قرر مجلس الأمن استخدام القوة، فإنه قبل أن يطلب من عضو غير ممثل فيه تقديم القوات المسلحة وفاءً بالالتزامات المنصوص عليها في المادة 43، ينبغي له أن يدعو هذا العضو إلى أن يشترك إذا شاء في القرارات التي يصدرها فيما يختص باستخدام وحدات من قوات هذا العضو المسلحة.

The noun واجب, i.e. '*duty*' can be used in Arabic legal discourse to assign duties as in these two examples taken from the Omani Constitution (articles 12 no 2 and 38):

What is your opinion about the translation of تعاضد *into* 'collaboration'? *Is it accurate? If not, what do you suggest?*

The lexical item فتنة *can be translated into* 'sedition'. *Try to find the difference between* 'discord' *and* 'sedition'

> التعاضد والتراحم صلة وثيقة بين المواطنين، وتعزيز الوحدة الوطنية واجب. وتمنع الدولة كل ما يؤدي للفرقة أو الفتنة أو المساس بالوحدة الوطنية.

> Collaboration and compassion are intimate bonds amongst the Citizens. The reinforcement of the national unity is a duty. The State shall prevent anything that might lead to division, discord, or disruption of the national unity.

> الحفاظ على الوحدة الوطنية وصيانة أسرار الدولة واجب على كل مواطن.

Preserving the national unity and safeguarding the secrets of the State is a duty incumbent upon every Citizen.

In these two examples the noun واجب lends itself to the lexical item '*duty*'. To rewrite, for instance, تعزيز الوحدة الوطنية واجب by using the preposition على or يجب على, those on whom the duty is imposed, i.e. citizens' are foregrounded, as in على جميع المواطنين تعزيز الوحدة الوطنية. When this new version is translated into English, actionalizing, i.e. changing the noun تعزيز '*reinforcement*' to a verb '*to reinforce*' takes place in addition to foregrounding those on whom the duty is imposed, as shown in this table:

Re-write the Arabic article by using the modalized preposition على with or without يجب or يتعيّن. Then, re-write it by using the verb يلتزم.

The *reinforcement* of the national unity is a duty.	تعزيز الوحدة الوطنية واجب.
All citizens [foregrounded by mentioning and fronting] *shall reinforce* [actionalizing] the national unity.	على جميع المواطنين تعزيز الوحدة الوطنية.

In Arabic, مُلْزَم, which is اسم مفعول, can be used to assign duties, as in this example extracted from Hatim et al. (1995: 170–1):

Re-write the Arabic article without using من قبل.

إن الطرف الثاني ملزم باحترام الأنظمة الداخلية التي يضعها الطرف الأول والمصدق عليها من قبل السلطات المعنية بمقتضى القانون.

The Second Party is obliged to respect the internal regulations laid down by the first party and endorsed by the competent authorities in accordance with the law.

Here, مُلزَم is translated into '*be obliged to*', which can be replaced with '*shall*', as in:

The Second Party shall respect the internal regulations laid down by the first party and endorsed by the competent authorities in accordance with the law.

3. Conditional obligations

In Arabic, conditional legal obligations are usually expressed by the conditional markers إذا or في حالـ(ة) along with the past tense or present tense in the main clause, as shown in this example taken from the Jordanian Constitution (article 28, d) along with its official translation:

Note that a disjunctive hamza همزة قطع *should be used in* إلى *and* أمة.

وإذا توفي آخر ملك بدون وارث على نحو ما ذكر يرجع الملك الى من يختاره مجلس الامة من سلالة مؤسس النهضة العربية المغفور له الملك حسين بن علي.

Learn how to translate المغفور له *in such a context.*

Should the last King die without an heir in the manner prescribed above, the Throne shall devolve upon the person selected by the Parliament from amongst the descendants of the founder of the Arab Renaissance, the late King Hussein Bin Ali.

Here, the conditional legal obligation in Arabic is expressed by the conditional marker إذ along with the present simple يرجع in the main clause to refer to a case/situation in the future that instates an obligation when such a condition is realized. As can be seen, this present simple lends itself to '*shall*' in English. As regards '*should*' used in the conditional clause, it has nothing to do with 'futurity', but rather it can be replaced with '*if*', thus functioning as a conditional marker.

In the following example extracted from the Omani Constitution (article 45), the present simple يفوض is used in the main clause along with the conditional marker في حالة:

Note that يتولى رئاسة *can be shortened to* يترأس.

يتولى رئيس مجلس الوزراء رئاسة جلسات المجلس وله إسناد إدارة الجلسات التي لا يحضرها إلى أحد نواب رئيس الوزراء. وفي حالة غياب رئيس الوزراء ونوابه يفوض السلطان من يراه مناسبا لإدارة الجلسات.

The phrasal verb 'to preside over' *means to be in charge of something, such as a meeting, session, etc.*

The Prime Minister shall preside over the meetings of the Council of Ministers and may entrust one of his Deputies to conduct the meetings which he does not attend. If the Prime Minister and his Deputies are absent His Majesty the Sultan shall authorise whom His Majesty sees appropriate to conduct the meetings.

Note that the noun غياب *lends itself to the adjective* 'absent', *thus resulting in transposition. Try to find another example of transposition in the translation of this article.*

Here, the conditional legal obligation in Arabic is expressed by the conditional marker في حالة along with the present simple يفوض in the main clause to refer to a case/situation in the future that instates an obligation when such a condition is realized. This present simple lends itself to '*shall*' in English. As regards يتولى, it is an example of an action obligation that is why it lends itself to '*shall*'.

Rights, Benefits, and Entitlements

Rights

Generally, in grating rights, the relationship between the grantor المانح and grantee الممنوح is not equal, but rather the grantor is characterized by being-able-to-grant rights (powerfulness) while the grantee is characterized by being-able-not-to-give, but just to receive (powerlessness). To grant rights in Arabic legal discourse, the modalized particle لـ is frequently employed in these three main structures in Arabic, namely'

1. لـ + الشخص/الجهة، إلخ + الحق/حق في ...

... ولكل مواطن الحق في ممارسة العمل الذي يختاره لنفسه في حدود القانون.

Every Citizen has the right to engage in the work of his choice within the limits of the Law. (the Omani Constitution, article 12)

You need to learn the differences among المتهم, المدان, المشتبه به *and* المحكوم عليه.

للمتهم الحق في أن يوكل من يملك القدرة في الدفاع عنه أثناء المحكمة.

The accused has the right to appoint a person capable of undertaking his defence during the trial. (the Omani Constitution, article 23)

للمواطنين الحق في مخاطبة السلطات العامة فيما ينوبهم من أمور شخصية أو فيما له صلة بالشؤون العامة بالشروط والكيفية التي يعينها القانون.

The Citizens have the right to address public authorities on personal matters or matters in connection with public affairs, in the manner and conditions specified by the Law. (the Omani Constitution, article 34)

Note that a disjunctive hamza همزة قطع *should be used in words like* أو *and* أنظمة.

لكل أردني حق في تولي المناصب العامة بالشروط المعينة في القانون او الانظمة.

Every Jordanian shall be entitled to hold public offices under the conditions prescribed in law or regulations. (the Jordanian Constitution, article 22)

Identify any spelling mistake in the Arabic texts concerning the use of the conjunctive hamza همزة الوصل *and disjunctive hamza* همزة القطع.

يعرض رئيس الوزراء مشروع كل قانون على مجلس النواب الذي له حق قبول المشروع او تعديله او رفضه وفي جميع الحالات يرفع المشروع الى مجلس الاعيان ولا يصدر قانون الا إذا اقره المجلسان وصدق عليه الملك.

The Prime Minister shall refer the draft of every law to the House of Representatives which shall have the right to accept, amend, or reject the draft; in all cases the draft shall be referred to the Senate. No law may be promulgated unless passed by both Houses and ratified by the King. (the Jordanian Constitution, article 91)

Note that على أن *can be replaced with* شريطة أن, بشرط, على شرط *etc., thus lending itself to* 'provided (that)', 'providing (that)', 'on (the) condition that', *etc.*

2. يحق + لـ + الشخص/الجهة، إلخ + اسم ...

يحق للجماعات تأسيس مدارسها والقيام عليها لتعليم افرادها على ان تراعي الاحكام العامة المنصوص عليها في القانون وتخضع لرقابة الحكومة في برامجها وتوجيهها.

Congregations shall have the right to establish and maintain their own schools for the education of their own members provided that they comply with the general provisions of the law and be subject to the Government control in their curricula and orientation. (the Jordanian Constitution, article 19)

How would you translate وفقًا للشروط المعتمدة للترشح أو لممارسة حق الانتخاب?

يحق لكل عماني وعمانية الترشح لعضوية مجلس الشورى والمشاركة في انتخاب أعضائه وفقًا للشروط المعتمدة للترشح أو لممارسة حق الانتخاب.

Every Omani man or woman has the right to be a member in the Shura Council or vote for a member. (the Omani Constitution, article 35)

The word قوانين *here is* منصوبة *'accusative'. Why is it without* تنوين *'nunation'?*

3. يحق + لـ + الشخص/الجهة، إلخ + أن + فعل ...

عندما يكون مجلس النواب منحلاً يحق لمجلس الوزراء بموافقة الملك أن يضع قوانين مؤقتة لمواجهة الأمور الآتي بيانها:

When the House of Representatives is dissolved, the Council of Ministers- with the approval of the King- shall have the right to issue provisional laws to cover the following matters: (the Jordanian Constitution, article 94)

It is worth noting that the modalized لـ can be used without the noun حق or the verb يحق, in particular when the grantee is characterized by powerfulness, such as a king, president, minister, sultan, prince, UN, etc. as in these illustrative examples:

Note that بقصد *in article 105 no 3 can be replaced with* بهدف, بغرض, بغية, من أجل, *etc. However,* بقصد *is rhymed phonetically with* توصيات, خاصة *and* تفاصيل.

للجمعية العامة أن تقدم التوصيات بقصد تحديد التفاصيل الخاصة بتطبيق الفقرتين 1 و 2 من هذه المادة، ولها أن تقترح على أعضاء الهيئة عقد اتفاقات لهذا الغرض.

The General Assembly may make recommendations with a view to determining the details of the application of paragraphs 1 and 2 of this Article or may propose conventions to the Members of the United Nations for this purpose. (the United Nations Charter, Chapter XVI: Miscellaneous Provisions, article 105 no 3)

Is there any example of reduction and/or shift in the translation of article 58 no 29?

لجلالة السلطان دعوة مجلس عمان للاجتماع في الحالات التي يقدرها.

His Majesty the Sultan may summon Majlis Oman, outside the regular session … (the Omani Constitution, article 58 no 29)

Is there any example of expansion and/or shift in the translation of article 58 no 36?

لمجلس عمان اقتراح مشروعات قوانين وإحالتها إلى الحكومة لدراستها ثم إعادتها إلى المجلس.

Majlis Oman may propose draft laws and refer them to the Government for review, and then the Government shall return the same to the Majlis. (the Omani Constitution article 58 no 36)

As one may observe, in these three examples the modalized لـ lends itself to '*may*' to show that the General Assembly, His Majesty the Sultan, and Majlis Oman are characterized by authority and powerfulness, i.e. being-able-to-do.

Benefits and Entitlements

Benefits and entitlements can be expressed by a variety of different ways. In Arabic, to begin with, it can be expressed by verbs, such as يتمتع, يستحق and يُمنح as shown in these examples:

يتمتع الطرف الثاني، أثناء العقد، بكل الامتيازات والحقوق التي يقرها نظام العمل في المملكة العربية السعودية …

During the period of this contract, the Second Party shall enjoy all the privileges and rights recognized by the Labour Law … (Hatim et al. 1995: 170–1)

تتمتع الهيئة في أرض كل عضو من أعضائها بالمزايا والإعفاءات التي يتطلبها تحقيق مقاصدها.

The Organization shall enjoy in the territory of each of its Members such privileges and immunities as are necessary for the fulfilment of its purposes. (the Jordanian Constitution, article 105 no1)

The phrase بصفة قانونية *in article 35 was translated into* 'legally'. *What do we call this strategy?*

يتمتع كل أجنبي موجود في السلطنة بصفة قانونية بحماية شخصه وأملاكه طبقا للقانون. وعليه مراعاة قيم المجتمع واحترام تقاليده ومشاعره.

Every foreigner who is legally present in the Sultanate shall enjoy protection for himself and his property in accordance with the Law. He shall observe the values of the Society and respect the traditions and sentiments thereof. (the Constitution of Oman, article 35)

As one may notice the verb يتمتع lends itself to '*shall enjoy*' in all these examples. It is worth noting that in contracts the verbs يستحق and يمنح are frequently used. To explain, let us discuss these examples quoted from Hatim et al. (1995)

One of the synonyms of the verb استحق is استأهل. *Can we use it here to say* يستأهل المتعاقد إجازة عادية براتب كامل؟ *Discuss.*

يستحق المتعاقد إجازة عادية براتب كامل مقدارها خمسة وأربعون يومًا عن كل سنة كاملة من سنوات الخدمة.

The Contracted Party shall be entitled to a fully paid normal leave of forty-five days for each full year of service. (pp. 177–8)

تستحق المتعاقدة إجازة وضع براتب كامل مدتها خمسة وأربعون يومًا بما في ذلك أيام العطل الرسمية.

A female Contracted Party shall be entitled to a fully paid maternity leave of forty-five days including official holidays. (pp. 197–90)

Here يمنح المتعاقد *was translated into* 'he shall receive'. *Can it be considered an example of modulation?*

يمنح المتعاقد بعقد شخصي عند انتهاء الخدمة مكافأة تعادل راتب نصف شهر عن كل سنة كاملة من سنوات خدمته بشرط أن يكون قد أمضى خمس سنوات متوالية على الأقل في الخدمة بموجب العقد وبحد أقصى مقداره 30,000 (ثلاثون ألف ريال).

Upon termination of the service of the Contracted Party engaged by an individual contract, he shall receive a payment equivalent to half a month's salary for every full year of service, provided that he has remained in service for at least five consecutive years under the contract. This payment shall not exceed 30,000 SR (thirty thousand Riyals) (pp. 180–1).

To negate these entitlements from a contracted party, for example, one may opt for structures, such as لا يستحق or يسقط حقه في, as in these illustrative examples extracted from Hatim et al. (1995):

Note that a conjunctive hamza همزة وصل, *not a disjunctive hamza* همزة قطع, *should be used in* انقطاع. *What about* انتهت and ادانته? *Are they correct?*

أ- إذا انتهت خدمة المتعاقد بسبب الإنقطاع عن العمل سقط حقه في تذاكر العودة المستحقة له ولعائلته.
ث- إذا انتهت خدمة المتعاقد بسبب الإنقطاع أو فصله بقرار من مجلس المحاكمة أو ادانته جنائيًا سقط حقه في التعويض عن مدة الإجازة وفي مكافأة نهاية الخدمة.

a. If the service of the Contracted Party is terminated due to absence from work, he shall forfeit his right to the return tickets due to him and his dependents.
b. If the service of the Contracted Party is terminated due to absence from work, dismissal due to a court council decision or criminal conviction, he shall forfeit his right to the compensation for the period of leave and to the end-of-service payment. (pp. 180–1)

Note that إذا انتهت خدمة المتعاقد *was translated into* 'If the service of the Contracted Party is terminated'. *Is there any type of modulation here? Discuss.*

تدفع الوزارة إلى المتعاقد بدل سكن مقداره ثلاثة رواتب ويدفع هذا البدل دفعة واحدة سنويًا ومقدمًا في بداية مدة العقد ثم في بداية كل سنة من سنوات التجديد ولا يستحق المتعاقد بدل سكن إذا أمنّت الوزارة مسكنًا مؤثثًا.

The Ministry shall pay the Contracted Party a housing allowance equivalent to three months salary. This allowance shall be paid in a lump sum annually and in advance at the commencement of the contract, then at the beginning of each renewal year. The Contracted Party shall not be entitled to housing allowance when the Ministry provides him with furnished accommodation. (pp. 176–7)

Giving Permissions

To give permission in Arabic, the modalized verbs يجوز and جاز can be used, as shown in these examples taken from the Constitution of Jordan:

What about the modalized phrase من الجائز? *Can it be used in legislative texts? Support your answer with an authentic example.*

مدينة عمان عاصمة المملكة ويجوز نقلها الى مكان آخر بقانون خاص.

The City of Amman is the capital of the Kingdom, and it may be transferred to another place by a special law. (article 3)

لا يفرض التشغيل الالزامي على أحد غير أنه يجوز بمقتضى القانون فرض شغل أو خدمة على أي شخص:

Compulsory labour shall not be imposed on any person, but pursuant to law, work, or service may be imposed on any person: (article 13)

يجوز في حالة إعلان الأحكام العرفية أو الطوارئ أن يفرض القانون على الصحف والنشرات والمؤلفات ووسائل الإعلام والاتصال رقابة محدودة في الأمور التي تتصل بالسلامة العامة وأغراض الدفاع الوطني.

Identify any spelling mistake in the Arabic texts concerning the use of the conjunctive hamza همزة الوصل *and disjunctive hamza* همزة القطع.

In the event of the declaration of martial law or an emergency, the law may impose a limited censorship on newspapers, publications, books, and information and communication media in matters related to public safety and national defence purposes. (article 15, 5)

تنتقل ولاية الملك من صاحب العرش الى اكبر ابنائه سناً ثم الى اكبر ابناء ذلك الابن الاكبر، وهكذا طبقة بعد طبقة، واذا توفى اكبر الابناء قبل ان ينتقل اليه الملك كانت الولاية الى اكبر ابنائه ولو كان للمتوفى اخوة على انه يجوز للملك ان يختار احد اخوته الذكور ولياً للعهد وفي هذه الحالة تنتقل ولاية الملك من صاحب العرش اليه.

The Royal title shall pass from the holder of the Throne to his eldest son, then to the eldest son of that eldest son, and in linear succession in a similar process thereafter. Should the eldest son die before the Throne devolves upon him, his eldest son shall inherit the Throne, even if the deceased has brothers. The King may, however, select one of his brothers as heir apparent. In this event, the title to the Throne shall pass to him from the holder of the Throne. (article 28, a)

يجوز ان يعهد الى الوزير بمهام وزارة او اكثر حسب ما يذكر في مرسوم التعيين.

The Minister may be entrusted with the functions of one or more Ministries, as stated in the decree of appointment. (article 46)

In the Arabic version of article 60 no 2, there are two grammatical mistakes. Identify them.

في الدعوى المنظورة أمام المحاكم يجوز لأي من أطراف الدعوى إثارة الدفع بعدم الدستورية وعلى المحكمة إن وجدت أن الدفع جدياً تحيله إلى المحكمة التي يحددها القانون لغايات البت في أمر إحالته إلى المحكمة الدستورية.

In the case viewed by courts, any of the parties of the case may raise the issue of the non-constitutionality; the court shall—if it finds that the plea is serious-refer it to the court specified by the law for the purposes of the determination of its referral to the Constitutional Court. (article 60, 2)

In article 65, can we replace the word اعادة *with* تكرار*? If not, what is the difference between them? Further, is it* اعادة or إعادة*? What about* اعيان, اعضاء, اربع and انتهت*? Are they spelt correctly?*

1. مدة العضوية في مجلس الاعيان اربع سنوات ويتجدد تعيين الاعضاء كل اربع سنوات ويجوز اعادة تعيين من انتهت مدته منهم.
2. مدة رئيس مجلس الاعيان سنتان ويجوز اعادة تعيينه.

1. The term of membership in the Senate shall be four years; the 47 appointment of members shall be renewed every four years; and those of them whose term expired may be reappointed.
2. The term of office of the Speaker of the Senate shall be two years and he may be reappointed. (article 65)

'to resign his seat' *can be replaced with* 'to resign his post', 'to resign his position' *or* 'to resign his office'. *What about shortening it to* 'to resign'?

يجوز لاي عضو من اعضاء مجلس النواب ان يستقيل بكتاب يقدمه الى رئيس المجلس وعلى الرئيس ان يعرض الاستقالة على المجلس ليقرر قبولها او رفضها.

Any member of the House of Representatives may resign his seat by addressing the Speaker of the House in writing, and the Speaker shall place the resignation before the House to decide to accept it or reject it. (article 72)

As regards جاز, it is also used as in this example:

Identify any spelling mistake in the Arabic texts.

إذا رأى مجلس الأمن أن التدابير المنصوص عليها في المادة 41 لا تفي بالغرض أو ثبت أنها لم تف به، جاز له أن يتخذ بطريق القوات الجوية والبحرية والبرية من الأعمال ما يلزم لحفظ السلم والأمن الدولي أو لإعادته إلى نصابه.

Should the Security Council consider that measures provided for in Article 41 would be inadequate or have proved to be inadequate, it may take such action by air, sea, or land forces as may be necessary to maintain or restore international peace and security. (Charter of the United Nations, Chapter VII, article 42)

Prohibition

Another important function of modality is 'prohibition', which indicates forbidding something. In Arabic, prohibition can be expressed by the prohibitive لا, which indicates forbidding and demand, as in لا تسخر من الأطفال that can lend itself to '*Do not make fun of children*'. Here, in this example, by virtue of the grammatical form and content specification used, the Sayer is characterized by being-able-to-give-advice/order. In Arabic legal discourse, this prohibitive لا is frequently used with the modalized verb يجوز as in لا يجوز meaning it is not allowed to do. By way of example, let us consider these three articles taken from the Jordanian Constitution (articles 8, 9, and 10):

Here, we can also say لا يجوز القبض على أحد أو توقيفه أو حبسه أو تقييد حريته.

1. لا يجوز أن يقبض على أحد أو يوقف أو يحبس أو تقيد حريته إلا وفق أحكام القانون.
2. كل من يقبض عليه أو يوقف أو يحبس أو تقيد حريته تجب معاملته بما يحفظ عليه كرامة الإنسان، ولا يجوز تعذيبه، بأي شكل من الأشكال، أو إيذاؤه بدنياً أو معنوياً، كما لا يجوز حجزه في غير الأماكن التي تجيزها القوانين، وكل قول يصدر عن أي شخص تحت وطأة أي تعذيب أو إيذاء أو تهديد لا يعتد به.

Can we use the absolute object المفعول المطلق *in place of* تجب *to say* كل من يقبض عليه ... يعامل معاملة?

The verb يقبض عليه *was translated into* 'to seize'. *Can we use* 'to arrest'? *Discuss.*

1. No person may be seized, detained, imprisoned, or the freedom thereof restricted except in accordance with the provisions of the law.
2. Every person seized, detained, imprisoned, or the freedom thereof restricted should be treated in a manner that preserves human dignity; may not be tortured, in any manner, bodily or morally harmed; and may not be detained in other than the places permitted by laws; and every statement uttered by any person under any torture, harm or threat shall not be regarded.

Identify any spelling mistake in the Arabic texts concerning the use of the conjunctive hamza همزة الوصل *and disjunctive hamza* همزة القطع.

1. لا يجوز ابعاد اردني من ديار المملكة.
2. لا يجوز أن يحظر على اردني الاقامة في جهة ما أو يمنع من التنقل ولا أن يلزم بالاقامة في مكان معين الا في الاحوال المبينة في القانون.

1. No Jordanian may be deported from the territory of the Kingdom.
2. No Jordanian may be prohibited from residing at any place; be prevented from movement; or be compelled to reside in a specified place, except in the circumstances prescribed by law.

Note that the noun حرمة *was translated into an adjective* 'inviolable', *thus resulting in transposition.*

للمساكن حرمة فلا يجوز دخولها الا في الأحوال المبينة في القانون، وبالكيفية المنصوص عليها فيه.

Dwelling houses shall be inviolable and may not be entered except in the circumstances prescribed by law, and in the manner provided for therein.

It is worth noting that لا يجوز can be replaced with يُحظر in Arabic legal discourse, as shown in this example:

للمساكن حرمة فلا يجوز/فيحظر دخولها الا في الأحوال المبينة في القانون، وبالكيفية المنصوص عليها فيه.

To reinforce this point, the following examples where يُحظر is used in place of لا يجوز can be discussed:

المتهم برئ حتى تثبت إدانته في محاكمة قانونية تؤمن له فيها الضمانات الضرورية لممارسة حق الدفاع وفقًا للقانون ويحظر إيذاء المتهم جسمانيًا أو معنويًا.

The accused is innocent until proven guilty in a legal trial in which the essential guarantees to exercise his right of defence in accordance with the Law are guaranteed. It is not permissible to harm an accused either bodily or mentally. (the Omani Constitution, article 22).

The verb يحظر *was translated into* 'it is not permissible', *thus resulting in modulation. Can we avoid this modulation?*

حرية تكوين الجمعيات على أسس وطنية ولأهداف مشروعة وبوسائل سلمية وبما لا يتعارض مع نصوص وأهداف هذا النظام الأساسي مكفولة وفقًا للشروط والأوضاع التي يبينها القانون. ويحظر إنشاء جمعيات يكون نشاطها معاديًا لنظام المجتمع أو سريًا أو ذا طابع عسكري، ولا يجوز إجبار أحد على الانضمام إلى أية جمعية.

لا يجوز *here was translated into* 'it is not permissible'. *Use* 'may' *to have another version.*

The freedom of forming societies on national basis, for legitimate objectives, by peaceful means, and in a manner that does not conflict with the provisions and objectives of this Basic Statute, is guaranteed in accordance with the terms and conditions prescribed by the Law. It is prohibited to form societies the activity of which is adverse to the order of society, secretive, or of a military nature. It is not permissible to force anyone to join any society. (the Omani Constitution, article 33).

The noun محظور derived from the verb يحظر can be also used in equational sentences as in this example:

Use يحظر or لا يجوز *in place of* محظورة *to have another version.*

المصادرة العامة للأموال محظورة، ولا تكون عقوبة المصادرة الخاصة إلا بحكم قضائي في الأحوال المبينة بالقانون.

General confiscation of property is prohibited. The penalty of specific confiscation shall only be imposed by virtue of a judicial decision and in such circumstances as prescribed in the Law. (the Omani Constitution, article 11 no 6).

Is it 'as prescribed in the law' *or* 'as prescribed by (the) law'?

Further, *la* of absolute negation لا النافية للجنس can be used in this regard, as in these examples:

لا جريمة ولا عقوبة إلا بناء على قانون، ولا عقاب إلا بناء على الأفعال اللاحقة للعمل بالقانون الذي ينص عليها. والعقوبة شخصية.

There shall be no crime except by virtue of a Law. There shall be no punishment, except for acts subsequent to the entry into force of the Law wherein such acts are stated. Punishment shall be personal. (the Omani Constitution, article 21).

لا سلطان على القضاة في قضائهم لغير القانون.

There shall be no power over judges in their ruling except for the Law. (the Omani Constitution, article 61).

As can be seen, in these examples, *la* of absolute negation is used four times لا جريمة, لا عقوبة, لا عقاب and لا سلطان indicating the absolute denial of the species in the circumstance(s) defined by the sentences. In these examples, as one may notice, *at all*-frame is invoked in our mind by virtue of the use of *la* of absolute negation. With this in mind, لا جريمة ولا عقوبة إلا بناء على قانون, for instance, can be read in this way لا جريمة على الإطلاق ولا عقوبة على الإطلاق إلا بناء على قانون. This *la* of absolute negation lends itself in English legal discourse into an existing process expressed by 'there shall be no + noun'.

Exercise 1

Re-write the following sentences as required. Then, translate them into English:

1. يُسمحُ باستحداث هيئات مستقلة أخرى حسب الحاجة والضرورة في حدود القانون.

Use يجوز

2. يجب أن ينشر هذا القانون في الجريدة الرسمية ويتعيّن العمل به من تاريخ نشره على شرط لا يوجد ما ينص على خلاف ذلك.

Use simple present without يجب and يتعيّن

Use ما لم in place of على شرط

Note that the word هيئة *is spelt* هيأة *in some countries, such as Iraq.*

3. لمجلس النواب الحق في حلّ أي هيأة بعد انتهاء مهمتها بالأغلبية المطلقة.

Use يحق

4. إبعاد أي مواطن عن البلاد، أو منعه من العودة إليها محظور.

Use لا يجوز

5. للأموال العامة حرمة، وحمايتها واجب على الجميع وفقًا للقانون.

Use لا يجوز and replace the noun واجب with the verb يجب

Exercise 2

Re-write the following sentences as required. Then, translate them into Arabic:

1. Everyone has the right to hold opinions without interference. (use '*be entitled to*')
2. Anyone who is deprived of liberty by arrest or detention is entitled to take proceedings before a court in order that the court may decide without delay on the lawfulness of the detention. (use '*have the right to*')
3. Judgment shall be pronounced publicly but the press and public may be excluded from all or any part of the trial to the extent strictly necessary in the opinion of the court. (change the first finite clause to active)
4. The local authority applied for care orders according to section 31 of the Children Act 1989. (use '*pursuant to*')
5. Commission has the duty to encourage an understanding and acceptance of, and compliance with, the fundamental rights and freedoms guaranteed by the Bill of Rights. (use '*shall*')

Assignment 1

The following passage along with its translation is taken from Al-Murshidi (2012: 19–20). Your task is to

1. identify any spelling or grammatical mistakes in Arabic and correct them,
2. identify the type of modality used (for example obligations imposed, duties or responsibilities assigned, permissions given, rights conferred, etc.),
3. comment on the translation, paying special attention to modality, and

4. re-translate the text into English.

وإذا لم يقم الطرف الثاني "المشتري" بسداد الثمن الاجمالي المشار اليه في المواعيد له فانه يستحق على المبلغ المتأخر سداده فائدة تأخير من تاريخ الاستحقاق الفعلي للبائع بواقع 10 % (عشرة بالمائة) من قيمة المبلغ المستحق عليه...
وفي حالة قيام الطرف الثاني "المشتري" باستلام الوحدة يطبق عليه ذات الشروط وتعتبر يده غاصبة للوحدة موضوع البيع ويجب طرده.

If the Second Party (the buyer) delays paying the total price on its due payment an interest to be determined from the due date until the date of the actual payment to the seller at 10% (ten percentage) of the value of the amount owed. ...

In case of the second party (the buyer) received the unit, thus he will be applied to the same conditions, and therefore, he will be considered by usurper for the unit subject to this sale contract and thus must be expelled.

Assignment 2

The following articles along with their translations are extracted from the Iraqi Constitution (articles 8, 10, 15, 16, 20, 24, 25, 26, 33, and 36).

Your task is to

1. identify any spelling or grammatical mistakes in Arabic and correct them,
2. identify the type of modality used (for example obligations imposed, duties or responsibilities assigned, permissions given, rights conferred, etc.),
3. comment on the translation, paying special attention to modality, and
4. suggest changes if you are not quite happy with any.

يرعى العراق مبدأ حسن الجوار، ويلتزم عدم التدخل في الشؤون الداخلية للدول الاخرى، ويسعى لحل النزاعات بالوسائل السلمية، ويقيم علاقاته على اساس المصالح المشتركة والتعامل بالمثل، ويحترم التزاماته الدولية.

Iraq shall observe the principles of good neighborliness, adhere to the principle of noninterference in the internal affairs of other states, seek to settle disputes by peaceful means, establish relations on the basis of mutual interests and reciprocity, and respect its international obligations.

العتبات المقدسة والمقامات الدينية في العراق كيانات دينية وحضارية، وتلتزم الدولة بتأكيد وصيانة حرمتها، وضمان ممارسة الشعائر بحرية فيها.

The holy shrines and religious sites in Iraq are religious and civilizational entities. The State is committed to assuring and maintaining their sanctity, and to guaranteeing the free practice of rituals in them.

لكل فرد الحق في الحياة والأمن والحرية، ولا يجوز الحرمان من هذه الحقوق أو تقييدها إلا وفقاً للقانون، وبناءً على قرار صادر من جهة قضائية مختصة.

Every individual has the right to enjoy life, security and liberty. Deprivation or restriction of these rights is prohibited except in accordance with the law and based on a decision issued by a competent judicial authority.

تكافؤ الفرص حق مكفول لجميع العراقيين، وتكفل الدولة اتخاذ الاجراءات اللازمة لتحقيق ذلك.

Equal opportunities shall be guaranteed to all Iraqis, and the state shall ensure that the necessary measures to achieve this are taken.

للمواطنين، رجالاً ونساءً حق المشاركة في الشؤون العامة، والتمتع بالحقوق السياسية بما فيها حق التصويت والانتخاب والترشيح.

Iraqi citizens, men and women, shall have the right to participate in public affairs and to enjoy political rights including the right to vote, elect, and run for office.

تكفل الدولة حرية الانتقال للأيدي العاملة والبضائع ورؤوس الاموال العراقية بين الاقاليم والمحافظات، وينظم ذلك بقانون.

The State shall guarantee freedom of movement of Iraqi manpower, goods, and capital between regions and governorates, and this shall be regulated by law.

تكفل الدولة اصلاح الاقتصاد العراقي وفق اسس اقتصادية حديثة وبما يضمن استثمار كامل موارده وتنويع مصادره وتشجيع القطاع الخاص وتنميته.

The State shall guarantee the reform of the Iraqi economy in accordance with modern economic principles to insure the full investment of its resources, diversification of its sources, and the encouragement and development of the private sector.

تكفل الدولة تشجيع الاستثمارات في القطاعات المختلفة وينظم ذلك بقانون.

The State shall guarantee the encouragement of investment in the various sectors, and this shall be regulated by law.

ترعى الدولة المعاقين وذوي الاحتياجات الخاصة وتكفل تأهيلهم بغية دمجهم في المجتمع وينظم ذلك بقانون.

The State shall care for the handicapped and those with special needs, and shall ensure their rehabilitation in order to reintegrate them into society, and this shall be regulated by law.

ممارسة الرياضة حق لكل فرد وعلى الدولة تشجيع أنشطتها ورعايتها وتوفير مستلزماتها

Practising sports is a right of every Iraqi and the state shall encourage and care for such activities and shall provide for their requirements.

Assignment 3

The following articles are taken from the UK Constitution. Your task is to

1. discuss the strategic decisions that you have to take before embarking on translating the text,
2. translate the text into Arabic, paying special attention to the modalized verbs, prepositions, particles and phrases used, and
3. comment on at least four local strategies opted for by you while translating the text.

45.1 The Prime Minister shall keep Parliament and the Head of State fully informed about all matters pertaining to the conduct of government.

45.2 A Minister shall—

1. exercise general direction and control over all matters within the area of responsibility assigned to that Minister; and
2. render a full and regular account to Parliament and its committees concerning those matters.

45.3.1 As soon as practicable after appointment, a Minister shall—

1. lay before Parliament a full description of the responsibilities assigned to the Minister; and
2. indicate, with reasons, any matter concerning which the Minister may be unwilling to give a full account to Parliament. 2 A Minister shall inform Parliament of any significant change in those responsibilities or with respect to any matter for which the Minister may be unwilling to give such an account. …

55.1 Parliament may make laws with respect to any matter that is within the legislative powers of the Assemblies under Article 54, if—.

1. that matter cannot be adequately regulated by an individual Assembly; or
2. the regulation of a matter by an Assembly would prejudice the interests or interfere with the rights of residents of other parts of the United Kingdom.

55.2 Unless Act of Parliament otherwise expressly provides, a matter with respect to which Parliament has made a law under this Article shall be within the executive powers of national, regional, or local authorities. …

70.1 A Constitutional Bill shall not be presented to the Head of State for Assent unless it is passed, at its final reading in both the House of Commons and the Second Chamber, by a majority of all the members of the House.

70.2 If a Constitutional Bill, which has been passed by one House of Parliament, is not passed by the other House, the Bill shall be returned to the House by which it was passed, endorsed with the certificate of the Speaker of the other House, signed by the Speaker, that the B ill is a Constitutional Bill.

70.3 For the purposes of this Constitution, the expression "Constitutional Bill" means a public Bill which, in the opinion of the Speaker of the Second Chamber, whilst not containing an amendment to the Constitution,

1. is required by or under this Constitution to be enacted; or
2. gives detailed effect to any Article of the Constitution; or
3. affects any Article of the Bill of Rights, contained in Chap. 2; or
4. affects the functions of the Head of State or the composition, powers, or jurisdiction of the House of Commons, the Second Chamber, the Assemblies, the Supreme Court or the judiciary; and the expression "Constitutional legislation" shall be construed accordingly.

Assignment 4

The following text is taken from محاماة نت (www.mohamah.net). Your task is to

1. discuss the strategic decisions that you have to take before embarking on translating the text,
2. translate the text into English, paying special attention to the modalized verbs, prepositions, particles and phrases used, and
3. comment on at least four local strategies opted for by you while translating the text.

البند الأول: الوظيفة ومكان العمل:

أ. يقر الطرف الثاني أنه بناء على طلبه وموافقة الطرف الأول قبل العمل لدى الطرف الأول وتحت إدارته وإشرافه بوظيفة ... في مدينة ... أو بأي جهة أخرى يمارس فيها الطرف الأول نشاطه داخل المملكة وأن يقوم بكافة ما يدخل في اختصاص هذه الوظيفة مستخدماً في ذلك كفاءته ومؤهلاته وخبراته.

ب. لا يجوز للطرف الأول تكليف الموظف بعمل يختلف اختلافاً جوهرياً عن مهام الوظيفة المتفق عليها في هذا العقد بغير موافقته الكتابية، إلا في حالات الضرورة التي قد تقتضيها ظروف عارضة ولمدة لا تتجاوز ثلاثين يوماً في السنة وفقاً للمادة رقم (60) من نظام العمل.

البند الثاني: مدة العقد وفترة التجربة:

أ. أبرم هذا العقد لمدة غير محددة تبدأ من تاريخ بداية ... هـ الموافق ... م.

ب. يخضع الطرف الثاني لفترة تجربة مدتها ثلاثة أشهر ابتداءً من تاريخ بداية العقد الموضحة في الفقرة (أ) أعلاه ولا تدخل في حساب فترة التجربة إجازة عيدي الفطر والأضحى والإجازة المرضية، ويكون للطرفين إنهاء هذا العقد خلال هذه الفترة وفقاً للمادة.

ت. لا يجوز وضع الموظف تحت التجربة أكثر من مرة واحدة لدى الطرف الأول، واستثناء من ذلك يجوز باتفاق طرفي العقد إخضاع الموظف لفترة تجربة ثانية لا تتجاوز مدتها تسعين يوماً بشرط أن تكون في وظيفة أخرى أو عمل آخر، وإذا انتهى العقد خلال فترة التجربة فإن أياً من الطرفين لا يستحق تعويضاً كما لا يستحق الموظف مكافأة نهاية الخدمة وفقاً للمادة رقم (54) من نظام العمل.

ث. يخضع الطرف الثاني للبرنامج التدريبي الذي يحدده الطرف الأول لمدة ... شهراً بهدف تأهيله لمهام وظيفته، ويلتزم الطرف الثاني بالعمل لدى الطرف الأول لمدة لا تقل عن مدة التدريب أو سنة أيهما أطول.

البند الثالث: الأجر والمزايا:

يستحق الطرف الثاني الراتب والبدلات والمزايا التالية:

أ. يستحق الطرف الثاني خلال مدة التدريب راتباً شهرياً مقداره ...ريال.

البند الرابع: ساعات العمل والراحة الأسبوعية:

أ. يلتزم الطرف الثاني بأن يعمل لدى الطرف الأول ولمدة ثماني ساعات عمل يومياً ولا تزيد عن ثماني وأربعين ساعة أسبوعياً، وتخفض إلى ست ساعات عمل في شهر رمضان المبارك بحيث لا تزيد عن ست وثلاثين ساعة أسبوعياً.

ب. يثبت الطرف الثاني حضوره وانصرافه حسب الطريقة التي يحددها الطرف الأول لمتابعة ساعات الدوام وكذلك عليه الامتثال للتفتيش متى طلب منه ذلك.

البند الخامس: نسخ العقد:

حرر هذا العقد من نسخة، وتسلم الطرف الثاني صورة من العقد مختومة بختم الطرف الأول، واحتفظ الطرف الأول بأصل العقد.

الطرف الأول

الطرف الثاني

References

Abdel-Fattah, M.M. 2005. On the Translation of Modals from English into Arabic and Vice Versa: The Case of Deontic Modality. *Babel* 51 (1): 31–48.

Almanna, A. 2016a. *The Routledge Course in Translation Annotation: Arabic-English-Arabic*. London/New York: Routledge.

———. 2016b. *Semantics for Translation Students. Arabic-English-Arabic*. Oxford: Peter Lang.

———. 2018. *The Nuts and Bolts of Arabic-English Translation: An Introduction to Applied Contrastive Linguistics*. Newcastle upon Tyne, England: Cambridge Scholars Publishing.

Al-Murshidi, M. M. 2012. ترجمة العقود المدنية *Translating Civil Contracts*. Egypt: Dār Aj-Jami'a Aj-Jadīda for Publication.

Bell, R.T. 1991. *Translation and Translating: Theory and Practice*. London/New York: Longman.

Downing, A., and P. Locke. 1992. *A University Course in English Grammar*. Hemel Hempstead: Phoenix ELT.

Farghal, M. 2019. A Case Study of Modality in Legal Translation: The Omani constitution. In *Discourse in Translation*, ed. S. Faiq, 163–183. London/New York: Routledge.

Farghal, M., and A. Shunnaq. 1999. Major Problems in Students' Translations of English Legal Texts into Arabic. *Babel* 38 (4): 203–210.

Halliday, M.A.K. 1970. Functional Diversity in Language as Seen from a Consideration of Modality and Mood in English. *Foundation of Language* 6 (3): 322–361.
Hatim, B., A. Shunnaq, and R. Buckley. 1995. *The Legal Translator at Work: A Practical Guide.* Jordan: Dār al-Hilāl for Translating and Publishing.
Huddleston, R. 1984. *Introduction to the Grammar of English.* Cambridge University Press.
Jarjour, M. 2006. *A Relevance-Theoretic Account of the Translation of Ideological Assumptions in the Language of the News with Specific Reference to Translation from English into Arabic.* Unpublished doctoral dissertation. Salford: University of Salford.
Lyons, J. 1977. *Semantics.* Cambridge: Cambridge University Press.
Perkins, M.R. 1983. *Modal Expressions in English.* London: Frances Pinter.

PART II

Practice

CHAPTER 6

Legal Rights

Warming up ...

Before making a start, be familiar with the area by listening to the following videos:

Real vs personal property
https://www.youtube.com/watch?v=jnix8T3OM1M
Property law
https://www.youtube.com/watch?v=1bq7daBmjN0
Easement
https://www.youtube.com/watch?v=X99egMZf8t4
Mortgage
https://www.youtube.com/watch?v=CBIJwb37O_4&t=9s
Pledge, mortgage and hypothecation
https://www.youtube.com/watch?v=3b_rCbHu1Ho

A. Almanna, *Legal Translation between English and Arabic*,
https://doi.org/10.1007/978-3-031-14838-5_6

Exercise 1

Dear instructors: go through the following text adapted from Al-Aqaileh (2015: 205–211) to evaluate with your students the two translations (A and B) in terms of accuracy and acceptability.

Re-write the Arabic sentence without using من قبل.

A: Generally speaking, a right is an interest recognized and protected by the rules of law. B: In general, a right is an interest recognized and protected by the rules of law.	بشكل عام، فإن الحق هو مصلحة معترف بها ومحمية من قبل قواعد القانون.
A: The object of the right may be a material thing, such as the right of ownership over a piece of land, or immaterial thing, such as patent rights, copyrights and trademarks. B: The object of the right may be material (tangible), such as the right of ownership over a plot of land or immaterial (i.e. intangible), such as franchise, copyright or trademarks	محل الحق قد يكون شيئاً مادياً (ملموساً) مثل حق الملكية المقرر على قطعة من الأرض أو شيئاً غير مادي (غير ملموس) مثل حقوق الامتياز وحقوق النشر وحقوق العلامات التّجارية.

Note that in Arabic we can say تقسيم الشيء إلى *or* تقسيم الشيء على.

A: In general, legal rights can be categorized into: perfect and imperfect rights; positive and negative rights; rights in rem and rights *in personam*; and public and private rights. B: In general, legal rights can be classified into perfect or inchoate rights; positive or negative rights; *in rem* rights or *in personam* rights; and public or private rights.	إجمالًا، يمكن تقسيم الحقوق القانونية إلى حقوق كاملة وحقوق ناقصة، وحقوق إيجابية وحقوق سلبية، وحقوق عينية وحقوق شخصيّة، وحقوق عامة وحقوق خاصة.
A: A right *in rem* is enforceable against the public in general, but a right *in personam* is enforceable against one person in particular. B: An *in rem* right is a right enforceable against the entire world. A *personam* right, however, is a right enforceable against a particular person.	الحق العيني هو حق قابل للتنفيذ في مواجهة جميع الناس بشكل عام، لكن الحق الشّخصي هو حق قابل للتنفيذ في مواجهة شخص معين على وجه التّحديد.

Exercise 2

Dear instructors: evaluate with your students the translation of the following English text adapted from (www.coursehero.com), paying extra attention to the technical terms and syntactic structures.

Legal rights	الحقوق القانونية
When a person has legal rights, these rights can be either rights *in personam* (personal rights) or rights *in rem* (real rights).	عندما يكون للشخصِ حقوق/حقوقاً قانونيّة، فإن هذه الحقوق تكون إما حقوقٌ/ حقوقاً شخصيّة أو حقوقٌ/حقوقاً عينيّة.
To start with rights *in personam*, they are rights enforceable against another person, such as the rights arising from a contract—these rights can only be enforced against the other person in the contract. A license, for example, is an example of rights *in personam* because it belongs to a specific person.	فالحقوق الشّخصيّة هي حقوق يمكن محاججة شخص آخر بها، كالحقوق الناشئة عن عقد، على سبيل المثال، فتلك الحقوق لا يمكن محاججة شخص آخر غير الطرف الأخر في العقد. فالرخصة، على سبيل المثال، ما هي إلا حقٌ شخصيٌ لأنها ممنوحة لشخص بعينه.
Rights *in rem*, however, refer to the rights which are enforceable against the entire world. So, when a tenancy agreement is signed between a tenant and a landlord, for instance, the tenant has an *in rem* right to the house, and accordingly, this right is enforceable against not just the landlord with whom the contract is signed, but against anyone in the world who trespasses.	أما الحقوق العينية، فهي حقوقٌ يمكن المحاججة بها ضد العالم برمته، فلو تمّ توقيع عقد إيجار بين مُستأجر ومؤجّر، على سبيل المثال، فسيكون للمُستأجر حقٌ عينيّ في البيت، وهذا الحق العيني يمكنّه من محاججة ليس صاحب البيت الذي وقع معه عقد إيجارٍ فحسب، بل كلٌ من يحاول التعدي على حرمة البيت أيضا.

Is it حقوقٌ *or* حقوقًا*? Discuss.*

Note that the complex adjective ‘enforceable’ *collocates well with the noun* ‘right’. *It can be translated into Arabic as* قابل للتنفيذ, يمكن المحاججة به ضد,ملزم, *etc. Can you suggest something else?*

Note that the word ‘trespass’ *as a verb means to go onto someone’s private land without permission, as in:* ‘The man was arrested for trespassing on my property’.

Is it يُعرّفُ الحقُ *or* يُعرّفُ الحقَ?

Exercise 3

Translate the following text adapted from (elawpedia.com) into English paying, extra attention to the technical terms used and differences between Arabic and English.

الحقوق العينيّة

يعرّف الحق العيني بأنه سلطة مباشرة على شيء مادي معين بالذات يقرّها القانون لشخص معين. ويتبيّن من هذا التّعريف أن الحق العيني ينصبُ على شيء مادي، أي محسوس، معين بذاته، بحيث توجد صلة مباشرة بين صاحب الحق والشّيء.

وتنقسم الحقوق العينية إلى نوعين، هما:

1. **حقوق عينية أصلية،** كحق الملكية والحقوق المتفرعة عنها مثل حق الارتفاق، والذي يشمل حق المرور وغيرها من الحقوق، وحق الانتفاع، وحق المساطحة، وحق الشّفعة، وغيرها من الحقوق.
2. **حقوق عينية تبعية** وهي حقوق لا تكون مستقلة بذاتها بل تستند في وجودها إلى حق آخر، وعادة ما تستند إلى حق شخصيّ، فحق الرّهن هو حقّ عيني تبعي لأنه يوجد لضمان الوفاء بحق شخصي.

Some notes

1. The phrase الحق العيني can be translated as '*a right in rem*' or just '*a real (property) right*'.
2. The word مادي or محسوس can be rendered into material or tangible while its opposite غير مادي or غير محسوس lends itself to '*immaterial*' or '*intangible*'.
3. The adjectives أصلية and فرعية can be rendered into '*principal*' (or '*primary*') and '*accessory*' respectively.
4. The verb ينصبّ can be translated in this context as '*to be attached to*'.
5. Look at the translations of these technical terms:

the right of ownership	حق الملكية
an easement	حق الارتفاق
the right of way	حق المرور
the right of usufruct (or just simply 'the right of profit')	حق الانتفاع
the right of superficies	حق المساطحة
the right of preemption (or 'the preemptive right').	حق الشفعة

6. حق شخصي can be translated as '*personal right*' or more technically as '*in personam right*' or '*right in personam*'.
7. حق الرّهن can be rendered into '*a pledge*' رهن حيازي, '*hypothecation*' رهن مال منقول or '*mortgage*' رهن عقاري.
8. The noun ضمان can be translated as '*security*'. However, when it lends itself to a verb such as '*to secure*', there will be an example of what is called class shift (Catford 1965) or transposition (Vinay and Darbelnet 1958/1995).

Note that 'in one's possession' *means held by, or under the (safe) custody of someone, thus lending itself to* في حيازة. *Now, translate this example into Arabic.*

'The policemen have made every possible effort to know how long the victim's car had been in the suspect's possession (or under the custody of the suspect)'.

Exercise 4

Listen to the video suggested in this chapter that explains the differences among a pledge رهن حيازي, hypothecation رهن مال منقول and mortgage رهن عقاري to translate the following text adapted from (www.quora.com) into Arabic.

Pledge, hypothecation, and mortgage are three methods used by lenders to create a charge (i.e. an interest or right) on the asset. To begin with, a pledge is used when the lender takes actual possession of the property. Say for example you pledge your gold with the bank for a loan. The bank takes the possession of the gold and gives you the money. So a pledge is used only in case of 'movable' assets, and the pledgee/pawnee (i.e. lender) retains the possession of the goods until the pledger/pawnor (i.e. borrower) repays the entire debt. In case there is default by the borrower, the pledgee has the right to sell the goods in his possession. Hypothecation, however, is creating a charge against the security of 'movable' assets, but here the possession of the security remains with the borrower. When you take a car loan, for instance, the car is hypothecated to the bank (i.e. lender). Here it is a 'movable' asset and you (i.e. borrower) have the possession of the asset. Thus, in case of default by the borrower, the lender will have to first take possession of the security and then sell it. A mortgage, by contrast, is used for creating a charge against an immovable property which includes a land, a building, etc. (i.e. anything that is permanently attached to earth).

Exercise 5

Listen to the video that explains property law to translate the following text into English.

عندما تقوم بشراء بيتٍ ما، فإن فعل الشراء هذا يمنحك جملةً من الحقوق العينية. فيحق لكَ، على سبيل المثال لا الحصر، أن تستحدث حوضَ سباحةٍ فيه، ولكَ أيضًا أن تؤجرّ العقارَ أو جزءاً منه أو تبيعه.

ولكن السؤال الذي يطرح نفسه في هذا الصّدد، هل ستترتب لك حقوق عينية مطلقة تجاه العقار الذي اشتريته؟ في الحقيقة إن حقوقك ليست مطلقة، فليس من حقك، على سبيل المثال، أن تحوّل العقار إلى حديقة حيوانات أو مطعم متى ما تشاء.

وأفضلُ طريقة لفهم حقوق المالك العينيّة فيما يتعلّق بالعقار الذي يملكه هو أن نحدّدَ علاقة الآخرين بالعقار ذاته، فلو أجرّ مالكُ العقار عقارَهُ أو جزءاً منه لشخص آخر، فإن بعضَ الحقوق ستنتقل من المالك إلى المستأجر، ومن هذه الحقوق حق الانتفاع مثلا.

Note that على سبيل المثال لا الحصر *lends itself to* 'for example, but not limited to' *or* 'including but not limited to'.

Note that السؤال الذي يطرح نفسه في هذا الصّدد *can be translated into* 'but the question that may arise/jump into/spring into is'.

Exercise 6

Translate the following text taken from *Dutch Civil Law* (www.dutchcivillaw.com) into Arabic, paying extra attention to the technical terms used and differences between Arabic and English.

Easement

An easement is a real property right with which a land plot ('the servient land') is encumbered on behalf of the owner of a neighbouring land ('the dominant land') and which forces the owner of the encumbered land to tolerate that the owner of the neighbouring land makes use of his property in a certain way or that the owner of the neighbouring property is allowed to do something on his own land which the owner of 'the servient land' otherwise could have stopped (Article 5:70 (1) DCC).

The owner of the neighbouring—dominant—land has consequently a number of rights and powers to be exercised with respect to 'the servient land' of someone else. For this reason, the owner of 'the servient land' has no longer a full right of ownership. He isn't able, as a normal owner

Transition markers such as فيما يتعلّق، فيما يخصّ، بالنسبة إلى*, etc. can be rendered as* 'with respect to', 'in respect of', 'as regards', 'concerning', 'regarding', *etc.*

would, to stop his neighbour from using the servient or dominant land in accordance with the easement. To this point his right of ownership has been stripped with certain rights, that now belong to the proprietor of the easement.

Some notes

1. The term '*easement*' lends itself to حقوق الارتفاق.
2. The phrase '*the servient land*' lends itself in Arabic to العقار الخادم or العقار المرتفق به. As for '*the dominant land*' in this context, it can be translated functionally as العقار المخدوم or العقار المرتفق.
3. The verb '*to encumber*' in this context can be translated as يحمّل or يفرض, etc.
4. The word '*proprietor*' meaning '*right holder*' can be rendered as صاحب الحق (العينيّ).
5. The adjective '*immovable*' lends itself to (أموال) غير منقولة. Its opposite is '*movable*' (أموال منقولة).
6. The phrase '*a full right of ownership*' can be rendered as (حق) ملكية مطلقة or (حق) ملكية تامة.

Exercise 7

Complete the translation of the following text adapted from (almerja.com) into English, paying extra attention to the technical terms used:

حق الارتفاق

إن حق الارتفاق هو حق عينيّ يتقرّر على عقار يسمى بالعقار الخادم أو المرتفق به لمصلحة عقار آخر مجاور يسمى بـالعقار المخدوم أو المرتفق، وعليه فإنَّ حق الارتفاق لا يتقرّر إلا على عقار، فالمنقول لا يصلح أن يكون محلاً لهذا الحق. ويتميّز حق الارتفاق بحجته على الكافة، فحق الارتفاق حق عينيّ، فهو بهذا الاعتبار لا يحتج به في مواجهة مالك العقار الخادم فحسب ، وإنما يحتج به في مواجهة الكافة. كذلك يتميّز حق الارتفاق بكونه لا ينفصل عن العقار فهو يتبع العقار الخادم والمخدوم وينتقل معه.

An easement

An easement is a right *in rem* with which a property called a servient property is encumbered on behalf of a neighbouring property called a dominant property. Therefore,

Some notes

1. The verb يتميّز can be ignored while translating the sentence يتميّز حق الارتفاق بحجته على الكافة, as in '*An easement is enforceable against the entire world*'.
2. في هذا الاعتبار can be translated as '*in this respect*', '*in this regard*', '*in this connection*', etc.
3. The correlative conjunction... لا ... فحسب، وإنما (also لا ... فحسب، بل ... أيضًا) lends itself to '*not only ..., but ... as well*' or '*not only ..., but also ...*'

Reflect on these words: 'pledger & pledgee', 'mortgagor & mortgagee', 'pawner & pawnee', and 'bailer & bailee'

Exercise 8

In modern semantics, antonymy is divided into three types, viz. gradable antonyms (e.g. '*tall*' and '*short*'), nongradable antonyms (e.g. '*dead*' and '*alive*'), and relational antonyms (e.g. '*give*' and '*receive*'; for more details, see Almanna (2006b: 105–6). One of the features of legal writing in English is the use of the prefixes '*–er*' (or '*–or*') and '*–ee*' to indicate the flow of energy (Alcaraz and Hughes 2014, p. 22). The following legal text adapted from (www.coursehero.com) and translated into Arabic. Your task is to (1) find any example of this usage, (2) evaluate the translation, paying extra attention to the technical terms and syntactic structures, and (3) identify as many examples as you can of (a) shift and (b) non-finite clauses. Then, skim the book to find as many examples as you can of this usage.

Note that in Arabic, it is better to say من دون *or* بدون.

Licenses and Third Parties	الرخص والطّرف الثالث
A license is permission given by the landlord (legally known as licensor) to someone (legally known as licensee or license holder) to do specific acts on the licensor's land which would otherwise constitute a trespass.	إن الرّخصة هي إذنٌ يمنحه صاحب الأرض (يسمّى قانوناً مانح الرّخصة) لشخص آخر (يسمّى قانوناً الممنوح) ليقوم بأعمال محددة على أرض مانح الرّخصة، وإن هذه الأعمال تعدّ تعديًا من دون هذه الرّخصة.

Exercise 9

Translate the following text adapted from Al-Aqaileh (2015: 221) into English paying, extra attention to the technical terms used and differences between Arabic and English.

الحقوق العامة والحقوق الخاصة

عندما تكون العلاقة القانونية بين الدولة (بوصفها ممثلاً للمجتمع بشكل عام وليس بوصفها فردًا عاديًا) وبين الفرد، عندها يكون الحق عامًا. ولكن عندما تكون العلاقة القانونية بين الأفراد أنفسهم أو بين الأفراد وبين الدولة (بوصفها فردًا عاديًا)، عندها يكون الحق خاصًا.

Exercise 10

Translate the following text taken from *Dutch Civil Law* (www.dutchcivillaw.com) into Arabic, paying extra attention to the technical terms used and differences between Arabic and English.

Right of superficies

The right of superficies is a real property right which enables its proprietor—the superficiary—to have or obtain for himself buildings, constructions or plants in, on, or above an immovable thing owned by someone else (Article 5:101 (1) DCC).

A right of superficies is, in other words, a limited property right that provides its proprietor the full ownership of a component of another person's immovable thing. This thing may be someone else's land, but it's possible as well to establish a right of superficies on just a part of a building on that land, for instance on the left wing of a castle. A right of superficies may in addition serve to obtain the ownership of pipes, cables, and tubes under or above someone else's land.

Some notes

1. The phrase '*right to superficies*' lends itself to حق المساطحة. Related words include '*superficiary*' which can be translated as مساطح.
2. The word '*proprietor*' can be rendered as صاحب الحق (العينيّ).
3. The adjective '*immovable*' lends itself to غير منقولة (أموال). Its opposite is '*movable*' (أموال منقولة).

References

Al-Aqaileh, Z. M. 2015. المصطلحات القانونية باللغة الإنجليزية مع ترجمة كاملة إلى اللغة العربية *'Legal Terms in English fully Translated into Arabic'*. Jordan: Dār Al-Thaqāfa for Publication & Distribution

Alcaraz Varó, E. & Hughes, B. 2014. *Legal Translation Explained*. London/New York: Routledge. Fist published in 2002.

Almanna, A. 2016. *Semantics for Translation Students. Arabic-English-Arabic*. Oxford: Peter Lang.

Catford, J.C. 1965. *A Linguistic Theory of Translation*. Oxford: Oxford University Press.

Vinay, J. P., and J. Darbelnet. 1958/1995. *Stylistique comparée du français et de l'anglais. Méthode de traduction*. Paris: Didier (trans. and ed.) J. C. Sager & M. J. Hamel, *Comparative Stylistics of French and English: A Methodology for Translation*. Amsterdam/Philadelphia: John Benjamins.

CHAPTER 7

Contractual Obligations

Warming up …

Before making a start, be familiar with the area by listening to the following videos:

Contracts
https://www.youtube.com/watch?v=6QWZXl-qWos
https://www.youtube.com/watch?v=lYOsbq-CCOQ
https://www.youtube.com/watch?v=VnChrJuX7xg

Powers of attorney
https://www.youtube.com/watch?v=DpPw4RVwclA&t=25s
https://www.youtube.com/watch?v=P7rvZV9QJrc
https://www.youtube.com/watch?v=Yd_l60SFmdY&t=3s
https://www.youtube.com/watch?v=JpxwNAekXyY&t=50s

A. Almanna, *Legal Translation between English and Arabic*, https://doi.org/10.1007/978-3-031-14838-5_7

Exercise 1

Go through this bilingual text written for the purposes of this course to translate the English text adapted from (www.srdlawnotes.com) into Arabic:

The sources of obligations	مصادر الالتزامات
The sources of obligations in civil law can be classified into two main types, namely voluntary obligations and involuntary obligations.	يمكن تقسيم مصادر الالتزام في القانون المدني إلى نوعين رئيسين، هما المصادر الإرادية والمصادر غير الإرادية.
Voluntary obligations are classified into two types. They are • Contract • Unilateral contract	وتُقسّم المصادر الإرادية إلى نوعين، هما • العقد • (العقد بـ) إرادة منفردة
Involuntary obligations, however, are classified into • Unjust enrichment • Injury-producing action or tortious liability • Law	أما الالتزامات غير الإرادية، فتُقسّم إلى: • الإثراء بلا سبب • الفعل الضار أو المسؤولية التقصيرية • القانون

Can we say المصادر الغير إرادية *in Arabic? Discuss.*

Can we say وتنقسم المصادر الإرادية *in place of* وتُقسّم المصادر الإرادية*? If no, what is the difference?*

There are four sources of an obligation which are as follows:

1. Contractual obligation (i.e. obligations arising from contract) are those which are created by contracts or agreements. These obligations create rights ***in personam*** between the parties.
2. Delictual Obligations (i.e. obligations arising from a civil wrong) arise from tortious liability.
3. Quasi-contractual obligations (i.e. obligations arising from quasi-contracts). The term ‘Quasi’ is a Latin word, which means ‘as if’ or ‘similarly’. Quasi-contract is not a real contract entered into by the parties intentionally, but resembles a contract based on the principle of equity, i.e. “a person shall not be allowed to enrich himself unjustly at the expense of another”.
4. Innominate obligations are all the obligations which are other than those falling under the heads of contractual obligations, delictual obligations and quasi-contractual obligations.

Exercise 2

Dear instructors: evaluate with your students the English translation of the following Arabic legal text written for the purposes of this course, paying extra attention to the technical terms and syntactic structures.

Contract	عقد
A contract is much more than just an agreement between two parties as an agreement must have certain elements in order to be considered a contract, such as an offer, an acceptance, intention to make a legally binding agreement, and a legal capacity.	إنَّ العقد هو أكثر من أن يكون مجرّد اتفاق بين طرفين؛ إذ لا بدّ من توفر بعض العناصر كي يُعدّ الاتفاق عقداً، نحو الإيجاب، والقبول، والنيّة في الدخول في اتفاق ملزم قانونيًا، والأهلية.
Thus, we can conclude that the elements of a contract are: ! An offer ! An acceptance ! The object of the contract ! Consideration ! The legal capacity of the contracting parties (a capacity to contract). ! Mutual obligation	من هذا نستخلص أن أركان العقد هي: ! الإيجاب ! القبول ! محل العقد ! المقابل/العوض ! أهلية المتعاقدين ! إلتزام متبادل
There are a variety of contracts. Some of them are conditional while some others are implied. In case of implied contracts, the court should determine based on certain circumstances that there is an implicit agreement between the two parties.	وهناك أنواع عديدة من العقود، فبعضها معلّق وآخر ضمني وغيرها. وفي حالة العقود الضمنية، فإنه يقع على عاتق المحكمة إثبات أنه ثمة تعاقد بين طرفين قد تمّ بناء على ظروف معينة.

Is the verb 'based' *underlined finite or non-finite?*

Exercise 3

Is it a legislative text, juridical text or academic legal text?

Listen to the videos suggested in this chapter to translate the following text into Arabic, paying extra attention to the technical terms used and the differences between Arabic and English.

How would you translate 'not unlawful'?

Remember you will have an example of modulation when translating a passive form into active one.

Replace the connector 'as' *(line 9) with one of its synonyms.*

Note that the discourse marker 'broadly speaking' *can be shortened to* 'broadly'. *Can you replace it with another discourse marker without affecting the meaning?*

A contract will be legally binding when an offer by one party is accepted by the other party and the object of the contract is not unlawful.

An offer must be distinguished from mere willingness to deal or negotiate. If a man, for instance, offers to sell his car to his brother, and his brother decides not to continue before discussing its colour, size, price, and so on, then there will be no legally binding contract between them as there is no definite offer. When a person, for example, does not explicitly reject an offer, this cannot be considered as acceptance.

Broadly speaking, the acceptance must reflect the terms of the offer. If not, the acceptance is viewed as a rejection or counter offer.

Exercise 4

Dear instructors: evaluate with your students the translation of the following Arabic legal text written for the purposes of this course, paying extra attention to the technical terms and syntactic structures.

Note that 'furthermore' *can be replaced with* 'further', 'moreover', *etc.*

The object of the contract	محل العقد
In any contract, there must be something agreed on between two parties, such as selling a car, renting a house, publishing a book, and so on.	في أيّ عقد لا بدّ أن يكون هناك شيءٌ ما يتمّ الاتفاق عليه بين طرفين كأن يكون بيع سيّارة أو تأجير بيت أو نشر كتاب وغيرها.
Furthermore, the object of the contract must be lawful; otherwise, the contract is void.	وعلاوة على ذلك، يجب أن يكون محل العقد مشروعاً وإلا يعدّ العقد باطلًا.

Is it اتّفق *or* إتّفق*?*
And why?

Learn how to deal with words and expressions such as علاوة على ذلك, وبالتالي, ألا وهو, كأن يكون, أما, *etc.*

Note that غير شرعي (*also* غير قانوني) *can be rendered into* 'illegal' *or* 'unlawful'.

Why is the word لابدّ *translated into* 'must'?

The object of the contract	محل العقد
If a person agrees with somebody else to sell his/her car for a certain amount of money, here the object of the contract, that is, selling a car, is legal, and thus, the contract is legally binding.	فلو اتّفق/إتّفق شخصٌ على بيع سيارته لشخصٍ آخر مقابل مبلغ معيّن فهنا محل العقد، ألا وهو بيع السيارة، مشروع، وبالتالي العقد ملزم قانوناً.
However, if a person agrees with somebody else to forge, for instance, a general power of attorney for a certain amount of money, here the object of the contract, that is, forging a general power of attorney, is illegal.	أما إذا اتّفق/إتّفق شخصٌ مع شخصٍ آخر على تزوير وكالة عامة مثلاً مقابل مبلغ معيّن، فهنا محل العقد، ألا وهو تزوير وكالة، غير مشروع.

Exercise 5

Go back to exercise 4 to replace the following words/expressions with their synonyms:

- *such as* (line 3)
- *and so on* (line 5)
- *furthermore* (line 6)
- *otherwise* (line 8)
- *if* (line 10)
- *that is* (line 14)
- *and thus* (line 15)
- *however* (line 17)

Exercise 6

Translate the following text written for the purposes of this course into Arabic, paying extra attention to the technical terms used and differences between Arabic and English.

In some countries, the first stage in a contractual dispute is to enter into arbitration. Arbitration is a term used to describe the process by which the parties to a dispute submit their differences to the judgment of an impartial person appointed with the agreement of both sides. To be impartial means you have to treat both sides fairly and equally.

Arbitration can be either binding or non-binding. When it is binding, then the decision made by the arbitrator must be followed by the two disputing parties. By contrast, when it is non-binding, then the arbitrator's decision cannot be enforced by law.

Some notes

1. The word '*dispute*' can be translated into نزاع, خصومة, and the like.
2. The word '*arbitration*', which collocates well with verbs such as '*to enter into*' or '*to go to*', lends itself to تحكيم.
3. The adjective '*impartial*' means not supporting any of the sides involved in an argument. With this in mind, how would you translate the word '*impartial*'? Related words include '*impartiality*' and '*impartially*'.
4. The adjective '*binding*' lends itself to مُلزِم. Its opposite '*non-binding*' can be translated into غير مُلزِم.
5. The verb '*to enforce*' in such a context can be rendered as يُنفِّذ.

Exercise 7

Re-write the following sentence as required before translating it into Arabic:

When it is binding, then the decision made by the arbitrator must be followed by the two disputing parties.

a. Change the non-finite clause '*made by the arbitrator*' to a finite clause:

____

____

b. Change the passive form in '*the decision made by the arbitrator must be followed by the two disputing parties*' to active:

____

____

Exercise 8

Translate the following text written for the purpose of this course into English, paying extra attention to the technical terms used and differences between Arabic and English.

عندما يخلّ أحدُ أطرافِ العقد ببنود العقد المتّفق عليه، عليه أن يلجأ إلى المحكمة الابتدائية في منطقته ويرفع دعوى ضد الطرف الثاني. يحق للمدّعى عليه أن يطلب نقل الدعوى إلى المحكمة الابتدائية القريبة من سكنه. وعند النظر في الدعوى سيتحقق القاضي من العقد وأركانه. فإن كان محل التعاقد أو المقابل مخالفاً للقانون أو الآداب العامة فسيعدّ العقد باطلاً. وإن تبيّن أن العقدَ صحيح وملزم قانونيا للطرفين سيطلب من المدّعى عليه أن يوفي بالتزاماته المنصوص عليها في العقد.

Some notes

1. The verb أخلّ/يخلّ can be translated into '*to breach*', '*to break*', '*to commit a breach of*', '*to fail to meet*', '*to fail to perform*', and so on.
2. The word بنود, which is normally translated into '*clause*' in other types of agreements, can be rendered into '*term*'.
3. المحكمة الإبتدائية (also محكمة البداءة) lends itself to '*court of first instance*'.
4. المدعّى عليه can be translated into '*defendant*'. المدّعي can be rendered here into '*plaintiff*' or '*the complaining party*'.
5. The phrase وعند النظر في الدعوى can be translated into '*when the case is looked into*'.
6. The phrase محل التعاقد (also محل العقد) lends itself to '*the object of the contract*'.
7. The word مقابل (also العوض) can be rendered into '*consideration*'.
8. The word مخالف can be translated into '*at variance with*', '*contrary to*', etc. Alternatively, it can be lexically adjusted to يخالف, thus lending itself to '*to breach*', '*to infringe*', etc.
9. The phrase آداب عامة, which is commonly used in law, lends itself to '*public morals*'.
10. The lexical item باطل (also لاغٍ) lends itself to '*void*' or '*invalid*'.

11. The verb يوفي, which means '*to pay off*' in another context, lends itself here to '*to fulfil*' as it collocates well with the noun '*obligation*'.
12. The phrase المنصوص عليها can be translated into '*set forth in*', '*provided for in*', or '*stipulated in*'. Alternatively, one can make some syntactic adjustments, as in يوفي التزاماته التعاقدية, thus lending itself to '*to fulfil his contractual obligations*'.

Exercise 9

Translate the following text adapted from *Judicial Education Centre* (jec.unm.edu) into Arabic, paying extra attention to the technical terms used and differences between Arabic and English. Then, replace the following expressions with their synonyms:

- *complaining party*
- *by way of*
- *in other words*
- *in exchange for*

When you file a suit claiming a breach of contract, you, as a complaining party, must prove four elements to show that a contract existed. They are

- *An offer*, that is, one of the contracting parties made a promise to do or refrain from doing some specified action in the future.
- *Acceptance*, that is, the offer made by one party was accepted unambiguously by the second party by way of words, actions, etc.
- *Consideration*, that is, the value that induces the two parties to enter into a contract. In other words, it is something of value which was promised in exchange for doing or refraining from doing some specified action in the future.
- *Legal capacity*, that is, you are legally qualified for entering into a contract.

Some notes

1. The verb '*to file a suit*', which can be replaced with '*to file a lawsuit*', '*to bring a lawsuit*', '*to bring an action to court*', '*to bring a civil case to court*', '*to sue somebody for/over*', and the like, lends itself to يقيم دعوى, يرفع دعوى, يشتكي, and the like. In a similar vein, '*to drop a lawsuit*' or '*to drop a case*', which means to decide not to pursue a lawsuit, lends itself to يتنازل عن القضيّة/الدعوى/الشكوى.
2. The verb '*to refrain*' can be translated into احجم عن, امتنع عن, etc.
3. The verb '*to enter (into a contract)*' can be translated into يتعاقد or يلزم نفسه عقديًا.
4. The verb '*to induce*', which can be replaced with the verb '*to motivate*', can be translated as حثّ, حفزّ, شجّع, etc.
5. The phrase '*legal capacity*' can be translated into أهلية. Related words include '*incapacitate*' يجعله غير قادر *or* يعيق, '*incapacity*' فقدان الأهلية and '*incapacitated*' فاقد الأهلية.

Exercise 10

Translate the following text adapted from *Armstrong Legal* (www.armstronglegal.com) into Arabic, paying extra attention to the technical terms used.

Is the verb 'paid' *(line 7) finite or not finite? Discuss*

The word 'forbearance' *refers to the act of refraining from exercising a legal right, especially enforcing the payment of a debt.*

The word 'detriment' *means harm or damage, as in: 'You can follow this diet without detriment to your health'.*

For a valid contract to exist, five elements must be present. These elements are offer, acceptance, consideration, intention to create legal relations and certainty. This article outlines consideration in contract law.

What Is Consideration?

There must be a price paid by one party for the promise of the other party. The price legally called 'consideration' must be something of value, although it need not be money. Consideration may be some right, interest, or benefit going to one party or some forbearance, detriment, loss or

(*continued*)

responsibility given, suffered or undertaken by the other party.

So long as consideration exists, the court will not question its adequacy, provided that it is of some value. For example, the promise to pay a peppercorn rent in return for the lease of a house would be good consideration. Of course, the consideration must not be illegal or impossible to perform.

Note that the noun phrase 'a peppercorn rent' *means a very small amount of money paid as rent.*

Exercise 11

Translate the following text adapted from *Investopedia* (www.investopedia.com) into Arabic to a professional level:

A power of attorney is a legal document giving one person (the agent or attorney-in-fact) the power to act for another person (principal). The agent can have broad legal authority or limited authority to make legal decisions about the principal's property, finance, or medical care.

A power of attorney can end for a number of reasons, such as

- the principal dies,
- the principal evokes it,
- a court invalidates it,
- the principal divorces his/her spouse who happens to be the agent,
- the agent can no longer carry out the outlined responsibilities.

The complex word 'invalidate' *consists of three morphemes. What are they?*

A power of attorney should be considered when planning for long-term care. There are different types of power of attorney that fall under either a general power of attorney or limited power of attorney.

Replace 'to begin with' *with one of its synonyms.*

Replace the transition marker 'with respect to' *with one of its synonyms.*

To begin with a general power of attorney, the agent under a general power of attorney may be authorized to take care of issues such as handling bank accounts, signing checks, selling properties and assets like stocks, filing taxes, etc.

With respect to a limited power of attorney, it gives the agent the power to act on behalf of the principal in specific matters or events. For example, the limited power of attorney may explicitly state that the agent is only allowed to manage the principal's retirement accounts.

Some notes

1. '*A power of attorney*' lends itself to وكالة or توكيل.
2. While '*the agent*' (or '*attorney-in-fact*') can be translated as وكيل, '*the principal*' can be translated into موكّل.
3. '*broad authority*' and '*limited authority*' can be translated as صلاحيات واسعة and صلاحيات محدودة respectively.

Exercise 12

Go back to the text used in exercise 11 to

1. Identify the non-finite verbs used in the above text.
2. Change this sentence '*A power of attorney should be considered when planning for long-term care*' to a complex one.

Exercise 13

Listen to the videos suggested in this chapter to translate the following text adapted from (ar.wikipedia.org) into English:

الوكالة قانوناً عقد تفويض، أي توكيل، بمقتضاه يلتزم الوكيل بأن يقوم بعمل قانوني لحساب الموكل كما عرفته المادة (699) من القانون المدني المصري، والمادة (665) من القانون المدني السوري، والمادة (699) من القانون المدني الليبي، والمادة (716) من القانون المدني القطري.

وتقسّم الوكالات إلى عدّة أنواع:

الوكالة العامة

هي وكالةٌ تخوّل الشّخص الذي تُمنِح له حقَ التّصرف بكافة الممتلكات الخاصة بالمُوكّل. لذلك فأن منحها يجب أن يكون بشكل دقيق. وهذه الوكالة لا ينتهي مفعولها إلا بالغائها/بإلغاءها عن طريق المُوكّل. والوكالة العامة على نوعين:

Is it بالغائها *or* بإلغاءها? *Discuss.*

1. توكيل أحد الأشخاص
2. توكيل إلى محامٍ.

Why is it محام?

الوكالة الخاصة

هي وكالة تُمنِح للوكيل في مسألة أو عدة مسائل معيّنة، وهي لا تخوّله حق التّصرّف إلا فيما بيّنته من المسائل أو الاعمال وحسبما يقتضيه نوع العمل أو العرف. وتنتهي بانتهاء موضوعها.

Exercise 14

Before translating the following text taken from Almanna (2018: 229–30), try to be familiar with the technical terms used in this text and similar texts:

! to rent, to lease, to hire	إستأجر !
! to rent, to lease, to hire	أجّر !
! tenant, lessee, leasee, leaseholder	مستأجر !
! lessor	مؤجّر !
! rent	الأجرة/الإيجار !
to pay the rent	يدفع الإيجار
to fall behind/to lag behind/to be delay ...	يتأخر في دفع الإيجار

! lease contract, rent contract, contract of lease, contract of rent, leasehold, tenancy agreement	! عقد إيجار
to renew …	يجدّد عقداً
to terminate …, to rescind …, to revoke…	يفسخ عقداً
to sign …	يوقّع عقداً
to conduct …, to enter into …	يبرم عقداً
! term of lease, term of rent, rental period,	! مدة الإيجار
! rented property/estate/house leased property/estate/house	! المأجور/العين المستأجرة
to view …, to check …, to examine …, to inspect	يعاين العين المستأجرة
to repair …, to fix …,	يرمم العين المستأجرة
to quit …	يخلي العين المستأجرة
to hand … over	يسلّم العين المستأجرة

عقد إيجار

أبرِم هذا العقد بين كل من السيد ______________ (المشار إليه فيما بعد "المؤجّر") والسيد ______________ (المشار إليه فيما بعد "المستأجر"). ويعتبر عقد الإيجار هذا ساري المفعول من تاريخ توقيعه.

1. يقرّ المستأجر أنه قام بمعاينة الشقة موضوع العقد وتسلّم مفاتيحها.
2. يقرّ المؤجّر أنه تسلّم عند توقيع هذا العقد الأجرة المتّفق عليها لمدة ثلاثة أشهر.
3. ليس للمستأجر الحق في إستئجار الشقة أو جزء منها للغير بدون موافقة خطيّة من المؤجّر.
4. لا يحق للمستأجر أن يحدث أي تغيير في المأجور/الشقة، من هدم أو بناء أو تغيير في الأبواب إلا بموافقة المؤجّر الخطيّة.
5. إذا تأخّر المستأجر عن دفع الإيجار لأكثر من ثلاثة أشهر، فيحق للمؤجّر أن يفسخ العقد.
6. للمُستأجر أن يُرمِّم الشقة وإستقطاع نفقات الترميم من أجرة البيت شريطة أن يتمّ إبلاغ صاحب العقار قبل البدء بالترميمات.

تحرر هذا العقد بنسختين.

Some notes

1. The verb أبرم is in the passive voice, thus lending itself to '*this contract is made between* …' or '*this contract is conducted between* …'.

2. The expression المشار إليه فيما بعد (also المشار إليه في هذا العقد or المشار إليه أدناه) lends itself to '*hereinafter referred to as* …'. Compare it with المشار إليه أعلاه which lends itself to '*hereinabove referred to as* …'.
3. The expression ساري المفعول lends itself to '*enter into force*', '*effective*', '*valid*', and the like, as in '*This contract shall enter into force/be effective/be valid* ….'.
4. The verb يقرّ lends itself to '*to acknowledge*'.
5. لا يحق للمستأجر or ليس للمستأجر الحق في lends itself to '*the tenant has no right to* …' or '*the tenant may not* …'.
6. The particle إذا (also في حالة) can be translated here into '*in case* …', '*in the event that* …', or just '*if* …'.
7. The conditional clause ... إذا تأخر المستأجر عن دفع lends itself to '*in case of default of payment of the rent…*' or '*if the tenant falls behind paying the rent* …', etc.
8. The verb يستقطع can be translated into '*to deduct*'.
9. The expression شريطة (also على شرط, بشرط) lends itself to '*provided*', '*provided that*', '*providing*', '*providing that*', '*on condition that*', and so forth.
10. The expression تحرر هذا العقد can be translated into '*this contract has been made*', '*this contract has been written*', '*this contract has been drawn up*', and the like.

Exercise 15

Translate the following text adapted from Almanna and Almanna (2008: 181) into English, paying extra attention to the technical terms used and differences between Arabic and English.

عقد بيع

إنه في يوم ____ الموافق ____ تحرر هذا العقد بين كل من:

أولاً: السيد ________ ، عراقي الجنسية، يحمل بطاقة رقم ________
والمقيم في ________ والمشار إليه فيما بعد بالطرف الأول/البائع.
ثانياً: السيد ________ ، عراقي الجنسية، يحمل بطاقة رقم ________
والمقيم في ________ والمشار إليه فيما بعد بالطرف الثاني/المشتري.
أقر الطرفان بكامل أهليتهما القانونية للتعاقد واتفقا على ما يلي:

1. باع وتنازل الطرف الأول/البائع في هذا العقد للطرف الثاني/المشتري الشقة رقم ________ والكائنة في منطقة ________ عمارة ________ الدور الأرضي والتي تبلغ مساحتها ________ متر مربع وتتكوّن من غرفتين نوم، وصالة، ومطبخ وحمام.
2. تم هذا البيع نظير ثمن إجمالي قدره ________ فقط لا غير وقد تسلّم الطرف الثاني/المشتري الثمن بالكامل، ويعدّ توقيعه على هذا العقد مخالصة نهائية بالثمن.
3. يقرّ الطرف الثاني/المشتري بأنه قد عاين الشقة موضوع البيع معاينة تامة.
4. من المتفق عليه أن الطرف الثاني/المشتري قد أصبح بموجب هذا العقد مالكا للشقة محل العقد ملكية خالصة وبذلك يحق له التصرف بالشقة تصرفا كاملا، كالإيجار، والبيع، وغيرها من التصرفات القانونية.
5. يلتزم الطرف الأول/البائع بتمكين الطرف الثاني/المشتري من الانتفاع من الشقة وعدم التعرّض في انتفاعه بالشقة المباعة.
6. يلتزم الطرف الأول/البائع أن يرد الثمن الذي قبضه من الطرف الثاني/المشتري في حالة ثبت أن للغير حقاً في الشقة محل التعاقد.
7. يلتزم الطرف الأول/البائع بالحضور أمام محكمة البداءة لإقرار صحة التعاقد، وكذلك الحضور أمام الشهر العقاري لإنهاء إجراءات العقد النهائي .

حُـرّر هذا العقد من نسختين، لكل طرف نسخة للعمل بموجبها عند اللزوم.
وبناء على ما تقدّم، مهر الطرفان هذا العقد بإمضائهما، وبصماه بخاتميهما في اليوم والسنة المذكورين أعلاه.

طرف أول/بائع:	طرف ثانٍ/مشتري:
توقيع:	توقيع:
شاهد أول	شاهد ثانٍ
توقيع:	توقيع:

Why is it ثانٍ*?*

The word 'acquittance' *means a written receipt attesting the settlement of a fine or debt.*

Some notes

1. The verb تحرر in تحرر هذا العقد means أبرم هذا العقد, thus lending itself to '*this contract is made and enter into …*'.
2. The phrase بين كلّ من can be translated into '*by and between*'.
3. The verb يحمل in such a context lends itself to '*to hold*'.
4. The phrase والمشار إليه فيما بعد can be translated into '*hereinafter referred to as*'.
5. The legal sentence أقر الطرفان بكامل أهليتهما القانونية للتعاقد واتفقا على ما يلي, which is commonly used in contracts, can be rendered into

   '*the two contracting parties hereto declare that they are legally competent to enter into this contract and hereby agreed upon the following*'
   Or: '*the two contracting parties hereto declare that they have the legal capacity to enter into this contract and hereby agreed upon the following*'.

6. The word نظير, which means مقابل, lends itself to '*in consideration of*', '*for*', or '*in consideration of and for*'.
7. The expression يعدّ مخالصة نهائية can be rendered into '*to be considered an acknowledgement of the safe receipt of*' or '*to be considered an acquittance of*'.
8. The verb يلتزم can be translated into '*shall comply with*', '*shall undertake*', or just '*shall*'.
9. The phrase بموجب هذا العقد (also بمقتضى هذا العقد) lends itself to '*as per*', '*under*', '*in accordance with*', '*by virtue of*', and the like.
10. The phrase الشهر العقاري (also دائرة العقاري or مصلحة الشهر العقاري) lends itself to '*Real Estate Publicity Department*'.
11. لكلّ طرف نسخة للعمل بموجبها عند اللزوم can be rendered into '*one (copy) per each party for necessary action*'.
12. The sentence وبناء على ما تقدّم، مهر الطرفان هذا العقد بإمضائهما، وبصماه بخاتميهما في اليوم والسنة المذكورين أعلاه can be translated as '*In witness whereof, the said parties have hereunto set their hands and sealed on the day and year first hereinabove mentioned*'.

Exercise 16

Translate the following text taken from Almanna and Almanna (2008: 184) into Arabic, paying extra attention to the technical terms used:

Contract for Sale of Land

This agreement made and entered into this day of ______ by and between, the party of the first part and the party of the second part,

Witnesseth:

1. The said party of the first part, for and in consideration of the sum ______ to be paid as hereinafter provided, hereby agrees to sell unto the party of the second part the following tract of land.
2. The said party of the second part hereby agrees to purchase said premises at said consideration of ______ and to pay the same as follows.
3. The said party of the first part, upon receiving the final payment mentioned hereinabove, shall execute and deliver to the said party of the second part, or to his assigns, a duly acknowledged Warranty Deed, conveying to him or them the fee simple title to said premises, free and clear from all encumbrances.

In witness whereof, the said parties have hereunto set their hands and sealed on the day and year first hereinabove mentioned.

References

Almanna, A. 2018. *The Nuts and Bolts of Arabic-English Translation: An Introduction to Applied Contrastive Linguistics*. Newcastle upon Tyne, England: Cambridge Scholars Publishing.

Almanna, A., and Almanna, F. 2008. الترجمة: تاريخها، نظرياتها، تطبيقاتها *Translation: History, Theory & Practice*. London: Sayyab Books Ltd.

CHAPTER 8

Torts

Warming up …

Before making a start, be familiar with the area by listening to the following videos:

Torts https://www.youtube.com/watch?v=B3EZzJ0oSqI https://www.youtube.com/watch?v=jQ6smN3lcnY&t=200s https://www.youtube.com/watch?v=7qYcbohlou4 https://www.youtube.com/watch?v=mnPakaCc-Ys https://www.youtube.com/watch?v=YB7gK5eyydI

A. Almanna, *Legal Translation between English and Arabic*, https://doi.org/10.1007/978-3-031-14838-5_8

Exercise 1

Dear instructors: evaluate with your students the English translation of the following legal text written for the purposes of this course, paying extra attention to the technical terms and syntactic structures.

Negligence liability	المسؤولية التقصيرية
In civil cases based on negligence liability, there must have been a civil wrong committed by a person against another.	في القضايا المدنية المبنية على المسؤولية التقصيرية لا بدّ أن يكون هناك خطأً مدني إرتكبه شخصٌ ما بحق شخصٍ آخر.
In civil law, the injured person has the right to bring a civil case to court, asking for compensation for an injury that s/he suffers from.	ففي القانون المدني، يحق للشخص المتضرر اللجوء إلى القضاء وذلك برفع دعوى مدنية يطالب فيها بالتعويض جراء الضرر الذي لحقه.
For example, if you walk in a grocery store and slip on a banana fallen on the ground, then you will be considered the injured person legally called 'plaintiff', and the shop owner is the negligent person legally called 'tortfeasor'.	فلو دخلت محلاً لبيع الفواكه والخضار، مثلاً، وتزحلقت بموزة سقطت على الأرض، فهنا ستكون أنت بحكم القانون الشخص المتضرر ويطلق عليك "المدّعي" وصاحب المحل هو الشخص المهمل ويطلق عليه "المدّعى عليه".
As a result, you are entitled to take a civil action against the defendant, asking for suitable compensation for the medical bills, etc. that you may spend money on.	وعليه، يحق لك أن ترفع دعوى مدنية تطالب فيها المدّعى عليه بالتعويض المناسب لما قد تُصرفه على العلاج وغيرها.

Replace 'to bring a civil case to court' *with one of its synonyms.*

The word 'tortfeasor' can be replaced with the word 'defendant', *i.e.* المدّعى عليه; *it is the opposite of 'plaintiff'* المدّعي.

Replace 'to take a civil action against' *with one of its synonyms.*

The phrase بحكم القانون *lends itself here to the adverb* 'legally'.

The expression يحق لـ *(also* له الحق في*) can be translated into* 'somebody has the right to …', 'somebody is entitled to …', *and the like.*

Exercise 2

Translate the following text adapted from *Wadaq.info* into English, paying extra attention to the technical terms used and differences between Arabic and English.

المسؤولية التقصيرية

المسؤولية التقصيرية بشكل عام هي حالة تنشأ خارج دائرة العقد ويكون مصدرُ الالتزام فيها هو القانون، فإذا سلك الشخص سلوكًا ما وسبّب ضررًا للغير، ففي هذه الحالة يلتزم بحكم القانون بالتعويض. وهنالك ثلاثة أركان للمسؤولية التقصيرية وهي:

1. الخطأ التقصيري (الفعل الضار)
2. الضرر
3. العلاقة السببية بين الخطأ والضرر.

وتجدر الإشارة إلى أن هنالك بعض الظروف لو حدثت لن تكون هناك علاقة سببية بين الخطأ والضرر، ومن هذه الظروف نذكر، على سبيل المثال لا الحصر، القوة القاهرة، والقضاء والقدر، وعمل الشخص المتضرر أو تصرفه.

The term 'tort' in law refers to a civil wrong committed by a person who is legally obligated to provide a certain amount of carefulness in behaviour to another person, thus resulting in injury to another person's property or reputation.

Some notes

(1) The discourse marker بشكل عام can be translated into '*generally*', '*in general*', '*broadly*', '*by and large*', and the like.
(2) The phrase مصدر الالتزام lends itself to '*the source of obligation*'.
(3) The absolute object سلك سلوكاً can be translated into '*to behave in a way that*', '*to act in a certain way that*', etc.
(4) The word ضرر in such a context lends itself to '*injury*' or '*harm*'.
(5) The phrase الخطأ التقصيري can be translated into '*tort*'
(6) The phrase فعل ضار can be rendered into '*injury-producing action*'.
(7) The phrase العلاقة السببية lends itself to '*causation*'.
(8) The phrase على سبيل المثال لا الحصر lends itself to '*for example but not limited to*' or just '*for example*', '*for instance*', etc.
(9) The phrase القوة القاهرة can be rendered into '*force majeure*',
(10) The phrase القضاء والقدر can be translated into '*Act of God*'.

Is it ذو*,* ذا *or* ذي*?*
And why?

Is it فعلٌ ضارٌ *or* فعلاً ضارًا*?*
And why?

The pronoun ـه
attached to يستحق *was not translated? Why?*

Exercise 3

Dear instructors: evaluate with your students the translation of the following English legal text written for the purposes of this course, paying extra attention to the technical terms and syntactic structures.

The elements of negligence liability	أركان المسؤولية التقصيرية
Generally speaking, in some civil cases, the injured person is entitled to sue for damages.	إجمالاً، في بعض القضايا المدنية، يحق للشخص المتضرر أن يقيم دعوى مدنية يطالب فيها بالتعويض.
For a claim to be well-founded, there must have been an injury-producing action made by the defendant against the plaintiff, which resulted in an injury.	ولكي يكون الادعاء ذو/ذا/ذي أساس من الصحة، يجب أن يكون هناك فعلٌ ضارٌ/فعلاً ضارًا قام به المدّعى عليه وتسبب في ضرر للمدعي.
More importantly, there must have been causation between an injury—producing action and the injury.	والأهم من ذلك، يجب أن تكون هنالك علاقة سببية بين الفعل الضار والضرر.
Then, the court will determine as whether the defendant should be held legally accountable for the injuries or not.	ستقرر المحكمة، عندئذ، فيما إذا كان المدعّى عليه يتحمّل المسؤولية القانونية عن الأضرار أم لا.
Further, the court will determine what type of compensation the injured person is entitled to.	وكذلك ستقرر نوع التعويض الذي يستحقه الشخص المتضرر.

Exercise 4

Translate the following sentences into Arabic, paying extra attention to the technical terms used.

1. Our company has been recently sued for damages by the injured workers.
2. If you decide to enter into litigation with her, you need to consult a lawyer.
3. In some civil cases, the court may order the defendant to pay some money called 'damages' to the plaintiff for being harmed by the defendant.
4. In some cases, a judge may issue a judicial order demanding the defendant to stop infringing the plaintiff's legal rights. Such a judicial order is called an 'injunction'.

Exercise 5

Re-write the following sentences without changing their meaning, and then translate them into Arabic:

1. Due to the high cost of legal action and complexity of many civil cases, both parties may well try to reach a settlement. (use '*because*')

2. The court will ask witnesses to provide their testimony. (change it to passive)

Exercise 6

Translate the following civil case written for the purpose of this course into English, paying extra attention to the technical terms used.

How many finite verbs are used in the first sentence?

Re-write وتمّ تشخيص حالته على أنه....

Can we use the verb يعاني *without the preposition* من*, thus saying* يعاني ارتجاجًا*?*

Is there any time gap between the act of walking and the act of falling in the second sentence?

قرّرَ رجلٌ في الحادية والثّلاثين من العمر أن يتمشّى ليلاً في الشّارع الذي يسكُن فيه. وبينما كان يتمشّى وقعتْ على رأسِهِ طابوقة وسبّبت له أضراراً جسدية. نُقِل على أثرها إلى المستشفى وتمّ تشخيص حالته على أنه يعاني من ارتجاج في الجّمجمة.

بعد أن خرجَ من المستشفى، تحقق من الأمر وتبيّن أن جارَهُ كان قد ربط الطابوقة لسياج بيته كي تُسمك حبل الغسيل الذي تنشر عليه زوجته الملابس. عندها قرّر أن يقيم دعوى مدنية بحق جارِهِ مطالباً إياه بالتعويض.

Some notes

1. ضرر جسدي can be translated into '*bodily injury*'.
2. The phrase ارتجاج في الجمجمة can be rendered into '*concussion of the brain*' or more technically into '*cerebral commotion*'.
3. The word سياج can be translated into '*brick fence*'.
4. The phrase حبل الغسيل lends itself to '*clothes line*'.
5. The verb نشر/ينشر (غسيلاً) in such a context lends itself to '*to hang (clothes)*'.

Exercise 7

Translate the following case written for the purpose of this course into English, paying extra attention to the technical terms used and differences between Arabic and English.

Is there any difference between أشهر *and* شهور*? If yes, which one is correct here?*

Is it اختارت *or* إختارت*? And why?*

قبل أربعة شهور/أشهر، قررتْ سيدة في الخمسين من العمر أن تحضرَ سباق مارثون أقيم في أحد شوارع المدينة. اختارت/إختارت أن تقف في المنطقة التي يضيق فيها الشّارع كي ترى الجميع بوضوح. ما إن اقترب أحد العدائين منها، حتى فقد توازنه وسقط عليها مسببًا لها أضراراً في ساقها اليمنى.

لم تمض أيامٌ قليلة حتى بدأتْ تعاني من آلام شديدة في ساقها اليمنى، الأمر الذي أضطرّها إلى زيارة المستشفى. في المستشفى، تمّ تشخيصُ حالتها على أنها تعاني من رضوض في الركبة.

Why is it حاولتِ *not* حاولتْ التّخلص التّخلص*?*

بعد أسبوع قررتْ أن تقيم دعوى بحق العدّاء لما لحقها من أضرار بسبب الاعتداء المتعمّد مدعية أنها حاولتِ التّخلّص من العدّاء إلا إنه تعمّد الوقوع عليها. وعند النظر في القضيّة وملابساتها تبيّن أن العدّاء لم يقصد، بأي حال من الأحوال، الحاق الأذى بالسيدة.

Some notes

1. أقيم lends itself to '*to hold*', as it collocates well with words like '*race*' سباق, '*marathon*' ماراثون, etc.
2. The correlative conjunction ما إن ... حتى can be translated into '*no sooner … than …*', '*hardly … when …*', '*scarcely … when …*', '*barely … when …*', and the like.
3. The word عدّاء lends itself to '*runner*'.
4. فقد توازنه can be translated into '*to lose his footing*', '*to lose his balance*', and the like.
5. مسبباً lends itself to '*causing*' or '*thus causing*'.
6. The correlative conjunction لم تمضِ أيام قليلة حتى ... lends itself to '*it wasn't long before/when …*', '*no sooner had a few days passed than …*', etc.
7. تم تشخيص lends itself to a passive form: '*it was diagnosed that …*'.
8. The word رضوض can be translated into '*bruises*'.
9. بحق can be translated into '*against*', in particular when verbs like '*to take*' or '*to bring*' (an action against the negligent person) are

used. However, when the verb '*to sue*' (somebody for ...) is used, it is ignored.

10. مدعيّة lends itself to '*claiming*'.
11. The verb (الوقوع) تعمّد can be translated as '*to intend to fall*', '*to fall deliberately*', '*to fall willfully*', etc.
12. بأي حال من الأحوال can be translated as '*at any rate*', '*in no way*', etc.
13. عند النظر في القضيّة وملابساتها can be translated into '*when the case along with its accompanying circumstances was looked into (by the judge)*'.

Exercise 8

Translate the following text adapted from *FindLaw* into Arabic, paying extra attention to the technical terms used and differences between Arabic and English.

Replace 'with the aim of' *with one of its synonyms.*

Intentional Torts

An intentional tort is an act that is intentionally committed against another person with the aim of causing harm. There are several intentional torts that fall into this category, such as assault, battery, conversion, fraud, false imprisonment, trespassing, and invasion of privacy. Not every injury-producing action is cause for an intentional tort lawsuit. However, the court will look into the case brought by the plaintiff to determine whether the action committed by the defendant is, in fact, an intentional act or just mere wanton act not specifically meant to cause fear or injury, but is considered reckless.

Some notes

1. The phrase '*an intentional tort*' lends itself to تقصير متعمّد.
2. Although '*assault*' and '*battery*' are often paired together as one offense, there is a slight difference between them. If the victim has not actually been touched by the offender, but only threatened, then the crime is assault and thus can be translated into التلويح بالاعتداء. However, if the victim has been touched by the offender in an offensive way, then the crime is battery and thus can be translated into اعتداء (فعلي).
3. Look at the translations of these technical terms:

conversion	استيلاء بالباطل على مواد منقولة
fraud	غش/نصب/احتيال
false imprisonment	الحبس بالخطأ
trespassing	الاعتداء على أملاك الغير
invasion of privacy	انتهاك الخصوصية

4. The phrase '*injury-producing action*', which means an action that produces an injury, lends itself to فعل ضار.
5. The adjective '*wanton*', which means showing no thought or care for the rights, feelings, or safety of other people, lends itself in such a context to فعل ينطوي على استهتار, فعل ينمّ عن استهتار or just فعل مستهتر.
6. The word '*reckless*' lends itself literally to إهمال.

Exercise 9

Translate the following text adapted from *Harvard Business Review* into Arabic, paying extra attention to the technical terms used and differences between Arabic and English.

Replace 'due to' *with* 'as' *meaning* 'because' *without changing the meaning.*

Note that 'thus' *in the first paragraph can be replaced with* 'thereby'.

Due to the high cost of legal action and complexity of many civil cases, both parties may well try to reach a settlement, that is, an agreement to resolve a dispute before being taken to court, thus saving their time, money, and energy.

If the parties do not settle the case out of court, then a court hearing organized in a similar fashion

In a group of two, identify the non-finite clauses used in the text.

to criminal cases will be held. There, each side can state his/her case and present evidence. The court will ask witnesses to provide their testimony. After the plaintiff and the defendant have presented their cases, a jury or judge will decide the verdict. If they do not find that the plaintiff has proven his/her case, then the case will be dismissed. Alternatively, if the plaintiff has proven his/her case, then damages are awarded.

However, if the defendant disagrees with the verdict, then s/he might choose to file an appeal to have the verdict overturned or to reduce the amount of damages that s/he is liable for.

Exercise 10

Listen to the videos suggested in this chapter to translate the following text written for the purpose of this course into English, paying extra attention to the technical terms used:

Can we say تقسيم الضّرر على ثلاثة أنواع*?*

Is there any difference between الضّرر *and* الأذى *in Arabic?*

Is it اجتماعي *or* إجتماعي*? And why?*

أنواع الضّرر في المسؤولية التّقصيرية

ذهب القسم الأكبر من فقهاء القانون المدني إلى تقسيم الضّرر إلى ثلاثة أنواع: ضرر شخصي، وضرر مالي، وضرر معنوي.

1. الضّرر الشّخصي. هو أذى يصيب جسد الإنسان فيؤدي إلى موته أو قد لا يؤدي إلى موته، ولكن يسبب عاهة مستديمة، على سبيل المثال.
2. الضّرر المالي. هو ضرر يصيب عقارات الشخص وممتلكاته الشّخصية، وخير مثال على ذلك تلف المحاصيل الزّراعية أو الضّرر الذي يصيب السّيّارة وغيرها.
3. الضّرر المعنوي. هو ضرر يصيب الإنسان في شرفه أو حريته أو شعوره أو مركزه الاجتماعي/الإجتماعي.

Some notes

1. The verb ذهب here lends itself to '*to hold*', '*to argue*', and the like.
2. The word فقهاء can be translated into '*scholars*'.

3. The phrases ضرر مالي ,ضرر شخصي and ضرر معنوي can be rendered as '*personal damage*', '*property damage*' and '*damage to reputation*' respectively.
4. The verb يصيب in وهو ضرر يصيب شيئاً can be ignored as in '*a harm to something*'.
5. The word عقار (also عين) can be rendered as '*real*' or '*real estate*'.
6. The phrase المحاصيل الزراعية can be translated as '*agricultural products*', '*crops*', etc.
7. The phrase عاهة مستديمة can be translated as '*bodily infirmity*', '*permanent disability*', etc.
8. الممتلكات الشخصيّة (also الأملاك الشخصيّة) can be translated as '*personal properties*'.

Note that the term 'defamation' *can be also translated into* تشويه السّمعة.

Note that يرفع دعوى *in Arabic can be translated into* 'to bring a case', 'to sue (somebody) for/over', 'to take an action against', 'to take a legal action against', 'to bring a civil case to court', 'to bring a case against', 'to file a suit (claiming a breach of a contract)', 'to litigate', 'to enter into litigation', *etc.*

Exercise 11

Dear instructors: evaluate with your students the Arabic translation of the following legal text adapted from *Legal Information Institute*, paying extra attention to the technical terms and syntactic structures.

Defamation	تشويه السمعة
The term 'defamation' legally refers to the act of publishing false expressions and pictures with a view to defaming somebody else's reputation.	إنَّ مصطلح "التّشهير" قانوناً يشمل نشر عبارات وصورٍ غير صحيحة بغية تشويه سمعة شخص آخر.
To prove prima facie defamation, a plaintiff must show four things: (1) a false statement purporting to be fact; (2) publication or communication of that statement to a third person; (3) fault amounting to at least negligence; and (4) damages caused to the person or entity who is the subject of the statement.	ولكي يُثبت، مبدئيًا، التّشهير، على المدّعي تقديم أربعة أشياء، هي (1) بيان كاذب روّج له على أنه حقيقي، و(2) نشر البيان أو نقله إلى شخص ثالث، (3) وخطأ ينطوي، كحد أدنى، على تقصير، (4) وأضرار لحقت بالشخص أو الكيان الموجه ضده البيان.
There are two forms of defamation, namely libel, that is a written defamation, and slander, that is a spoken defamation.	وهناك نوعان من التّشهير، وهما القذف، بمعنى التشهير الكتابي، والسّب، بمعنى التشهير الكلامي.
In such cases, the injured person has the right to bring a civil action against the defendant seeking compensation.	وفي مثل هذه الحالات، يحق للشخص المتضرر أن يرفع دعوى مدنية ضد المدعّى عليه مطالباً بالتعويض.

CHAPTER 9

People and Law

Warming up …

Before making a start, be familiar with the area by listening to the following videos:

At the court
https://www.youtube.com/watch?v=UetYqtMzW5I
https://www.youtube.com/watch?v=tZYvv_s5R-s
Organization of courts
https://www.youtube.com/watch?v=fAqisNivrXk
https://www.youtube.com/watch?v=hh5pIZtv1gw
Family law
https://www.youtube.com/watch?v=STz_P89OKdg
Declaration of parentage
https://www.youtube.com/watch?v=6fVo1MngEWQ
Family court orientation
https://www.youtube.com/watch?v=4ODqAbjeWI4

A. Almanna, *Legal Translation between English and Arabic*,
https://doi.org/10.1007/978-3-031-14838-5_9

Exercise 1

Dear instructors: evaluate with your students the Arabic translation of the following legal text, paying extra attention to the technical terms and syntactic structures.

At the court room	في قاعة المحكمة
Once the case begins, both the lawyer for defence and prosecution will present their evidence and ask witnesses to answer certain questions related to the crime.	عندما تبدأ المحاكمة يقدّم كلٌّ من محامي الدفاع والادعاء العام أدلتهما ويقومان بطرح بعض الأسئلة المتعلّقة بالجريمة على الشهود.
Then the witnesses one by one will testify to what they know about the case and its accompanying circumstances. Actually, they will provide the court with a statement under oath of what they saw or knew about the case—such a statement provided by the witness is legally called 'the testimony'.	ثم يدلي كلُّ شاهدٍ بشهادته على انفراد/ إنفراد بما يعرفه عن القضية وملابساتها. في الحقيقة إنهم/أنهم سيزودون المحكمة تحت القسم بما شاهدوا أو عرفوا عن القضية، وهذه المعلومات التي يزوّد بها الشاهد المحكمة تسمّى قانونا "الشهادة".
When the judge and jury hear all the witnesses' testimonies, and the lawyer for defence and prosecution summarize their cases, the jury members then retire to deliberate on the case and reach a decision.	وعندما يفرغ القاضي وهيئة/هيأة المحلفين من سماع جميع شهادات الشهود، وينتهي كلٌّ من محامي الدفاع والادعاء العام من تلخيص قضاياهم، تختلي هيئة المحلفين، عندئذ، للمداولة في القضية والتوّصل إلى حكم.
When they reach a decision, they return to the court room to pass their verdict.	وعندما يتوصلون إلى حكم، يعودون إلى قاعة المحكمة ليدلون/ليدلوا بحكمهم.
If their verdict states that defendant is guilty, the judge then will convict the defendant of the crime thus, publically pronouncing the sentence against the convicted person.	إن كان حكمُهم يقضي بإدانة المتّهم، فسيدين القاضي المتّهم وبالتالي يصدر حكمًا علنيًا بحق المدان.

Note that the verb 'to retire', *which means to leave the court room and go to the jury room to decide the case, lends itself to* رفع الجلسة*. However, in the Arab world the decision is made by the judge. With this in mind, the verb* 'to retire' *can be translated into* يختلون بأنفسهم.

Is it على انفراد *or* على إنفراد*?*

Is it إنهم *or* أنهم*?*

Is it هيئة *or* هيأة*?*

Is it ليدلون *or* ليدلوا*?*

Note that the verb 'to deliberate' *here means to discuss and consider the case with members of the jury, thus lending itself to* يتداول*, as in* رفعت الجلسة للمداولة.

Note that the verb 'to pronounce', *which lends itself to* يصدر*, collocates well in legal English with the noun* 'sentence' حكم*; therefore, it can be replaced here with the verb* 'to deliver'.

Exercise 2

Translate the following text adapted from *Mawdoo3.com* into English, paying special attention to the technical words used.

أنواع المحاكم

عندما يحدث نزاعٌ أو سوءُ تفاهم بين أفراد المجتمع، فإن على الطرف المتضرر اللجوء إلى المحكمة. وعليه أن يعرف أن هناك أنواعٌ/أنواعًا مختلفة من المحاكم، فقد نصت المادة 11 من قانون التنظيم القضائي العراقي رقم 160 لسنة 1979م على أنّ أنواع المحاكم في التنظيم القضائي العراقي كالآتي:

Is it أن هناك أنواعٌ *or* أن هناك أنوعًا? *And why?*

1. المحكمة الابتدائية وهي المحكمة الأولى التي يلجأ إليها الشخص المتضرر وتتفرّع إلى

- محكمة الأحوال الشخصية، وهي محكمة تُعني بقضايا الأحوال الشّخصية كقضايا الميراث، والطلاق، ونفقة زوجية، ونفقة قاصرين، وإثبات النسب، وحضانة الطّفل، ومشاهدة الطفل، وغيرها من القضايا.
- المحكمة المدنية وهي محكمة تنظر في القضايا المدنية كالقضايا الناجمة عن المسؤولية التقصيرية أو التعاقدية، كنزاعات الملكية، وغيرها.
- المحكمة الجزائية وهي محكمة تنظر في قضايا المشاجرات، والاعتداء، والنصب، والتزوير، والسرقة، وغيرها.

2. محكمة الاستئناف وهي محكمة تنظر في الاستئنافات التي يقدّمها المتضرر من قرارات المحكمة الابتدائية.
3. محكمة التمييز وهي المحكمة العليا والتي تنظر في بعض القضايا القابلة للتمييز.

Some notes

1. The word نزاع can be translated into '*dispute*'.
2. The phrase الشخص المتضرر (also الطرف المتضرر) can be translated into '*the affected party*'.
3. The phrase المحكمة الابتدائية (also محكمة البداءة) can be translated into '*the court of first instance*'.
4. محكمة الأحوال الشخصية can be translated literally into '*court of personal status*' or functionally into '*family court*'.
5. The verb تُعنى/يُعنى can be translated into '*to deal with*', '*to be concerned with*', etc.
6. قضايا الأحوال الشخصية lends itself to '*personal status cases*'.
7. The technical terms ميراث (also إرث or تركة), طلاق, نفقة زوجية, نفقة قاصرين, إثبات نسب, حضانة الطفل and مشاهدة (الطفل) lend themselves to '*inheri-*

tance/legacy', '*divorce*', '*alimony*' (also known as '*spousal maintenance*', '*child support*' (also called '*child maintenance*'), '*declaration of parentage*', '*child custody*' and '*child visitation*'.

8. The verb ينظر/تنظر في lends itself in such a context into '*to hear*'.
9. القضايا المدنية can be translated into '*civil cases*'.
10. The phrases مسؤولية تقصيرية and مسؤولية تعاقدية can be translated into '*negligence liability*' and '*contractual liability*' (for more details on '*negligence liability*', see the previous chapter).
11. The phrase المحكمة الجزائية (also محكمة الجزاء) lends itself to '*criminal court*'.
12. The technical terms مشاجرة, اعتداء, نصب,تزوير and سرقة can be translated respectively into '*fight*', '*assault*', '*fraud*', '*forgery*', and '*theft*' (for more details, see next chapter).
13. The phrase محكمة الاستئناف can be translated as '*the court of appeal*'.
14. محكمة التمييز (also known as محكمة النقض or المحكمة العليا) can be translated as '*court of cassation*' (for more details, see Chap. 1 of this book).

Exercise 3

Dear instructors: evaluate with your students the translation of the following Arabic text adapted from Hatim et al. (1995: 114–5), paying extra attention to the technical terms and syntactic structures.

To the court of appeal …	إلى محكمة استئناف …
The appellant: The appellee: Subject of appeal On …, decision No. … was issued against me in case No. … brought to the court of first instance in the area of … by the plaintiff …	المستأنف: المستأنف ضده: موضوع الإستئناف بتاريخ … صدر بحقي القرار المرقم … في الدعوى رقم … التي أقامها المدّعي … أمام المحكمة الابتدائية في منطقة …

Note that a conjunctive hamza همزة وصل *should be used in* استئناف, *not a disjunctive hamza* همزة قطع.

(*continued*)

To the court of appeal ...	إلى محكمة استئناف ...
Whereas I am innocent of the charge which I have been charged with and I have been convicted of, I, within the legal period, hereby request the following:	وبما إنني بريء من التهمة المنسوبة إليّ والتي صدر حكم إدانة بحقي، فإني أقدّم استئنافي هذا وضمن المدة القانونية مطالباً بالآتي:
! My appeal shall be accepted formally and substantively.	! قبول استئنافي شكلًا وموضوعًا
! The decision issued by the aforementioned court of first instance shall be rescinded.	! فسخ القرار الصادر من المحكمة الابتدائية أعلاه.
! The appellee shall be made to bear the fees and costs of the case.	! تحمّل المستأنف ضده كافة رسوم القضية ومصاريفها.
Appellant's name and signature:	اسم المستأنف وتوقيعه:
Date:	التاريخ:

Exercise 4

Go through the meaning of the word '*witness*' before translating the following sentences into Arabic.

witness (n.)

a. is a person who provides testimony يدلي بشهادته in a court case. شاهد

b. is a person who is asked to be present at a particular event and sign his/her name in order to prove that things have been done correctly. شاهد

witness (v.)

a. to see something happen, especially an accident or a crime. شاهد/يشاهد

b. to be present at an event and sign your name as a proof that something was done correctly. شهد، يشهد

1. According to the witnesses who provided testimony in the law case, the robbery was carried out by three young people.
2. You have to sign the contract in the presence of two witnesses.
3. More witnesses are expected to testify at the trail today.
4. A doctor was called as an expert witness for the defence شاهد نفي/دفاع.

The word 'clemency' *means kindness when giving a punishment. If someone is granted clemency, they are punished less severely than they could be, thus lending itself to* الرأفة بالمتهم.

5. The jury passed a verdict of guilty حكم الإدانة, appealing to the judge for clemency.
6. While I was in the city at the time of the riots أعمال شغب, I witnessed many street battles.
7. New witnesses have cast doubt on some of the evidence دليل/أدلة that sent the 25-year-old to jail.
8. The key witness for the prosecution شاهد إثبات/ شاهد الادعاء العام was offered police protection after receiving death threats.
9. There must be at least two witnesses present when you sign the contract.
10. The judge reminded the witness for prosecution that she was under oath.

Exercise 5

Go through the meaning of the word '*judge*' before translating the following sentences into Arabic.

Judge (n.)

a. is a person who is responsible for running a trail in court. In the criminal court, s/he often makes a decision as to whether the crime has been committed by the offender or not. However, in some countries, the judge does not make this decision. Instead, a jury هيئة محلفين will make the decision.
b. a person who officially decides who is the winner of a competition. حَكَمٌ (في مسابقة)

Judge (v.)

a. to form, give, or have an opinion. يعبّر عن رأي or يصدر حكماً
b. to decide about something or somebody, especially after thinking carefully. يقرر (بشأن شيء ما أو شخص ما)
c. to decide who is the winner of a competition. يقرر (مَن الفائز)

The phrases 'eyewitness' *and* 'earwitness' *can be translated as* شاهد سماعي *and* شاهد عيان *respectively.*

1. Having examined the eyewitnesses and earwitnesses for the defence, the judge will pronounce sentence on the defendant this afternoon.
2. After being sentenced to 10-year imprisonment, he started shouting abuse at the judge.
3. So far, he's doing well, but it is really too soon to judge.
4. She has no right to judge other people because of what they believe.
5. I have been asked to judge the students' translations.

Exercise 6

Go through the meaning of the verb '*to prosecute*' before translating the following sentences into Arabic.

The verb '*to prosecute*' means
a. (as a public prosecutor) to officially accuse somebody of committing a crime in in court. يتهم/يوّجه اتهام
b. (as a lawyer) to try to prove that a person accused of committing a crime is guilty of a crime. يحاول أن يثبت تهمة

Grammatically, it is used in this way

subject	*verb*	*object*	*for*	*crime*
The lawyer The barrister The public prosecutor	prosecute(s)	somebody	for	theft robbery blackmail shoplifting fraud forgery murder manslaughter arson extortion

The phrase 'the public prosecutor' *can be translated into* نائب الادعاء العام. *Related words include* 'the public prosecution', *which can be translated into* النيابة العامة, الادعاء العام, جهة الادعاء العام, *and the like.*

1. The public prosecutor is an official who acts for the public and on behalf of the state against somebody accused of committing an important crime, such as murder, robbery, arson, drug trafficking, rape, kidnapping, etc.
2. The public prosecutor prosecuted the young man for committing the crime of shoplifting.
3. She was prosecuted by the barrister for theft.
4. Failure to pay the fine will lead to prosecution. So, it is better to pay it as soon as you can.
5. The public prosecutor claims that the driver was driving his car at 100 miles per hour.
6. The witness for prosecution explained to the judge what he saw in detail.

Exercise 7

Dear instructors: evaluate with your students the three translations of the following Arabic text in terms of accuracy, acceptability, readability, idiomaticity, authenticity and well-formedness.

Re-write the Arabic sentence starting with اِستُدعي...

تمّ استدعاء عددٍ من شهود النفي ليدلوا بشهادتهم في القضيّة. وفعلا حضر الشهود وشرحوا للقاضي ما حدث بالتفصيل. إلا إن أحدهم لم يتمكّن من الإجابة عن بعض أسئلة القاضي، مشكّكًا بذلك بشهادة الشهود. وبعد سماع شهود الإثبات والنفي واستجوابهم، أصدر القاضي حكمًا قضائيًا بسجن المتّهم خمسة سنوات.

Note that the words يدلي *and* شهادة *collocate well in Arabic.*

Can we say وبعد الاستماع*? If no, what is the difference between* سماع *and* إستماع*?*

Note that the lexical item حُكم *can be translated as (1)* 'verdict' *when it is reached and passed by jurors* مُحلفين *and (2)* 'sentence' *when it is pronounced by a judge* قاضٍ *in a criminal case. With this in mind, is there any divergence or convergence? Discuss.*

TT1 Human translation (MA student)	*TT2 Machine Translation (Reverso)*	*TT3 Machine Translation (Google)*
A number of witnesses for defence have been called to provide their testimony in the court case. Indeed, they attended and explained to the judge in detail what happened. However, one of them could not answer some of the judge's questions, thus casting some doubt on the witnesses' testimonies. Having listened to the witnesses for defence and prosecution and examined their testimonies, the judge pronounced a five-year imprisonment sentence on the defendant.	A number of exile witnesses were called to testify in the case. In fact, witnesses attended and explained to the judge what had happened in detail. However, one of them was unable to answer some of the judge's questions, questioning the witness testimony. After hearing and questioning the prosecution witnesses, the judge handed down a court sentence of five years' imprisonment.	A number of defence witnesses were called to testify in the case. Indeed, witnesses attended and explained to the judge what had happened in detail. However, one of them was unable to answer some of the judge's questions, casting doubt on the testimony of witnesses. After hearing and questioning the witnesses for the prosecution and denial, the judge issued a court ruling to imprison the accused for five years.

Re-write فإن تمّ إثبات أنه... starting with the passive form.

Exercise 8

Dear instructors: evaluate with your students the three translations of the following legal text written for the purposes of this course in terms of accuracy, acceptability, readability, idiomaticity, authenticity and well-formedness.

إن المشكو منه هو شخص أُتهم بارتكابه جريمة ما. والمتهم هو شخص بريء إلى أن تثبت إدانته. فإن تمّ إثبات أنه قد ارتكب الجريمة فعلاً، فهذا يعني أنه مذنب، ويسمّى قانوناً بالمدان. أما إذا تبيّن أنه لم يرتكب أيَّ فعلٍ يخالف القانون، فإنه، عندئذ، غير مذنب وبريء من التهم المنسوبة إليه.

TT1 Human translation (MA student)	*TT2 Machine Translation (Reverso)*	*TT3 Machine Translation (Google)*
The defendant is a person who has been accused of committing a crime. The accused person is innocent until proven guilty. If it has been proven that s/he has committed the crime, then, it means that s/he is found guilty, legally called 'the convicted person'. However, if it has been proven that s/he has not committed any wrong act, then it means that s/he is found not guilty, that is, innocent of the charges against him/her.	The complainant is a person charged with a crime. The accused is an innocent person until proven guilty. If it is established that he actually committed the offence, it means that he is guilty, legally called the convict. If it is found that he has not committed any act contrary to the law, then he is not guilty and innocent of the charges against him.	A defendant is someone who has been accused of a crime. The accused is an innocent person until proven guilty. If it is proven that he has actually committed the crime, then this means that he is guilty, and he is legally called a convict. But if it is found that he did not commit any act in violation of the law, then he is not guilty and innocent of the charges against him.

Some notes

1. Note that the lexical item '*defendant*' lends itself to مشكو منه in criminal cases and مدّعي عليه in civil cases.
2. The translator needs to distinguish among lexical items, such as المتّهم '*the accused person*', المشتبه به '*the suspected person*', and المدان '*the convicted person*'.
3. The verb ارتكب, which collocates well with the noun جريمة, can be translated as '*to commit*' (a crime).
4. The lexical item مذنب, which is the opposite of بريء '*innocent/not guilty*', lends itself to '*guilty*'.
5. The phrase المنسوبة إليه, which collocates well with the noun تهمة/تهم '*charges*', can be ignored in such a context as the adjective '*innocent*' in English is followed by the preposition '*of*', as in '*The court found him innocent of the crime*'. Such a sentence can be translated in this way:

برأتِ المحكمة ساحة المتّهم من الجريمة المتهم بها.
برأتِ المحكمة ساحة المتّهم من التهم المنسوبة إليه.
تبيّنَ للمحكمة أنه بريء من الجريمة.
ثبتَ للمحكمة أنه بريء من الجريمة.

Why is it برأتِ المحكمة, *not* برأتْ المحكمة؟

Exercise 9

Translate the following short texts written for the purpose of this course into Arabic, paying extra attention to the differences between the interfacing languages:

1. The word '*jury*' refers to a sworn body of people (usually 12) who have been chosen to hear the case and decide whether the defendant is guilty or innocent.

2. In his office, the lawyer warned his client that any manufacturer who does not conform to the standards could be prosecuted under the Consumer Protection Act, 1999.
3. Court ushers make sure that everyone involved with a court case is present. Further, they make sure that they have to know what they have to do during the hearing. In other words, they carry out various tasks to help the process run smoothly.

The word موكّل *can be translated into English as* 'client' *or* 'principal', *depending on the context. In this case, we have an example of divergence.*

Note that in English we say 'to conform to' *and* 'to comply with' *to mean to follow or adhere to a particular rule or regulation.*

Some notes

1. The lexical item '*jury*' can be translated into هيئة محلفين.
2. The word '*client*' here lends itself to موكّل.
3. The verb '*to conform*', which is followed by the preposition '*to*', can be rendered into يتقيّد بـ or يلتزم بـ. One of its synonyms is '*to comply with*'.
4. The word '*under*' can be translated into بموجب or بمقتضى.
5. The phrase '*the Consumer Protection Act*' lends itself to قانون حماية المستهلك.
6. The lexical item '*usher*', which is usually translated into حاجب (المحكمة), lends itself here to محضر الجلسة or معاون قضائي.

Exercise 10

Translate the following text written for the purpose of this course into Arabic, paying extra attention to the differences between the interfacing languages:

A solicitor is a qualified legal professional who provides legal advice to his clients. His clients can be individual people, private companies, or public sector organizations.

Replace the discourse marker 'broadly speaking' *with another one without affecting the meaning.*

Broadly speaking, solicitors deal with all the paperwork and communication involved with their clients' cases, such as

- writing important documents and contracts.
- ensuring the accuracy of legal advice and procedure.
- preparing papers for court on behalf of their clients.

Replace 'on the other hand' *with another discourse marker without affecting the meaning.*

A barrister, on the other hand, provides specialist legal advice and represents individual people, private companies, or public sector organizations in courts and through written legal advice.

Some notes

1. The word '*solicitor*' can be translated into محام مكتبي to differentiate it from the word '*barrister*' محام مترافع. In the USA, two different terms are used, namely '*counsellor*' and '*attorney*' to mean محام.
2. The lexical item '*professional*' as a noun can be translated into حرفي or مهني, but here it lends itself to شخص, as in شخص مؤهل قانوناً.
3. The discourse marker '*broadly speaking*' can be translated as عمومًا, إجمالًا, بشكل عام, etc.
4. The word '*procedure*' lends itself to إجراءات.
5. The verb '*to represent*' can be translated into يمثّل.

Reference

Hatim, B., A. Shunnaq, and R. Buckley. 1995. *The Legal Translator at Work: A Practical Guide*. Jordan: Dār al-Hilāl for Translating and Publishing.

CHAPTER 10

Crimes

Warming up …

Before making a start, be familiar with the area by listening to the following videos:

Crimes
https://www.youtube.com/watch?v=AVuC13JIumQ
https://www.youtube.com/watch?v=aMQR44byPm4
https://www.youtube.com/watch?v=nuMIRI8Ypi4
Types of crimes
https://www.youtube.com/watch?v=6kA0RjrE2ug
elements of crimes
https://www.youtube.com/watch?v=YyI5yy-Fc9U
https://www.youtube.com/watch?v=xzLAjG9rW4E
https://www.youtube.com/watch?v=mbXlaguHMm4

A. Almanna, *Legal Translation between English and Arabic*, https://doi.org/10.1007/978-3-031-14838-5_10

Exercise 1

Dear instructors: evaluate with your students the Arabic translation of the following text adapted from one of the videos suggested in this chapter.

Is it عناصرَ *or* عناصرِ? *And why?*

Note that in Arabic we say ينبغي لـ, *not* ينبغي على. *Now, can you replace it with* يتعيّن? *Is it* يتعيّن للادعاء العام *or* يتعيّن على الادعاء العام?

Is it خاطئٌ *or* خاطئًا? *And why?*

There are five elements that the prosecution must prove in order to convict somebody of a crime. They are:	هناك خمسة عناصرَ/عناصرِ ينبغي للادعاء العام إثباتها كي يدان شخص بارتكابه جريمة، وهي:
1. *Actus Reus*, i.e. a guilty act committed consciously and voluntarily.	1. السّلوك الإجرامي، وهو فعل جُرمي يرتكبه الجّاني وهو يعي ذلك وبشكل إرادي.
2. *Mens Rea* (guilty mind) is the mental element of a crime, i.e. the defendant knew what s/he was doing was wrong.	2. القصد الجنائي وهو الرّكن المعنوي للجريمة ويعني أن الجاني كان يعي أن ما يقوم به خاطئٌ/خاطئًا.
3. Concurrence of *Actus Reus* and *Mens Rea*.	3. تزامن السّلوك الإجرامي مع القصد الجنائي.
4. Causation	4. العلاقة السّببية
5. Resulting injury or crime.	5. الضّرر الناجم أو الجريمة المتحققة.

Exercise 2

Listen to the videos suggested in this chapter that explain the elements of crimes to translate the following text adapted from (specialties.bayt.com) into English:

أركان الجريمة التامة

إنَّ أركان الجريمة التّامة هما الرّكن المادي physical part والرّكن المعنوي mental part، إذ يتكوّن الرّكن المادي في الجريمة التامة من ثلاثة عناصر هي:

1. **السّلوك الإجرامي:** ويتنوّع إلى سلوك إيجابي وسلوك سلبي.

أ. السلوك الإيجابي: وهو كل حركة عضوية إرادية تصدر عن الجّاني ويتوصل بها إلى ارتكاب الجريمة.

ب. السلوك السلبي omission to act: وهو امتناع عن القيام بعمل يفرضه القانون، كما لو قام شخص بالامتناع عن دفع الضريبة المفروضة عليه أو عندما يتم التعاقد مع سبّاح محترف لإنقاذ حياة المتدربين الجدد، ولكنه انشغل بهاتفه النقّال وتسبب بغرق أحدهم.

2. **النتيجة الإجرامية**: يقصد بها الأثر الذي يحدث في العالم الخارجي كأثر للسلوك الإجرامي.
3. **العلاقة السّببية**: يقصد برابطة السّببية ضرورة توافر/توفّر رابطة بين سلوك الجاني والنتيجة الإجرامية بحيث يمكن القول إن/أن النتيجة حدثت بسبب سلوك الجاني لا غيره.

أما الركن المعنوي في الجريمة التامة فهو القصد الجنائي سواء أكان قصدًا عاماً أم قصدًا خاصًا

Is there any difference between الأثر *and* العلامة *in Arabic? Discuss.*

Is there any difference between توافر *and* توفّر*? If yes, which one do you prefer to be used here?*

Is it يمكن القول إن *or* يمكن القول أن*?*

Note that القصد الجنائي *can be translated into* 'criminal intention'.

Exercise 3

Complete the translation of the following text adapted from Al-Aqaileh (2015: 191).

Criminal law defines the acts that constitute crimes, thus imposing penalties on them. It commands abstention from certain acts and threatens punishment in default. It covers the whole range of criminal offences from minor contraventions to misdemeanours or felonies.

يحدّد القانونُ الجنائي ______________________

____

____

______________ المخالفات الصّغيرة إلى الجنح والجنايات.

Exercise 4

Listen to the videos suggested in this chapter that explain the elements of crimes to translate the following two cases adapted from one of them into English:

Case 1:

قام شخصٌ بأخذ حقيبة يدوية من محل لبيع الحقائب بنيّة حيازتها للأبد وتجريدِ صاحبِ المحل منها. فهنا تحقق الرّكنُ المادي والمتمثل بالسّلوك الإجرامي (فعل الأخذ) والنتيجةِ (تجريد صاحب المحل منها) والعلاقةِ السّببية بين فعل الأخذ وتجريد صاحب المحل من حاجتِهِ، وكذلك تحقق الرّكن المعنوي للجريمة ألا وهو القصد الجنائي المتمثل بنية حيازةِ الحقيبة للأبد وتجريدِ صاحبها منها.

Can we say أخذ *in place of* قام بأخذ*? If yes, which one do you prefer? And why?*

Is it ابنته *or* إبنته*?*

Case 2:

قرّرَ شخصٌ لا يعاني من أيِّ مشاكلَ صحيّةٍ قبل أيامٍ أن يزورَ ابنته/إبنته التي تقطن في إحدى القرى المجاورة، وفعلًا قاد سيارته متوجهًا صوب قريتها، ولكن قبل أن يصل إلى القرية تعرّض إلى سكتة دماغية مفاجئة مما تسبب بأضرار لإحدى السّيارات. وبعد التحقيق والاطلاع على التقرير الطّبي تبيّن أنه لم يقم بذلك بقصد جنائيّ، وإنما كان نتيجة تعرّضه لسكته دماغية

Exercise 5

Dear instructors: evaluate with your students the Arabic translation of the following legal text, paying extra attention to the technical terms and syntactic structures.

Is it أن هناك عنصرين *or* أن هناك عنصران*? And why?*

Is there any difference between الإذن *and* الرّضا*? Discuss.*

The denotative meaning of the lexical item مكتبة *in Arabic is wider and less specific than its counterparts in English as it refers to 'bookshop', 'library' and 'bookcase'. Therefore, translating the word bookshop into* مكتبة *is an example of convergence.*

Theft crimes The act of taking somebody's 'movable' property without his/her permission and consent with the intention of permanently depriving him/her of it is considered a crime of theft. This means there are two key elements in theft crimes. They are:	**جرائم السرقات** إن فعل أخذ مالٍ منقول من شخص آخر من دون إذنه ورضاه بنيّة تجريده منه بشكل دائم يُعدّ سرقة. هذا يعني أن هناك عنصرين أساسيين/عنصران أساسيان في جريمة السرقة، هما:
1. taking somebody's 'movable' property without his/her permission and consent. 2. depriving the owner of it permanently.	1. أخذ مال منقول مملوك لشخص آخر من دون إذنه ورضاه. 2. تجريد المالك منه إلى الأبد
For example, if somebody walks in a bookstore, puts a book in this handbag, and walks out of the bookstore with the intention of keeping it with him permanently, then it is a theft crime, and the person will be charged with theft, regardless of the price of the book. Similarly, he will be charged with theft if he steals a car from the parking lot.	فلو دخل شخصٌ إلى مكتبة لبيع الكتب، مثلاً، وأخذ كتاباً ووضعه في حقيبته وخرج من المكتبة بنيّة حيازته بشكل دائم، فهنا الفعل يعدّ سرقة وسيتّهم الشخص بجريمة السّرقة، بغض النظر عن ثمن الكتاب. كذلك سيتّهم بجريمة السّرقة لو سرق سيارة من مواقف السيّارات.

Exercise 6
Translate the following two texts written for the purposes of this course into English, paying attention to the linguistic and stylistic differences between the languages:

Text 1

أنواع السرقات

تجدر الإشارة إلى أن هناك نوعين/نوعان من السّرقات، وهي السّرقات البسيطة والسّرقات المقترنة بظروف مشددة. ومن الظروف المشددة، على سبيل المثال لا الحصر:

Is it أن هناك نوعين *or* أن هناك نوعان*? And why?*

- السرقة ليلًا
- سرقة دور العبادة
- حمل سلاح أو إرتداء قناع وغيرها
- تعدد مُرتكبي الجريمة

ومن جهة أخرى، يُمكن تصنيف جرائم السرقات إلى سرقة المحلات، والسطو المسلّح، والسرقة بالتهديد، والاختلاس.

Some notes

1. The phrase سرقات بسيطة can be translated as '*petty theft*'. Petty theft refers to the crime of stealing something that does not have a high value.
2. The phrase السّرقات المرتبطة بظروف مشددة can be translated functionally into '*grand theft*' or '*aggravated theft*' or ideationally into '*theft accompanied by aggravating circumstances*'.
3. دور العبادة means '*worshipping houses*'.
4. The lexical item مرتكب الجريمة can be rendered as '*perpetrator*', '*offender*', or '*wrongdoer*'.
5. The phrases السطو المسلّح, سرقة المحلات, and السرقة بالتهديد can be translated as '*burglary*', '*shoplifting*', and '*robbery*' respectively.
6. The lexical item اختلاس, which refers to the act of stealing money from one's employer, lends itself to '*embezzlement*'. Related words include '*to embezzle*' يختلس and '*embezzler*' مختلس.

Text 2

الاتجار بالمخدرات وتوزيعها

Is it على عواملَ *or* على عواملِ? *And why?*

تختلف عقوبة الاتجار بالمخدرات وتوزيعها وذلك بالاعتماد على عواملَ/عواملِ عديدة. نذكر منها هنا، على سبيل المثال لا الحصر:

1. نوع المخدر
2. كمية المخدر
3. الشخص المستهدف، فيما إذا كان طفلًا أم لا

Is it في جرائمَ *or* في جرائمِ? *And why?*

Replace إجمالًا *with another word without changing the meaning.*

وتتفاوت العقوبات في جرائمَ/جرائمِ الاتجار بالمخدرات وتوزيعها من بلد إلى آخر، ولكنها، إجمالاً، تتراوح من ثلاث سنوات سجن إلى خمس سنوات سجن.

Some notes

1. The phrases الاتجار بالمخدرات and توزيع المخدرات can be translated into '*drug trafficking*' and '*drug distribution*' respectively. The word '*traffic*' as a noun here refers to the activity of buying and selling goods or people illegally. Does it have another meaning?
2. The verb تختلف/يختلف can be translated here into '*to vary*'.
3. The noun عقوبة lends itself to '*punishment*' and '*sentence*', depending on the context.
4. The phrase على سبيل المثال لا الحصر can be rendered into '*for example but not limited to*'.
5. The verb تتفاوت/يتفاوت can be rendered into '*to range*'.

Exercise 7

Translate the following text adapted from *Elliott Kanter* (www.enkanter.com) into Arabic, paying attention to the linguistic and stylistic differences between the languages. Then, replace the following words and expressions with their synonyms:

- *unlawfully* (line 2)
- *including* (line 7)
- *to begin with* (line 12)
- *especially* (line 16)
- *however* (line 18)
- *finally* (line 22)

Identify the sentences in passive form.

Theft, also known as larceny, is a serious crime that involves unlawfully taking or using property that belongs to another person. If you have been arrested for theft, you have either been charged with petty theft or grand theft. Under these two main categories, there are many different types of theft, including embezzlement, shoplifting, fraud, and robbery. While all of these crimes have the same basic elements, they also have slight variations and different possible punishments if you are found guilty.

Shoplifting, to begin with, refers to the act of stealing items from shops. The person committed such a crime is called a shoplifter. When a person steals things, such as a wallet, purse, and the like out of people's pockets or bags, especially in a crowd, s/he is called a pickpocket.

However, when a deadly weapon, such as a gun, pistol, etc. is used by the offender, then it is a crime of robbery. Unlike burglary, the crime of robbery almost always requires the presence of a victim.

Finally, the crime of embezzlement refers to the act of secretly stealing money to which you are entrusted or money that belongs to a company you work for. The person committed such a crime is called an embezzler.

Some notes

1. The verb '*to steal*' lends itself to يسرق.
2. The lexical item '*item*' in this context can be translated into سلعة.
3. While the lexical item '*wallet*' lends itself to محفظة رجالية, the lexical item '*purse*' lends itself to محفظة نسائية.
4. The word '*pickpocket*' can be translated into نشال.

Exercise 8

Translate the following three cases into English to a professional level:

Case 1

لستُ سارِقاً

دخلَ رجلٌ في الثلاثين من عمرِهِ إلى محل لبيع الهواتف الذكيّة. ما إن مسكَ هاتفاً ذكيّا بيدِهِ حتى تلقّى اِتصالاً من أحدِ أقاربِهِ يخبره أن زوجتَهُ الآن في العناية المُركّزة. خرجَ من المحل مسرعًا وبيدِهِ الهاتف المحمول الجديد. عند باب المحل، مسكه رجلُ الأمن وبحيازته الهاتف وقيد إلى أقرب مركز شرطة. بعد إجراء التحقيق معه وثبوت أنه تلقّى اتّصالاً من أحدِ أقاربِهِ تبيّن أنه فعلاً أخذ الهاتف وحاول الخروج من المحل، ولكن لم يكن في نيته تجريد صاحب المحل من الهاتف بشكل دائم، وإنما حدث هذا بالخطأ.

Some notes

1. The verb دخل can be translated into '*to walk in*' in the past.
2. The correlative conjunction ... ما إن/أن ... حتى can be translated into '*no sooner … than …*', '*hardly … when …*', '*scarcely … when …*', '*barely … when …*', '*once*', '*as soon as*', '*the moment*', '*soon after*', and the like.
3. The phrase العناية المركّزة lends itself to '*intensive care*'.
4. The verb خرج which is followed by the adverb مسرعاً can be translated into '*to walk out of the shop quickly*', '*to dash out of the shop*', and so on.
5. The phrase رجل الأمن can be rendered into '*the security man*'.
6. The lexical item حيازة, which literally means '*possession*', lends itself here to '*holding*'.
7. The verb قيد can be translated into '*he was taken to*'.
8. بعد إجراء التّحقيق can be translated as '*After having investigated with*'.
9. لم يكن في نيته lends itself to '*he did not intend to*'.
10. The lexical item تجريد, which is derived from the verb جرّد, lends itself to '*to deprive of*', and the like.

Case 2

Is there any difference between أشهر *and* شهور*? If yes, which one is correct here?*

Is it إمرأة *or* امرأة*?*

Is it عشر سنوات *or* عشرة سنوات*?*

لم يمضِ وقتٌ طويلٌ على ... حتى *lends itself to* 'it wasn't long since … when/before …'. *With this in mind, how would you translate this?*
تزوّجَ رجلٌ في النصف الثاني من الثلاثين من امرأة في العشرين من عمرِها. لم تمضِ سنةٌ على زواجِهما حتى طلبت الطّلاق منه بِحجةِ أنه كثير الشّخير.

خيانةُ زوجٍ

قبل ثلاثةِ شهور/أشهر، قام رجلٌ متزوّجٌ من امرأة/إمرأة ثرية بتزوير توقيع زوجتِهِ على وكالة عامة تخولّه بيع جميع ممتلكاتها المنقولة وغير المنقولة. وفعلاً باعَ بموجب الوكالة المزوّرة إحدى الشقق التي تملكها. ولكن لسوء حظه أن المشتري قد عثر في اليوم التالي على حقيبة صغيرة وفيها رقم هاتف صاحبة الشقة. وعندما اِتّصل بها ليبلغها عن الحقيبة ذكر لها أنه المالك الجديد للشقة.
لم يمضِ وقتٌ طويلٌ على اكتشاف الجريمة حتى طلبتِ الزّوجةُ الطّلاقَ. ووجهت له المحكمة، فيما بعد، تهمة التّزوير وحُكم عليه بالسجن لمدة عشر/عشرة سنوات.

Some notes

1. قام بتزوير simply means زوّر, thus lending itself to '*to forge*'.
2. The phrase وكالة عامة can be translated into '*general power of attorney*'. Related words وكالة خاصة '*special/limited power of attorney*', موكّل '*principal*', وكيل '*agent*' or '*attorney-in-fact*'.
3. The verb يخوّل lends itself here '*to authorize*'.
4. The phrase ممتلكات منقولة وغير منقولة can be translated into '*movable and immovable properties*'. It is worth noting that الممتلكات غير المنقولة can be translated into '*real properties*' too.

Case 3

Is there any time gap between the act of walking out of his house and the act of opening fire on him? And which act happened before the other?

Can we say القتل الغير مُتعمّد *in Arabic? Discuss.*

لستُ قاتلًا

رجعَ مُزارِعٌ إلى بيتِهِ مُبكّراً على غير عادته فأخذَ بندقيتَهُ وخرجَ مسرعًا. انتظرَ خلف شجرةٍ بالقرب من منزل جارِهِ. وما إن خرج جارُهُ من منزلِهِ حتى أطلقَ عليه المزارعُ النّار وهربَ صوب الشّارع الذي يؤدي إلى المدينة. لم يمض وقتٌ طويل حتى فارق جارُهُ الحياة. بعد أيام، تمّ إلقاء القبض على المزارع وحيلت أوراقه إلى محكمة الجنايات. في المحكمة وجّه له نائب الادعاء العام تهمة القتل مع سبق الإصرار والترصد، لكن محامي المزارع أنكر التّهمة وطالب بتوجيه تهمة القتل غير المتعمّد لأن الجاني قد قتل المجني عليه بالخطأ.

Some notes

1. The verb أطلق النار can be translated into '*to open fire*', '*to shoot*', and the like.
2. The verb هرب lends itself to '*to run away*'.
3. The correlative conjunction لم يمض ... حتى can be translated into '*it was not long … before/when …*', '*no sooner …than …*', etc.
4. لقي or انتقل إلى الرّفيق الأعلى ,وافته المنيّة (also فارق الحياة, حتفه, etc.) simply means مات or توفي, thus lending itself to '*to die*', '*to pass away*', '*to breathe his last*', '*to meet his death*', and the like.
5. تمّ إلقاء القبض عليه can be shortened to أُلقي القبض عليه; therefore, it can be translated into a passive as in '*he was arrested*'.
6. The phrase محكمة الجنايات can be translated into '*the criminal court*'.
7. The verb (تهمة) وجّه in this context lends itself to '*to prosecute*'.
8. The phrase نائب الادعاء العام can be rendered into '*the public prosecutor*'.
9. مع سبق الإصرار والترصّد can be translated into '*willfully and premeditated*' or '*premeditated and lying in wait*'.
10. The verb أنكر lends itself to '*to deny*'.
11. The phrase القتل غير المتعمّد can be translated into '*manslaughter*'.

Is the quantity of the verb يتهرّب *made up of one element/*تهرّب *or more than one element? Discuss.*

Exercise 9

Dear instructors: evaluate with your students the English translation of the following legal text adapted from *Wadaq* (www.wadaq.info) paying extra attention to the technical terms and syntactic structures.

Crimes of scam and fraud	جرائم النصب والاحتيال
There are a wide range of crimes that cannot be considered legally theft crimes as the offender of such crimes takes the money by way of deceiving the victim.	هناك أنواع عديدة من الجرائم التي لا تعد بحكم القانون جرائم سرقة، لأن مرتكب مثل هذه الجرائم يأخذ المال عن طريق غش المجني عليه.
When a person attempts to take somebody's money by deceit, then it cannot be considered a theft crime, but rather a crime of scam or fraud. This is because the offender took the money with the victim's consent by way of deceit.	فعندما يحاول شخص ما أن يستحوذ على مال شخص آخر عن طريق الغش، فهنا لا تعدّ الجريمة جريمة سرقة، بل هي جريمة نصب أو احتيال لأن الجاني أخذ المال بإذن المجني عليه ولكن عن طريق الغش.
For the same reason, when a person attempts to avoid taxes, then it is not a theft crime, but rather it is a crime of tax evasion.	وللسبب نفسه، عندما يتهرّب شخصٌ من الضرائب، فهنا الجريمة ليست جريمة سرقة، بل هي جريمة تهرّب من ضرائب.

The idiom 'to air one's dirty laundry in public' *means to discuss very private matters, especially that which may be embarrassing in public. With this in mind, how would you translate this?*
'I wish you wouldn't air your dirty laundry in public in such a way'.

Exercise 10

Translate the following short texts into Arabic to a professional level

1. In the crime of money laundering, there are three main steps. They are:
   a. The money is deposited into a financial institution, such as a bank.
   b. The money is separated from its illegal origin by a number of complex transactions, thus making it difficult to trace the 'dirty' money.
   c. The 'dirty' money is mixed with legally obtained money.

Is there any difference between 'to burn' *and* 'to burn out'?

2. In the last few months, ten terrorists have murdered many local people, including a 12-year old boy. It wasn't long before the policemen caught three of them. They admitted they had committed many crimes, including several murders. A week later, the three terrorists were convicted of murder and sentenced to death.
3. A building in the heart of London was burnt out six months ago. The cause of the fire was not determined at that time, but the police suspected that somebody had intentionally set fire to the building. It was only two months since setting fire to the building before the police caught the offender. At the court, he was convicted of arson.

Some notes

1. The phrase '*money laundering*' lends itself to غسيل الأموال or جريمة غسيل الأموال.
2. The verb '*to deposit*', which is in the passive form, can be translated into يُودِع المال.
3. The phrase '*financial institution*' can be translated into مؤسسة مالية.
4. The adjective '*illegal*', which is the opposite of '*legal*', can be translated into غير شرعي or غير قانوني.
5. The phrase '*complex transaction*' lends itself to معاملات تجارية معقّدة.
6. The lexical item '*dirty*', which literally means وسخ or مُتّسخ, lends itself in such a context to مشبوه.
7. The verb '*to murder*' and its noun '*murder*' can be translated into قتل or قام بقتل and جريمة القتل respectively. Related words are '*murderer*' قاتل and '*manslaughter*' جريمة القتل غير المتعمّد.
8. The verb '*to admit*' lends itself to يقر, يعترف, etc.
9. The verb '*to convict*' can be translated into أُدين or تمت إدانته.

10. The verb '*to sentence*' lends itself to حُكِم عليه.
11. The word '*arson*' refers to the crime of intentionally setting fire to a building, thus lending itself to جريمة الحريق المتعمّد or حريق عمدًا, حريق متعمّد.
12. The verb '*to suspect*' can be translated as شكّ, ظنّ, اعتقد, etc.
13. The adverb '*intentionally*', which can be replaced with '*on purpose*', lends itself to عمدًا, عن قصد, متعمدًا, and the like.

Exercise 11

Translate the following sentences, paying extra attention to the technical terms used.

1. The accountant embezzled a huge amount of money while working for the wealthy family.
2. Yesterday evening, the policemen caught the armed robber who raided a supermarket a week ago.
3. The gang admitted they had committed two recent bank robberies. They have been convicted of robbery. As such, they will serve ten years in prison for robbery.
4. He broke into the house and stole the lady's jewelry. A week later, he was charged with burglary.
5. A 35-year old man was convicted of assaulting a police officer yesterday.
6. The government has undertaken a massive drive against drug trafficking.

7. دخل صبيٌ في الرابعة عشر من العمر إلى محل لبيع الهواتف وسرق هاتفًا ذكيًا منه.
8. اندلعت قبل أيامٍ النيران في بناية في وسط المدينة. وما إن وصل رجالُ الشّرطة وبدأوا إجراءات التحقيق، حتى توصلوا إلى أن الحريق لم يكن حادثًا عرضياً، بل تمّ بفعل فاعل.
9. اقتحم ثلاثةُ رجالٍ ملثمين بيتَ امرأة/إمراة عجوز ليلاً وسرقوا جميع مجوهراتها. وبعد أسبوع ألقت الشرطة القبض عليهم وتمت محاكمتهم بتهمة السّطو المُسلّح.

Is it امرأة *or* إمرأة?

10. زوّرَ محاسبُ الشّركة توقيع المدير وصرف لنفسه شيكًا بقيمة خمسين ألف دولارٍ أمريكي.
11. ألقت الشرطة قبل أسبوع القبض على عصابة تتاجر بالمخدرات، وتبيّن من سير التحقيق أنهم قد إرتكبوا جرائم أخرى، بما فيها السطو المسلّح.

Exercise 12

Go through the following text titled *bribery* (www.crimnal.findlaw/crimnal-charges/bribery.html) before translating the text titled أركان جريمة الرّشوة into English.

Bribery is the offer or acceptance of anything of value in exchange for influence on a governmental/public official or employee. In general, bribes can take the form of gifts or payments of money in exchange for favourable treatment, such as awards of government contracts.

At the most fundamental level, charges of bribery need only to prove that an agreement for the exchange of something of value (political influence, for example) for a sum of money or something else of value. There need not be a written agreement, but prosecutors must be able to prove that an agreement was actually made. For example, a taped phone call between a politician and the party offering the bribe may be sufficient evidence.

Broadly speaking, bribery can happen in many different spheres of influence. In the sporting world, for example, one boxer might offer another a payoff to 'throw' (deliberately lose) an important fight.

أركان جريمة الرّشوة

يعرّف قانون العقوبات المصري رقم47/1936 في المادة 106 الرّشوة على أنها قيام الموظف العام بالمتاجرة بالوظيفة العامة التي يؤديها من أجل تحقيق مصلحة خاصة. وبذلك، تتكون جريمة الرّشوة من طرفين، هما:

Is there any difference between العطية *and* الهدية*?*

Replace من أجل *and* مقابل *with one of their synonyms without affecting the meaning.*

1. **المرتشي:** وهو الموظف العام الذي يأخذ العطية من الرّاشي، أو يقبل الحصول عليها، أو يطلبها من الرّاشي، في مقابل قيامه بعمل من أعمال وظيفته أو امتناعه عن القيام بعمل من أعمال وظيفته.
2. **الرّاشي:** وهو صاحب المصلحة الذي يقدّم العطية للموظف العام، أو يعرضها عليه، أو يوافق على طلب الموظف لها، في مقابل قيام هذا الموظف بعمل من أعمال وظيفته أو الامتناع عن القيام بعمل من أعمال وظيفته.

Some notes

1. The verb '*to bribe*' means to make someone do something for you by giving him/her money, presents, or something else that they want, as in:

   He bribed immigration officials to let him enter the country illegally.

   The public official was accused of accepting/taking bribes from a businessman.
2. The noun '*bribe*' (n./c.) means money or a present that you give to someone else so that s/he will do something for you, usually something dishonest, thus lending itself to رشوّة. Related words include '*bribery*' جريمة الرّشوة, which is an uncountable noun, as in: *The company was rife with bribery and corruption.*
3. Related words, expressions, and sentences include ('*bribery*', '*bribe*', '*the bribing party*', '*the party offering the bribe*', '*somebody bribes a public official*', '*a public official was bribed*', etc.)

Reference

Al-Aqaileh, Z. M. 2015. المصطلحات القانونية باللغة الإنجليزية مع ترجمة كاملة إلى اللغة العربية *'Legal Terms in English fully Translated into Arabic'*. Jordan: Dār Al-Thaqāfa for Publication & Distribution

CHAPTER 11

Cybercrime

Warming up …

Before making a start, be familiar with the area by listening to the following videos:

In English

https://www.youtube.com/watch?v=dRKMlG0KTkY
https://www.youtube.com/watch?v=Ls8jyO46bmI
https://www.youtube.com/watch?v=NAcN93O8b6w

In Arabic

https://www.youtube.com/watch?v=9UA2VxZHHyc
https://www.youtube.com/watch?v=vmK_lfOBXA8

A. Almanna, *Legal Translation between English and Arabic*, https://doi.org/10.1007/978-3-031-14838-5_11

Exercise 1

Dear instructors: evaluate with your students the English translation of the following Arabic text written and translated for the purposes of this course:

Cybercrimes	الجرائم الإلكترونية
Cybercrime refers to any criminal activity that involves a computer or networked device.	تُشير الجريمةُ الإلكترونية إلى أيّ نشاطٍ إجراميّ يتضمن حاسوبًا، أو جهازًا مرتبطًا بشبكة ما.
Cybercrimes can be classified into three types, namely:	ويمكن تصنيف الجرائم الإلكترونية إلى ثلاثةِ أنواعٍ هي:
• Cybercrime targeting persons. This type of cybercrime, as the title suggests, targets people, especially children. Examples of this type of cybercrime include credit card fraud, and defamation through social media (be it libel or slander), and so on.	• الجريمة التي تستهدف الأشخاص. وهذا النوع من الجرائم الإلكترونية، كما يوحي العنوان، يستهدف الأشخاص وبخاصة الأطفال، ومن الأمثلة الشائعة لهذا النوع من الجرائم الإلكترونية هو الاحتيال على بطاقات الائتمان، والتّشهير عبر وسائل التواصل الاجتماعي، سواء أكان عن طريق السبّ أو القذف وغيرها من الأمثلة.
• Cybercrimes against property. This type does not attack people, but rather it attacks their properties as in violating their intellectual property rights, copyright infringement, computer vandalism, virus transmission, hacking, and so on.	• الجرائم التي تستهدف الأموال. وهذا النوع من الجرائم الإلكترونية لا يستهدف الأشخاص، بل يستهدف ممتلكاتهم كأن يستهدف حقوق الملكية الفكرية، أو انتهاك حقوق النشر، أو تخريب الكمبيوتر، أو نقل الفايروسات، أو القرصنة الإلكترونية وغيرها.
• Cybercrimes against governments. This type that attacks governments is considered an attack on state's sovereignty. Examples of this types include hacking, accessing confidential information, cyber warfare, cyber terrorism, pirated software, and the like.	• الجرائم التي تستهدف الحكومات وهذا النوع من الجرائم الذي يستهدف الحكومة يعدُّ تعدٍ/تعديًا ضد سيادة الدولة ومن الأمثلة لهذا النوع القرصنة، والوصول إلى معلومات سريّة، والحرب الإلكترونية، والإرهاب الإلكتروني، والبرامج المقرصنة، وغيرها.

Note that بخاصة *can be replaced with* خصوصًا *or* لا سيّما, *but you need to learn to use them correctly.*

Is it يُعدُّ تعدٍ *or* تعديًا*? And why?*

Exercise 2

Dear instructors: evaluate with your students the Arabic translations of the following English legal text taken from an article titled *'Cybercrime'* by Kate Brush (www.techtarget.com), paying extra attention to the technical terms and syntactic structures.

How cybercrime works

A	*B*
آلية الجريمة الإلكترونية	كيف تُنفَّذ الجرائم السيبرانية

Cybercrime attacks can begin wherever there is digital data, opportunity, and motive. Cybercriminals include everyone from the lone user engaged in cyberbullying to state-sponsored actors, like China's intelligence services. Cybercrimes generally do not occur in a vacuum; they are, in many ways, distributed in nature. That is, cybercriminals typically rely on other actors to complete the crime. This is whether it's the creator of malware using the dark web to sell code, the distributor of illegal pharmaceuticals using cryptocurrency brokers to hold virtual money in escrow or state threat actors relying on technology subcontractors to steal intellectual property (IP).

A	*B*
يمكن أن تُشن الهجمات الإلكترونية أينما وجدت بيانات رقمية، وأُتيحت الفرصة، وتوفرّت الدوافع. ومجرم الإنترنت هو كل شخص متورط سواء أكان متنمرًا إلكترونيًا يعمل بمفرده أو جهات فاعلة تحت رعاية دولة كأجهزة المخابرات الصينية. وهذه الجرائم لا تحدث عمومًا في فراغ؛ فهي، ومن عدة نواحٍ، موزّعة بطبيعتها، فمجرمو الإنترنت عادة ما يعتمدون على جهات أخرى لإتمام الجريمة، إن كانت هذه الجهات منشئ البرمجيات الخبيثة الذي يستخدم الشبكة الخفية لبيع التعليمات البرمجية، أو موزع المستحضرات الصيدلانية غير القانونية الذي يعتمد على وساطة العملة الرقمية للاحتفاظ بأموال افتراضية في سبيل الحراسة، أو الجهات الفاعلة التي تهدد الدولة وتعتمد على مقاولين فرعيين للتكنولوجيا بهدف سرقة الملكية الفكرية.	يمكن أن تُشَن الهجمات السيبرانية حيثما تتوفر البيانات الرقمية، والفرصة والدافع. وتتباين خطورة المدرجون على قائمة المجرمين السيبرانيين، من مستخدمين أفراد يتورطون في التنمر السيبراني إلى جهات فاعلة ترعاها دول، مثل جهاز المخابرات الصيني. والجرائم السيبرانية بشكل عام لا تحدث بشكل منفرد؛ فأدوارها موزعة بطرق متعددة بين أطرافها بشكل متأصل، أي أن المجرمين السيبرانيين يعتمدون عادة على جهات فاعلة أخرى لإتمام الجريمة، ابتداءً من مطوّر البرامج الخبيثة الذي يَستخدم الشبكة المظلمة لبيع شفرة البرمجة، إلى موزع المنتجات الدوائية غير القانونية الذي يَستخدم وسطاء العملات المشفرة للاحتفاظ بأموال افتراضية في حسابات الضمان، أو الجهات الفاعلة التي تهدد الدول بالاعتماد على متعاقدين من الباطن في مجال التكنولوجيا لسرقة حقوق الملكية الفكرية.

Cybercriminals use various attack vectors to carry out their cyberattacks and are constantly seeking new methods and techniques for achieving their goals, while avoiding detection and arrest.

A	*B*
فيستخدم مجرمو الإنترنت موجهات هجوم مختلفة لتنفيذ هجماتهم الإلكترونية ويبحثون باستمرار عن أساليب وتقنيات جديدة لتحقيق أهدافهم مع تفادي الاكتشاف والاعتقال.	ويَستخدم المجرمون السيبرانيون طُرق متنوعة لتنفيذ هجماتهم السيبرانية، ويبحثون باستمرار عن أساليب وتقنيات جديدة لتحقيق أهدافهم مع تجنب اكتشاف أمرهم والقبض عليهم.

Cybercriminals often carry out their activities using malware and other types of software, but social engineering is often an important component for executing most types of cybercrime. Phishing emails are another important component to many types of cybercrime but especially so for targeted attacks, like business email compromise (BEC), in which the attacker attempts to impersonate, via email, a business owner in order to convince employees to pay out bogus invoices.

A	*B*
وعادة ما ينفذ مجرمو الإنترنت أنشطتهم باستخدام البرمجيات الخبيثة وأنواع أخرى من البرامج، ولكن غالبًا ما تكون الهندسة الاجتماعية مكونًا مهمًا لتنفيذ معظم أنواع الجرائم الإلكترونية. وتعد رسائل التصيّد الإلكتروني مكونًا مهمًا آخر لأنواع مختلفة من هذه الجرائم وخاصة الهجمات المستهدفة، مثل اختراق البريد الإلكتروني للأعمال حيث يحاول المهاجم، عبر البريد الإلكتروني، انتحال شخصية رب العمل لإقناع الموظفين بدفع فواتير مزيفة.	وغالبًا ما يُنفِّذ المجرمون السيبرانيون أنشطتهم باستخدام البرامج الخبيثة وأنواع أخرى من البرمجيات، لكن الهندسة الاجتماعية غالبًا ما تكون مكونًا مهمًا في تنفيذ معظم أنواع الجرائم السيبرانية. وتُعد رسائل التصيد عبر البريد الإلكتروني مكونًا مهمًا آخر في العديد من أنواع الجرائم السيبرانية، ولكن بشكل خاص في حالة الهجمات محددة الأهداف، مثل اختراق البريد الإلكتروني للأعمال؛ حينما يحاول المهاجم انتحال شخصية صاحب العمل من خلال البريد الإلكتروني لإقناع الموظفين بدفع فواتير وهمية.

Exercise 3

Translate the following text adapted from one of my MA students' projects into English, paying extra attention to the technical terms used and differences between Arabic and English.

الجريمةُ الإلكترونية هي أيُّ نشاطٍ إجراميٍّ يتضمن جهاز كَمبيوتر، أو جهازًا مُتّصلاً بالشبكة، أو ربّما الشّبَكة نفسها، وفي حين أن معظم هذه الجرائم تُرتكب بدافع مادي بحت، فإنَّ بعضها يستهدف مباشرة الكمبيوتر أو الأجهزة لإتلافها أو تعطيلها، وبعضها الآخر يُنفّذ عبر استخدام أجهزة الكمبيوتر أو الشبكات لنشر برمجيات خبيثة، أو معلومات غير قانونية، أو صور، أو أي مواد أخرى. وقد تستهدف بعض الجرائم الإلكترونية الأمرين في آنٍ واحد كأن تستهدف أجهزة الكمبيوتر لإصابتها بفايروس، ومن ثم تستخدم هذه الفيروسات لنشرها في أجهزة أخرى أو في شبكات كاملة أحيانًا.

وتشمل الجرائم الإلكترونية أنواعًا مختلفة من الأنشطة الإجرامية بغية الربح المادي، بما في ذلك هجمات برمجيات انتزاع الفدية، والاحتيال عبر البريد الإلكتروني والإنترنت، وانتحال الهوية، فضلاً عن محاولات سرقة الحساب المالي أو بطاقة الائتمان أو معلومات أي بطاقة دفع أخرى. كما قد يستهدف مجرمو الإنترنت أيضًا المعلومات الشخصية للفرد أو بيانات الشركات لسرقتها وإعادة بيعها. ومع شروع العديد من الموظفين إلى العمل عن بعد بسبب كوفد-19، فإنه من المتوقع ازدياد الجرائم الإلكترونية وتكرارها في عام ٢٠٢١ وهنا تكمن أهمية حماية البيانات الاحتياطية.

Some notes

1. لنشر برمجيات خبيثة can lend itself here to '*to spread malware*'.
2. هجمات برمجيات انتزاع الفدية (also known as هجمات برامج الفدية) can be rendered as '*ransomware attacks*'.
3. الاحتيال عبر البريد الإلكتروني أو الإنترنت lends itself to '*email and internet fraud*'.
4. انتحال الهوية can be translated as '*identity fraud*'.
5. البيانات الاحتياطية here means '*backup data*'.

Exercise 4

Translate the following text taken from an article titled *'Cybercrime'* by Kate Brush (www.techtarget.com) into Arabic, paying extra attention to the technical terms used and differences between Arabic and English.

The U.S. Department of Justice (DOJ) divides cybercrime into three categories:

1. crimes in which the computing device is the target—for example, to gain network access;
2. crimes in which the computer is used as a weapon—for example, to launch a denial-of-service (DoS) attack; and
3. crimes in which the computer is used as an accessory to a crime—for example, using a computer to store illegally obtained data.

The Council of Europe Convention on Cybercrime, to which the United States is a signatory, defines cybercrime as a wide range of malicious activities, including the illegal interception of data, system interferences that compromise network integrity and availability, and copyright infringements.

The necessity of internet connectivity has enabled an increase in the volume and pace of cybercrime activities because the criminal no longer needs to be physically present when committing a crime. The internet's speed, convenience, anonymity and lack of borders make computer-based variations of financial crimes—such as ransomware, fraud and money laundering, as well as crimes such as stalking and bullying—easier to carry out.

Cybercriminal activity may be carried out by individuals or small groups with relatively little technical skill. Or, by highly organized global criminal groups that may include skilled developers and others with relevant expertise. To further reduce the chances of detection and prosecution, cybercriminals often choose to operate in countries with weak or nonexistent cybercrime laws.

Exercise 5

The following text is taken from an article titled *'Cybercrime'* by Kate Brush (www.techtarget.com). Your task is to compare the translation of the original text with the two translations given in TT1 and TT2 with the potential to comment on the translation of

1. the implicit and explicit conjunctions used in the original text;
2. the quantifiers (e.g. *'some'*) and indicators of expectancy (e.g. *'but'*) used in the original text; and
3. the model verbs (e.g. *'can'*, *'may'*, etc.) used in the original text.

Common examples of cybercrime

Some of the more commonly seen cybercrime attacks include distributed DoS (DDoS) attacks, which are often used to shut down systems and networks. This type of attack uses a network's own communications protocol against it by overwhelming its ability to respond to connection requests. DDoS attacks are sometimes carried out simply for malicious reasons or as part of a cyberextortion scheme, but they may also be used to distract the victim organization from some other attack or exploit carried out at the same time.

TT1	*TT2*
أمثلة شائعة للجرائم السيبرانية	**أمثلة شائعة على الجرائم السيبرانية**
من أكثر هجمات الجرائم السيبرانية شيوعًا هجمات "دوس" المُوزَّعة التي تُستخدم غالبًا لإغلاق الأنظمة والشبكات. ويَستخدِم هذا النوع من الهجوم بروتوكول الاتصال الخاص بالشبكة ضدها من خلال إضعاف قدرته على الاستجابة لطلبات الاتصال الزائدة. وقد تُنفذ هجمات "دوس" المُوزَّعة في بعض الأحيان ببساطة من أجل إحداث ضرر أو كجزء من مخطط ابتزاز سيبراني، ولكن يمكن أيضًا استخدامها لتشتيت انتباه المُنظَّمة الضحية عن هجوم أو استغلال آخر يُنفَّذ في نفس الوقت.	تتضمن بعض هجمات الجرائم السيبرانية الأكثرشيوعًا هجمات (DDoS) Dof، التي غالبًا ما تستخدم لإغلاق الأنظمة والشبكات، ويستخدم هذا النوع من الهجمات بروتوكول الاتصالات الخاص بالشبكة ضدها عن طريق إرباك قدرتها على الاستجابة لطلبات الاتصال، ويتم أحيانًا تنفيذ هجمات DDos ببساطة لأسباب خبيثة أو كجزء من مخطط ابتزاز سيبراني، ولكن يمكن أن تستخدم أيضًا لتشتيت انتباه المنظمة الضحية عن بعض الهجمات الأخرى أو استغلال يتم تنفيذه في الوقت ذاته.

Infecting systems and networks with malware is an example of an attack used to damage the system or harm users. This can be done by damaging the system, software, or data stored on the system. Ransomware attacks are similar, but the malware acts by encrypting or shutting down victim systems until a ransom is paid.

TT1	*TT2*
وتعدُّ إصابة الأنظمة والشبكات ببرامج خبيثة مثالاً على هجوم يُستخدم لإتلاف نظام ما أو إلحاق الضرر بالمستخدمين. ويمكن القيام بذلك من خلال إتلاف الجهاز، أو البرمجيات، أو البيانات المخزنة عليه. ولا تختلف هجمات برامج الفدية عن بعضها البعض، أما بالنسبة للبرامج الخبيثة فهي تعمل عن طريق تشفير أو إغلاق أجهزة الضحية حتى تُدفع الفدية.	وأحد أمثلة الهجوم الذي يستخدم لتدمير النظام أو إيذاء المستخدمين هو إصابة الأنظمة والشبكات ببرامج خبيثة، ويمكن أن يحدث ذلك عن طريق إتلاف النظام أو البرنامج أو البيانات التي تم تخزينها على النظام، وتعد هجمات برامج الفدية مشابهة لهذه، إلا أن البرامج الخبيثة هنا تعمل عن طريق تشفير أنظمة الضحية أو إيقاف تشغيلها إلى أن يتم دفع الفدية.

Phishing campaigns are used to infiltrate corporate networks. This can be by sending fraudulent emails to users in an organization, enticing them to download attachments or click on links that then spread viruses or malware to their systems and through their systems to their company's networks.

TT1	*TT2*
كما تستخدم حملات التصيد لاختراق شبكات الشركات، ويمكن أن يتم ذلك عن طريق إرسال رسائل بريد إلكتروني احتيالية إلى المستخدمين في إحدى المؤسسات وحثهم على تحميل المرفقات أو النقر على الروابط التي من ثم تنشر الفيروسات أو البرامج الخبيثة إلى أنظمتها أو من خلال أنظمتها إلى شبكات الشركات.	وبالنسبة لحملات التصيد فإنها تستخدم للتسلل إلى شبكات الشركات، ويمكن أن يحدث ذلك عن طريق إرسال رسائل بريد إلكتروني احتيالية إلى المستخدمين في منظمة ما، وجذب انتباههم لتحميل مرفقات أو الضغط على روابط تقوم بعدها بنشر فيروسات أو برامج خبيثة في أنظمتهم وفي شبكات شركتهم من خلال أنظمتهم.

A credentials attack is when a cybercriminal aims to steal or guess user IDs and passwords for the victim's systems or personal accounts. They can be carried out through the use of brute-force attacks by installing keylogger software or by exploiting vulnerabilities in software or hardware that can expose the victim's credentials.

TT1	*TT2*
ويقع الهجوم على بيانات الاعتماد عندما يحاول المجرم السيبراني سرقة أو تخمين مُعرّفات المستخدمين وكلمات المرور لأنظمة الضحية أو الحسابات الشخصية. ويمكن تنفيذ هذه الهجمات باستخدام القوة الغاشمة من خلال تثبيت برنامج راصد للوحة المفاتيح أو عن طريق استغلال نقاط ضعف في برمجيات أو مكونات بإمكانها أن تكشف عن بيانات الاعتماد الخاصة بالضحية.	وأما الهجوم الخاص بوثائق إثبات الشخصية فإنه يحدث عندما يهدف مجرم سيبراني إلى سرقة وثائق الهوية وكلمات السر الخاصة بأنظمة الضحية أو حساباتها الشخصية أو تخمينها، ويمكن أن تنفذ من خلال استخدام هجمات القوة العمياء عن طريق تثبيت برنامج رصد لوحة المفاتيح أو عن طريق استغلال الثغرات الأمنية في البرامج أو الأجهزة التي يمكن أن تكشف وثائق إثبات الشخصية الخاصة بالضحية.

Cybercriminals may also attempt to hijack a website to change or delete content or to access or modify databases without authorization. For example, an attacker may use a Structured Query Language (SQL) injection exploit to insert malicious code into a website, which can then be used to exploit vulnerabilities in the website's database, enabling a hacker to access and tamper with records or gain unauthorized access to sensitive information and data, such as customer passwords, credit card numbers, personally identifiable information (PII), trade secrets and IP.

TT1	*TT2*
وقد يحاول المجرمون السيبرانيون أيضًا اختطاف موقع إلكتروني لتغيير أو حذف محتواه أو الوصول إلى قواعد البيانات أو تعديلها دون إذن. على سبيل المثال، قد يستخدم المهاجم لغة البرمجيات "إس كيو إل" لإضافة شفرة ضارة إلى موقع إلكتروني؛ إذ يمكن استخدامه بعد ذلك في استغلال نقاط الضعف الخاصة بقاعدة بيانات الموقع، مما يُمكِّن المخترِق من الوصول إلى السجلات والتلاعب بها أو الوصول غير مصرح به إلى المعلومات والبيانات الحساسة، مثل كلمات مرور العملاء، وأرقام بطاقات الائتمان ومعلومات التعريف الشخصية، والأسرار التجارية وحقوق الملكية الفكرية.	وقد يحاول المجرمون السيبرانيون أيضًا اختطاف موقع ويب لتغيير محتوى أو حذفه أو لدخول قاعدة بيانات أو تعديلها بدون تصريح، فعلى سبيل المثال، يمكن أن يستخدم المهاجم استغلال حقنة "لغة الاستعلامات البنائية" (SQL) لإدخال رمز خبيث إلى موقع الويب، ويمكن أن يستخدم لاحقًا لاستغلال الثغرات في قاعدة بيانات موقع الويب، مما سيتيح للمخترق الوصول إلى السجلات والعبث بها أو الحصول على وصول غير مصرح به إلى المعلومات والبيانات الحساسة، مثل كلمات سر العملاء وأرقام البطاقات الائتمانية ومعلومات التعريف الشخصي (PII) والأسرار التجارية والملكية الفكرية (IP).

Here we have two styles, namely لتغيير أو حذف محتواه *and* لتغيير محتوى أو حذفه. *Which style do you prefer?*

Other common examples of cybercrime include illegal gambling, the sale of illegal items—like weapons, drugs, or counterfeit goods—and the solicitation, production, possession, or distribution of child pornography.

TT1	*TT2*
وتشمل قائمة الأمثلة الشائعة الأخرى للجرائم السيبرانية المقامرة غير القانونية، وبيع سلع غير قانونية مثل الأسلحة، أو المخدرات أو السلع المقلدة. وكذلك طلب، أو إنتاج، أو حيازة أو توزيع المواد الإباحية المتعلقة بالأطفال.	وتتضمن الأمثلة الشائعة الأخرى للجرائم السيبرانية المقامرة غير القانونية وبيع السلع غير القانونية -كالأسلحة أو المخدرات أو السلع المقلدة- وطلب المواد الإباحية المتعلقة بالأطفال أو إنتاجها أو حيازتها أو توزيعها.

Exercise 6

Dear instructors: evaluate with your students the MA students' translations of the following text titled '*Why remote working leaves us vulnerable to cyber-attacks*' by Bernd Debusmann Jr published on the BBC News website on July 26, 2021.

A cyber-crime group known as REvil took meticulous care when picking the timing for its most recent attack—US Independence Day, 4 July.

The word 'group' *can be translated into* جماعة, مجموعة, عصابة, *etc. Is there any difference between* مجموعة *and* جماعة *in terms of their connotative meaning?*

TT1	*TT2*	*TT3*
لقد اختار أفراد جماعة ريفيل (REvil) المعروفين بارتكاب جرائم سيبرانية توقيت تنفيذ هجمتهم الأخيرة بعناية فائقة ونفذوها تزامنا مع يوم استقلال الولايات المتحدة الأمريكية الموافق الرابع من شهر يوليو.	اختارت مجموعة الجرائم الإلكترونية المعروفة باسم "ريفيل" (REvil) توقيت هجومها الأخير بحذر شديد — يوم الاستقلال الأمريكي، الرابع من شهر يوليو.	جماعة جرائم سيبرانية تعرف بـ"ريفل" تتوخى الحذر الشديد عند اختيار توقيت هجومها الأخير — يوم استقلال الولايات المتحدة، الرابع من يوليو.

They knew many IT specialists and cyber-security experts would be on leave, enjoying a long weekend off work.

Is there any difference between العلم *and* الدراية*?*

TT1	TT2	TT3
فقد كانوا على دراية بأن العديد من مختصي تكنولوجيا المعلومات وخبراء الأمن السيبراني سيكونون في إجازة ويحظون بعطلة نهاية أسبوع طويلة بعيدا عن العمل.	حيث كانوا يعلمون ان العديد من اخصائي تكنولوجيا المعلومات وخبراء الأمن السيبراني سيكونون بعيداً عن مكاتبهم يتمتعون بعطلة نهاية أسبوع طويلة.	كانوا على دراية بأن العديد من متخصصي تكنولوجيا المعلومات وخبراء الأمن السيبراني سيكونون في إجازة يستمتعون بعطلة نهاية أسبوع طويلة خارج العمل.

Before long, more than 1,000 companies in the US, and at least 17 other countries, were under attack from hackers.

Is it بلدٍ *or* بلدًا*?*

TT1	TT2	TT3
ويذكر أنه قبل فترة ليست بالبعيدة، تعرضت أكثر من 1000 شركة في الولايات المتحدة الأمريكية وما لا يقل عن 17 دولة أخرى لهجمات شنها قراصنة الكترونيون (الهاكرز).	وفي مدة قليلة تمكنوا من قرصنة أكثر من 1000 شركة في الولايات المتحدة الأمريكية، وما لا يقل عن 17 دولة أخرى.	وقبل وقت طويل، كانت تتعرض أكثر من 1,000 شركة في الولايات المتحدة وعلى الأقل 17 بلد آخر لهجوم من المخترقين.

Many firms were forced into a costly downtime period as a result. Among those targeted during the incident was a well-known software provider, Kaseya.

By virtue of 'to force' *in the passive, the whole scene is characterized by having a force dynamic value of forcing those companies that usually work in normal circumstances to stop working. This has been reflected by the verb* اضطر*. Can you think of another verb?*

TT1	TT2	TT3
ونتيجة لهذا الهجوم، فلقد اضطرت العديد من الشركات إلى التوقف عن العمل لفترة تكبدت فيها الشركات خسائر مالية كبيرة ولقد كانت شركة (Kaseya) المشهورة في مجال البرمجيات من ضمن الشركات التي تم استهدافها في هذه الحادثة.	ونتيجة لذلك، اضطرت العديد من الشركات للدخول في انقطاع مكلف عن العمل .وكان من بين الشركات المستهدفة موفر البرمجيات المشهور "كاسيا"(Kaseya).	ونتيجة لذلك، اضطرت العديد من الشركات للخضوع لفترة من التعطل كلفتها الكثير. وكان من بين المستهدفين خلال الحادثة مزود برمجيات معروف جدًا يطلق عليه "كاسِيا".

Is there any difference between مشهور *and* معروف*? If yes, comment on the translation of* 'well-known' *in the three target texts.*

REvil used Kaseya as a conduit to spread its ransomware—a malware that can scramble and steal an organization's computer data—through other corporate and cloud-based networks that use the software.

TT1	TT2	TT3
فقد استخدم أفراد جماعة ريفيل شركة كاسيا كوسيلة لنشر برنامج الفدية الخاص بهم —وهو برنامج ضار يعمل على التسلل إلى بيانات الحاسوب الخاص بالمؤسسة وسرقتها— في شبكات المؤسسات التي تستخدم برامجها.	واستخدمت "ريفيل" "كاسيا" كقناة لنشر برنامج الفدية الخاص بها—وهو برنامج خبيث يمكنه التدافع وسرقة بيانات الحاسوب الخاصة بالمؤسسة-من خلال الشبكات القائمة على السحابة والشركات الأخرى التي تستخدم البرنامج.	واستخدمت "ريفل" "كاسِيا" كقناة لنشر برامج الفدية الخاصة بها— وهي برامج خبيثة يمكنها التدافع وسرقة بيانات الحاسوب الخاصة بالمنظمة —عن طريق شبكات سحابية ومؤسسية أخرى تستخدم البرنامج.

REvil took credit for the incident and claimed to have encrypted more than one million systems.

By virtue of the framing verb 'to claim', *the writer distances himself from the attributed material? Comment on the translation of this framing verb.*

TT1	TT2	TT3
وقد تبنت جماعة ريفيل هذا الهجوم وزعموا أنهم قد قاموا بتشفير أكثر من مليون نظام.	وأعلنت "ريفيل" انها المسؤولة عن هذا الهجوم وأنها أصابت أكثر من مليون جهاز ببرنامجها الخبيث.	وقد تحملت "ريفل" مسؤولية الحادثة وادعت بأنها قامت بتشفير أكثر من مليون نظام.

قام بتشفير *simply means* شفّر*? However, the text type and genre should be taken into account when translating. Which style do you prefer?*

The group then demanded a ransom of $70m (£50.5m) in Bitcoin for the release of a universal decryption tool that would allow those affected to recover their crucial files.

The evaluative word 'crucial' *was translated into* هام *and* مهم*. Is there any difference between* هام *and* مهم *in Arabic?*

TT1	TT2	TT3
ولقد طالبت المجموعة بفدية قدرها 70 مليون دولار أمريكي، أي ما يعادل 50.5 مليون جنيه إسترليني بعملة البيتكوين مقابل إصدارها لآلية عالمية لفك التشفير الذي قاموا به والسماح للمتضررين باستعادة ملفاتهم الهامة.	وطالبت "ريفيل" بفدية قدرها 70 مليون (50.5 مليون جنيه إسترليني) من عملة بيتكوين لإصدار أداة فك تشفير عالمية تسمح للمتضررين من استعادة ملفاتهم المهمة.	ثم طالبت الجماعة بفدية تقدر بـ 70 مليون دولار (50.5 مليون جنيه استرليني) من عملة البتكوين لكي تقوم بإطلاق أداة فك تشفير عالمية تسمح للمتضررين من استعادة ملفاتهم الهامة.

Hacking experts warn that such attacks are likely to become more frequent, and suggest businesses cannot afford to underestimate the hidden impact the pandemic has had on their vulnerability.

In Arabic, we say يتأثر بـ *and* يؤثر في*, not* على.

Is there any difference among من المحتمل*,* من المرجّح *and* من المُستبعد*? If yes, how would you translate* 'It is likely that …', 'It is possible that …', 'It is unlikely that …', *and* 'It is probable that …'?

TT1	*TT2*	*TT3*
كما وقد حذر عدد من الخبراء المختصون في التصدي لعميات القرصنة من التزايد المحتمل لمثل هذه الهجمات، مشيرين إلى أنه لا ينبغي على أصحاب الشركات الاستهانة بتأثير الجائحة الخفي ودوره في إضعاف نظم حمايتهم وجعلهم أكثر عرضة للهجوم.	وحذر خبراء القرصنة من تكرر هذا النوع من الهجوم، وأشاروا الى انه لا يمكن للأعمال التجارية ان تستخف بالأثر الوبائي على نقاط ضعفهم.	ويحذر خبراء الاختراق من أن هجمات كهذه من المرجح أن تصبح أكثر تواترًا، كما يشيرون بأن المشاريع التجارية لا تستطيع تحمل التقليل من أثر الوباء الخفي على ضعفها.

Exercise 7

Translate the following text taken from *SRD Law Notes* into Arabic to a professional level.

What is cybercrime?

Cybercrime is a crime that is done using technology whereas a computer is it tool for cybercrime. In simple words, cybercrime is an unlawful act that is done with the help of the Internet and electronic devices. Cybercrimes can involve criminal activities that are traditionally in nature such as theft fraud, forgery, mischief all of which are subject to the Indian penal code.

Types of cybercrime

There are different types of cybercrimes

1. **Identity theft**

In this type of crime personal information of a person is stolen with the purpose of using their financial resources or to take a loan or credit card in their name then such a crime is known as identity theft.

2. **Cyberbullying**

When a teenager or adolescent harasses, defames, or intimidate someone with the use of the Internet, phone, chat room, instant messaging or any other social network then the person is said to be committing the crime of cyberbullying.

3. **Cyber terrorism**

Cyber terrorism is a type of cybercrime when a three top extortion or any kind of harm is being subjected towards a person, group, or state, it is known as the crime of cyber terrorism. Generally, it includes the well-planned attack strategies on the government and corporate computer system.

4. **Hacking**

Hacking is the most common cybercrime in this type of crying the person gets access to another people's computer and password to use for their own wrongful gain.

Exercise 8

Translate the following text adapted from *the Legalist* to English

أركان الجريمة الإلكترونية

أركان الجرائم الإلكترونية تتمثل في ركنين، هما:

(1) **الركن المادي**

Is there any difference between توافر and توفّر? If yes, which one do you prefer in such a context?

Is there any difference between وجود and تواجد? If yes, which one do you prefer in such a context?

يتمثل هذا الركن في توافر/توفّر بيئة رقمية (الاتصال بالإنترنت، حاسب، إلخ) و/أو وجود/تواجد أحد البرامج الخارقة للمواقع أو الفيروسات على الحاسب. ولأن الجرائم الإلكترونية تفرض أنماطًا جديدة فقد تغيّر الركن المادي عن المألوف بعض الشيء، ففي بعض الجرائم، كجريمة "إعداد الفيروسات على الحاسب تمهيدًا لبثها" على سبيل المثال، فإنَّ الأعمال التحضيرية تدخل في ركن الجريمة المادي، بخلاف ما جري عليه القول في الجرائم العادية التي لا تعتبر الأعمال التحضيرية جزءًا من الركن المادي للجريمة.

(2) **الركن المعنوي**

أما فيما يتعلّق بالرّكن المعنوي، فإنّه يتمثل في العلم والإرادة، أي علم الجاني بالفعل الإجرامي. وهذا ما يطلق عليه بالحالة النفسية للجاني ونيته، وقد قنن القضاء الفرنسي مبدأ سوء النية في الاعتداء وأسس أنّه يتحقق بتوافر أدوات الجريمة على الحاسب أو على البريد الإلكتروني سواء أكان مغلقًا أم مفتوحًا، فالعبرة بوجود سوء النية.

Exercise 9

Translate the following text adapted from an article titled *'Cybercrime'* by Kate Brush (www.techtarget.com).

Types of cybercrime

There are many different types of cybercrime; most cybercrimes are carried out with the expectation of financial gain by the attackers, though the ways cybercriminals aim to get paid can vary. Some specific types of cybercrimes include the following:

Cyberextortion: A crime involving an attack or threat of an attack coupled with a demand for money to stop the attack. One form of cyberextortion is the ransomware attack. Here, the attacker gains access to an organization's systems and encrypts its documents and files—anything of potential value—making the data inaccessible until a ransom is paid. Usually, this is in some form of cryptocurrency, such as bitcoin.

Cryptojacking: An attack that uses scripts to mine cryptocurrencies within browsers without the user's consent. Cryptojacking attacks may involve loading cryptocurrency mining software to the victim's system. However, many attacks depend on JavaScript code that does in-browser mining if the user's browser has a tab or window open on the malicious site. No malware needs to be installed as loading the affected page executes the in-browser mining code.

Identity theft: An attack that occurs when an individual accesses a computer to glean a user's personal information, which they then use to steal that person's identity or access their valuable accounts, such as banking and credit cards. Cybercriminals buy and sell identity information on darknet markets, offering financial accounts, as well as other types of accounts, like video streaming services, webmail, video and audio streaming, online auctions and more. Personal health information is another frequent target for identity thieves.

Credit card fraud: An attack that occurs when hackers infiltrate retailers' systems to get the credit card and/or banking information of their customers. Stolen payment cards can be bought and sold in bulk on darknet markets, where hacking groups that have stolen mass quantities of credit cards profit by selling to lower-level cybercriminals who profit through credit card fraud against individual accounts.

Cyberespionage: A crime involving a cybercriminal who hacks into systems or networks to gain access to confidential information held by a government or other organization. Attacks may be motivated by profit or by ideology. Cyberespionage activities can include every type of cyberattack to gather, modify, or destroy data, as well as using network-connected devices, like webcams or closed-circuit TV (CCTV) cameras, to spy on a targeted individual or groups and monitoring communications, including emails, text messages and instant messages.

Software piracy: An attack that involves the unlawful copying, distribution and use of software programs with the intention of commercial or personal use. Trademark violations, copyright infringements and patent violations are often associated with this type of cybercrime.

Exit scam: The dark web, not surprisingly, has given rise to the digital version of an old crime known as the exit scam. In today's form, dark web administrators divert virtual currency held in marketplace escrow accounts to their own accounts—essentially, criminals stealing from other criminals.

Exercise 10

Translate the following text adapted from the Anti-Cybercrime Law No. 14 of 2014 published on Qatar Legal Portal (almeezan.qa) into English.

نحن تميم بن حمد آل ثاني أمير دولة قطر،
بعد الاطلاع على الدستور،
وعلى القانون رقم (3) لسنة 2004 بشأن مكافحة الإرهاب،
وعلى قانون العقوبات الصادر بالقانون رقم (11) لسنة 2004، والقوانين المعدلة له،
وعلى قانون الإجراءات الجنائية الصادر بالقانون رقم (23) لسنة 2004، المعدل بالقانون رقم (24) لسنة 2009،
وعلى قانون الاتصالات الصادر بالمرسوم بقانون رقم (34) لسنة 2006،
وعلى قانون مكافحة غسل الأموال وتمويل الإرهاب الصادر بالقانون رقم (4) لسنة 2010،
وعلى قانون المعاملات والتجارة الإلكترونية الصادر بالمرسوم بقانون رقم (16) لسنة 2010،
وعلى اقتراح وزير الداخلية،
وعلى مشروع القانون المقدم من مجلس الوزراء،
وبعد أخذ رأي مجلس الشورى،
قررنا القانون الآتي:

المادة 1

يُعمل بأحكام قانون مكافحة الجرائم الإلكترونية المرفق بهذا القانون.

المادة 2

على جميع مزودي الخدمة المخاطبين بأحكام القانون المرفق، القائمين في تاريخ العمل به، توفيق أوضاعهم بما يتفق وأحكام القانون المرفق، خلال ستة أشهر من تاريخ العمل به، ويجوز لوزير الداخلية في حالة الضرورة مد هذه المهلة لمدة أخرى.

المادة 3

يُصدر وزير الداخلية القرارات اللازمة لتنفيذ أحكام القانون المرفق.

المادة 4

يُلغى كل حكم يخالف أحكام القانون المرفق.

المادة 5

على جميع الجهات المختصة، كل فيما يخصه، تنفيذ هذا القانون. ويُنشر في الجريدة الرسمية [...]

المادة 11

يعاقب بالحبس مدة لا تجاوز ثلاث سنوات، وبالغرامة التي لا تزيد على (100,000) مائة ألف ريال، أو بإحدى هاتين العقوبتين، كل من ارتكب فعلاً من الأفعال التالية:

(1) استخدم الشبكة المعلوماتية أو إحدى وسائل تقنية المعلومات في انتحال هوية لشخص طبيعي أو معنوي.

(2) تمكن عن طريق الشبكة المعلوماتية أو إحدى وسائل تقنية المعلومات، من الاستيلاء لنفسه أو لغيره على مال منقول، أو على سند أو التوقيع عليه، بطريق الاحتيال، أو باتخاذ اسم كاذب، أو بانتحال صفة غير صحيحة.

References

Abdel-Fattah, M.M. 2005. On the Translation of Modals from English into Arabic and Vice Versa: The Case of Deontic Modality. *Babel* 51 (1): 31–48.

Adab, B. J. 1997. *Translation Strategies and Cross-Cultural Constraints: A Case Study of the Translation of Advertising Texts*. Unpublished doctoral dissertation. Aston: Aston University.

Al-Aqaileh, Z. M. 2015. المصطلحات القانونية باللغة الإنجليزية مع ترجمة كاملة إلى اللغة العربية *'Legal Terms in English fully Translated into Arabic'*. Jordan: Dār Al-Thaqāfa for Publication & Distribution

Alcaraz Varó, E. 2009. Isomorphism and Anisomorphism in the Translation of Legal Texts. In *Translation Issues in Language and Law*, ed. F. Olson, R.A. Lorz, and D. Stein, 182–192. London/New York: Palgrave Macmillan.

Alcaraz Varó, E. & Hughes, B. 2014. *Legal Translation Explained*. London/New York: Routledge. Fist published in 2002.

Almanna, A. 2005. *Aspects of Cohesion in Translating Legislative Texts from Arabic into English*. Unpublished master thesis. London: University of Westminster.

———. 2014. *Translation Theories Exemplified from Cicero to Pierre Bourdieu*. München: Lincom Europa Academic Publishers.

———. 2016a. *The Routledge Course in Translation Annotation: Arabic-English-Arabic*. London/New York: Routledge.

———. 2016b. *Semantics for Translation Students. Arabic-English-Arabic*. Oxford: Peter Lang.

———. 2018. *The Nuts and Bolts of Arabic-English Translation: An Introduction to Applied Contrastive Linguistics*. Newcastle upon Tyne, England: Cambridge Scholars Publishing.

Almanna, A., and Almanna, F. 2008. الترجمة: تاريخها، نظرياتها، تطبيقاتها *Translation: History, Theory & Practice*. London: Sayyab Books Ltd.

Al-Murshidi, M. M. 2012. ترجمة العقود المدنية *Translating Civil Contracts*. Egypt: Dār Aj-Jami'a Aj-Jadīda for Publication.

A. Almanna, *Legal Translation between English and Arabic*, https://doi.org/10.1007/978-3-031-14838-5

Al-Qinai, J. 2008. Translating Modals between English and Arabic. *Translation and Interpreting Studies* 3.1 (3.2): 30–67.
Altarabin, M. 2018. Translating English Legal Lexical Features into Arabic: Challenges and Possibilities. *AWEJ* 2 (2): 199–209.
Awe, B.I., and P.S. Fanokun. 2018. Archaisms in Legal Contracts- A Corpus-based Analysis. *European Journal of English Language and Literature Studies* 6 (4): 5–20.
Baaij, C.J.W. 2018. *Legal Interpretation and Language Diversity: Rethinking Translation in EU Law making*. Oxford: Oxford University Press.
Baker, M. 1992/2011. *In Other Words*. London/New York: Routledge.
Bell, R.T. 1991. *Translation and Translating: Theory and Practice*. London/New York: Longman.
Beveridge, B.J. 2002. Legal English, How it Developed and Why it is not Appropriate for International Commercial Contracts. In *The Development of Legal Language*, ed. H.E.S. Mattila, 55–79. Helsinki: Kauppakaari.
Bhatia, V. K. 1982. *An Investigation into Formal and Functional Characteristics of Qualifications in Legislative Writing and its Application to English for Academic Legal Purposes*. Unpublished doctoral dissertation. Aston: Aston University.
Bhatia, V.K. 1987. Language of the Law. *Language Teaching* 20: 227–234.
———. 1993. *Analysing Genre—Language Use in Professional Settings*, Applied Linguistics and Language Study Series. London: Longman.
———. 2006. Legal Genres. In *Encyclopedia of Language & Linguistics*, ed. K. Brown, vol. 7, 1–7. Boston: Elsevier.
———. 2010. Drafting Legislative Provisions: Challenges and Opportunities. *The Loophole* 12: 5–15.
———. 2014. *Worlds of Written Discourse: A Genre-based View*. London: Bloomsbury.
Biel, Ł. 2014. The Textual Fit of Translated EU Law: A Corpus-based Study of Deontic Modality. *The Translator* 20 (3): 332–355.
Cao, D. 2007. *Translating Law*. Clevedon: Multilingual Matters.
Castro, O. 2010. Non sexist-Translation and/in Social Change: Gender Issues in Translation. In *Compromiso socialy traducción/Interpretación translation/Interpreting and Social Activism*, ed. J. Boéri and C. Maier. Granada (ES): ECOS.
Catford, J.C. 1965. *A Linguistic Theory of Translation*. Oxford: Oxford University Press.
Chesterman, A. 1993. From 'is' to 'ought': Laws, Norms and Strategies in Translation Studies. *Target* 5: 1–20.
———. 1997/2000. *Memes of Translation: The Spread of Ideas in Translation Theory*. Amsterdam/Philadelphia: John Benjamins.
Coates, J. 1983. *The Semantics of the Modal Auxiliaries*. London: Croom Helm.
Crystal, D., and D. Davy. 1969. *Investigating English Style*. London: Longman.
Dámová, P. 2007. *The Language of Law-A Stylistic Analysis with a Focus on Lexical (Binomial) Expressions*. Unpublished doctoral dissertation. Brno: Masaryk University.
Danet, B. 1980. Language in the Legal Process. *Law and Society Review* 14 (3): 447–564.
———. 1984. Legal Discourse, *Text* 4: 1/3, special issue.
———. 1985. Legal Discourse. In *Handbook of Discourse Analysis*, ed. T. van Dijk, vol. 1, 273–291. London: Academic Press.
Dickins, J., and J.C.E. Watson. 1999. *Standard Arabic: An Advanced Course*. Cambridge: Cambridge University Press.
Dickins, J., S. Hervey, and I. Higgins. 2002. *Thinking Arabic Translation*. London/New York: Routledge.

Downing, A., and P. Locke. 1992. *A University Course in English Grammar*. Hemel Hempstead: Phoenix ELT.

El-Farahaty, H. 2015. *Arabic-English-Arabic Legal Translation*. London/New York: Routledge.

———. 2016. Translating Lexical Legal Terms between English and Arabic. *International Journal for the Semiotics of Law—Revue internationale de Sémiotique juridique*, 1–21. https://doi.org/10.1007/s11196-016-9460-2

Emery, P.G. 1989. Legal Arabic Text: Implications for Translation. *Babel* 35: 35–40.

Farghal, M. 2019. A Case Study of Modality in Legal Translation: The Omani constitution. In *Discourse in Translation*, ed. S. Faiq, 163–183. London/New York: Routledge.

Farghal, M., and A. Shunnaq. 1992. Major Problems in Students' Translations of English Legal Texts into Arabic. *Babel* 38 (4): 203–210.

Gémar, J.C., ed. 1982. *The Language of the Law and Translation: Essays on Jurilinguistics*. Montreal, Canada: Éditeur Officiel du Québec.

Goodrich, P. 1990. *Legal Discourse: Studies in Linguistics, Rhetoric and Legal Analysis*. London: Macmillan.

Haigh, R. 2004/2009. Legal English (2nd edition). London/New York: Routledge/Cavendish.

Hall. M. F. 2008. *Discourse Analysis of Fictional Dialogue in Arabic to English Translation*. Unpublished doctoral dissertation. London: University of London.

Halliday, M.A.K. 1970. Functional Diversity in Language as Seen from a Consideration of Modality and Mood in English. *Foundation of Language* 6 (3): 322–361.

Harvey, M. 2002. What's so Special About Legal Translation? *Meta* 47 (2): 177–185.

Hatim, B., A. Shunnaq, and R. Buckley. 1995. *The Legal Translator at Work: A Practical Guide*. Jordan: Dār al-Hilāl for Translating and Publishing.

Hellinger, M., and H. Bussmann, eds. 2001. *Gender Across Languages: The Linguistic Representation of Women and Men*. Vol. 1. John Benjamins Publishing.

Hjort-Pedersen, M. 1996. Legal Translation and the Principle of Relevance. *Metalingua* 15: 361–371.

Holmes, J. 1992/2013. *An Introduction to Sociolinguistics*, 4th edn. London/New York: Routledge.

Hu, P.-C., and L. Cheng. 2016. A Study of Legal Translation from the Perspective of Error Analysis. *International Journal of Legal Discourse* 1 (1): 235–253.

Huddleston, R. 1984. *Introduction to the Grammar of English*. Cambridge University Press.

Husni, R., and D. Newman. 2015. *Arabic-English-Arabic Translation*. London/New York: Routledge.

Janulevičienė, V., and S. Rackevičienė. 2011. Translation Strategies of English Legal Terms in the Bilingual Lithuanian and Norwegian Law Dictionaries. *Socialinių mokslų studijos/Societal Studies* 3 (3): 1073–1093.

Jarjour, M. 2006. *A Relevance-Theoretic Account of the Translation of Ideological Assumptions in the Language of the News with Specific Reference to Translation from English into Arabic*. Unpublished doctoral dissertation. Salford: University of Salford.

Kurzon, D. 1986. *It is Hereby Performed: Explorations in Legal Speech Acts*. Amsterdam/Philadelphia: John Benjamins Publishing Company.

Lyons, J. 1977. *Semantics*. Cambridge: Cambridge University Press.

Malone, J.L. 1988. *The Science of Linguistics in the Art of Translation*. Albany: State University of New York Press.

Mellinkoff, D. 1963. *The Language of the Law*. Boston: Little Brown.
Newmark, P. 1988. *A Textbook of Translation*. New York/London/Toronto/Sydney/ Tokyo: Prentice Hall.
Nida, E. 1964. *Towards a Science of Translation, with Special Reference to Principles and Procedures Involved in Bible Translating*. Leiden: E. J. Brill.
O'Barr, W.M. 1982. *Linguistic Evidence: Language, Power and Strategy in the Courtroom*. New York: Academic Press.
Perkins, M.R. 1983. *Modal Expressions in English*. London: Frances Pinter.
Prieto Ramos, F. 2014a. Legal Translation Studies as Interdiscipline: Scope and Evolution. *Meta* 59 (2): 260–277.
———. 2014b. International and Supranational Law in Translation: From Multilingual Law Making to Adjudication. *The Translator* 20 (3): 313–331. https://doi.org/10.1080/13556509.2014.904080.
Ramos, F. P. 2020. Translating Legal Terminology and Phraseology: Between Inter-systemic Incongruity and Multilingual Harmonization. *Perspective* (published online December 17) 29: 175–183.
Rylance, P. 1994. *Legal writing and Drafting*. London: Blackstone Press Limited.
Sabra, M. M. A. 2003. ترجمة العقود *Translation of Contracts*. Cairo: Dār Al-Kutub Al-Qānūniyya.
Šarčević, S. 1997. *New Approach to Legal Translation*. London/Boston: Kluwer Law International.
———. 2018. Challenges to Legal Translators in Institutional Settings. In *Institutional Translation for International Governance: Enhancing Quality in Multilingual Legal Communication*, ed. F. Prieto Ramos, 9–24. London: Bloomsbury.
Scott, J.W. 1986. Gender: A Useful Category of Historical Analysis. *The American Historical Review* 91 (5): 1053–1075.
Tiersma, P.M. 1999. *Legal Language*. Chicago: University of Chicago Press.
Trosborg, A. 1995a. Introduction: Special Issue on Laying Down the Law-discourse Analysis of Legal Institutions. *Journal of Pragmatics* 23 (1): 1–5.
———. 1995b. Statutes and Contracts: An Analysis of Legal Speech Acts in the English Language of Law. *Journal of Pragmatics* 23 (1): 31–53.
———. 1997. *Rhetorical Strategies in Legal Language: Discourse Analysis of Statutes and Contracts*. Tübingen: Gunter Narr Verlag Tubingen.
Veretina-Chiriac, I. 2012. Characteristics and Features of Legal English Vocabulary. Accessed January 18, 2018. studiamsu.eu/wp-content/uploads/20.-p.103-107.pdf
Vinay, J. P., and J. Darbelnet. 1958/1995. *Stylistique comparée du français et de l'anglais. Méthode de traduction*. Paris: Didier (trans. and ed.) J. C. Sager & M. J. Hamel, *Comparative Stylistics of French and English: A Methodology for Translation*. Amsterdam/Philadelphia: John Benjamins.
Weisflog, W. E. 1987. *Problems of Legal Translation*. Swiss Reports Presented to the XIIth International Congress of Comparative Law (pp. 179–218). Schulthess.
Wolff, L. 2011. Legal translation. In *The Oxford Handbook of Translation Studies*, Oxford Handbooks in Linguistics, ed. K. Windle and K. Malmkjaer, 228–242. Oxford University Press.

Index

A. Almanna, *Legal Translation between English and Arabic*,
https://doi.org/10.1007/978-3-031-14838-5

Index

A. Almanna, *Legal Translation between English and Arabic*,
https://doi.org/10.1007/978-3-031-14838-5

www.ingramcontent.com/pod-product-compliance
Ingram Content Group UK Ltd.
Pitfield, Milton Keynes, MK11 3LW, UK
UKHW020203290926
15471UKWH00005B/1032